ART CAREER GUIDE

ART CAREER GUIDE

Fourth Edition:
Revised and Enlarged
A Guidance Handbook
for Art Students, Teachers,
Vocational Counselors,
and Job Hunters

by Donald Holden

Watson-Guptill Publications/New York

N8350
.H6
1983

For Willi

Copyright © 1961, 1973, 1983 by Watson-Guptill Publications

Published 1983 in New York by Watson-Guptill Publications
a division of Billboard Publications, Inc.
1515 Broadway, New York, N.Y. 10036

Library of Congress Cataloging in Publication Data
Holden, Donald.
  Art career guide.
  Includes index.
  1. Art—Vocational guidance. I. Title.
N8350.H6 1983   702.3'73   82-24701
ISBN 0-8230-0252-7

Distributed in the United Kingdom by Phaidon Press Ltd., Littlegate
House, St. Ebbe's St., Oxford

Manufactured in U.S.A.

First Edition, 1961
  First Printing, 1961
  Second Printing, 1963
  Third Printing, 1965
Second Edition, 1967
  First Printing, 1967
  Second Printing, 1970
Third Edition, Revised, Enlarged, 1973
  First Printing, 1973
  Second Printing, 1974
  Third Printing, 1976
  Fourth Printing, 1977
Fourth Edition, Revised, Enlarged, 1983

Acknowledgments

Many distinguished men and women in the fields of art, design, architecture, crafts, education, and publishing played vital roles in the publication of *Art Career Guide*. They generously served as advisers, critics, and sources of material. The author is grateful for the time and patience of:

Damien Alexander
James M. Alexander, Jr.
Richard F. Bach
Robert Becker
Ralph G. Beelke
Regina Benedict
Gordon F. Bieberle
Phillip A. Bruno
Arnold Buchheimer
Margaret Burlin
John Canaday
Howard Conant
Beverly Jeanne Davis
Charles M. Dorn
Arthur S. Douglass, Jr.
Henry Dreyfuss

John Ebstein
Cyril Lee Ellison
Arpi Ermoyan
Yvonne Freund
Guy Fry
Millicent Hall Gaudieri
Edward U. Gips
William Goldsmith
Richard Grossman
Dione Guffey
Robert B. Hale
William D. Hamilton
Caroline Hightower
Deborah K. Holland
John E. Jamison
Stuart Kahan

Robert Kaupelis
Norman Kent
Lynn E. Klaskin
Stephen A. Kliment
Jean Koefoed
Boris Kroll
Ramah Larisch
Jack Lenor Larsen
George S. Lewis
Leo Lionni
John J. Mahlmann
Tran Mawicke
Gerald McConnell
Sterling McIlhany
Sol Mednick
Rodney P. Mercer
Diana Moore

Yina A. Moore
Lois Moran
Joyce Morrow
Elias Newman
Jules Perel
Barye Philips
Paul Reilly
Ben Rose
Beverly Russell
Susan Schreiber
Bonnie Silverstein
Gail Simmons
Deborah Trainer
Norman Ulrich
Polly Weaver
Eve Wilen
Brian J. Wynne

And for the exhausting job of assembling, checking, and rechecking the directory of art schools—certainly the hardest assignment of all—I'm indebted to my wife Willi.

Cooperating organizations

Art Career Guide was made possible by the aid of leading professional organizations, as well as one government agency. Many of these provided invaluable research material. Others gave advice and encouragement. Still others checked chapters for accuracy and completeness. The author is grateful for the cooperation of the following organizations:

American Association of Museums
American Association of University Professors
American Craft Council
American Institute of Architects
American Institute of Graphic Arts
American Personnel and Guidance Association
American Society of Interior Designers
American Society of Landscape Architects
American Society of Magazine Photographers
Art Directors Club of New York
Artists Equity Association
Association of Art Museum Directors
Association of Collegiate Schools of Architecture
Bureau of Labor Statistics, United States Department of Labor
Foundation for Interior Design Education Research
Graphic Artists Guild
Industrial Designers Society of America
Institute of Business Designers
Interior Design Educators Council
National Architectural Accrediting Board
National Art Education Association
National Council for Interior Design Qualification
National Council of Architectural Registration Boards
National Education Association
New York/Artists Equity Association
New York Chapter, American Institute of Architects
Professional Photographers of America
Society of Illustrators

Preface to fourth edition

Since *Art Career Guide* first appeared in 1961, the art professions have changed and so have the art schools.

The greatest changes have taken place in architecture and industrial design—and significant changes have been made in these chapters. The new edition of *Art Career Guide* also reflects the changing job patterns in teaching, art museums, and photography. And since statistics always change rapidly, there are substantial revisions in the chapter about earnings and job prospects.

Of course, the section that goes out of date most quickly is the art school directory that concludes the book. On the basis of a questionnaire survey of every art school, college, and university in America—conducted by the nation's largest art magazine, *American Artist*—this section has been updated for the fourth edition.

Contents

PART ONE
Planning Your Education

1
How to use this book

One Sunday evening toward the end of high school, I interrupted dinner with a startling announcement: I wanted to become an artist.

This was an uneasy moment for my parents. Like most people, they'd never really known any artists. The only artists they'd ever seen were in the movies. And the Hollywood version of the artist was no one to envy. He was skinny, unshaven, hungry. True, the script gave him his quota of beautiful models. But this didn't seem to make him any happier. His eyes were daubed with shadowy makeup to give him that haunted, doomed look. His masterpieces lay scattered about his dingy studio, unsold. If fame and fortune did reach him at last, they came too late. The prices of his pictures always soared the day after his funeral. Was *this* what I expected to do with my life? My parents shook their heads.

No, I was sure the movies were wrong. I just couldn't believe that all artists were penniless Bohemians who died before their time. Certainly there was *some* way for a young artist to earn a living. There *had* to be.

My family had no contact with the art world, but even *they* knew the names of a few artists who were said to command thousands of dollars for a single canvas, just to hang in someone's living room. What about the illustrations we saw in magazines and newspapers? Weren't artists paid to draw them? What about our furniture, our drapes, our wallpaper? Didn't somebody have to design them? Come to think of it, someone had to design our apartment house too. Even an architect was a kind of artist, though it had never occurred to us before.

My parents were encouraged. There was hope after all. It began to dawn on us, as we spoke, that there were many kinds of artists and all sorts of art careers. But how do you find out what these careers are? And how do you pick the right one? What do you study and how do you pick the right school? Then how do you find a job?

We hadn't the vaguest idea how to answer these questions. The next day, I went to the local library to look for a book that might help. There were plenty of books about jobs and schools. But amazingly enough, among those thousands of pages of advice, there was almost nothing about art careers. The branch librarian, who had worked hard to build up her guidance shelf, confirmed this. She told me there were lots of how-to-do-it books: richly illustrated textbooks on the techniques of drawing, painting, and various crafts. A few had chapters on job hunting. But my first job hunt was years off. There was no book to help me *now*.

Later that week, I tried the guidance counselor of my high school. He was a dedicated, overworked man, doing his best to keep up with all the printed matter that came across his desk. His walls were lined with books and college catalogs. He lent me catalogs he'd collected from nearby art schools. He'd made a point of visiting these schools periodically and talking to the instructors. He told me what he knew about art careers and art schools, but he frankly admitted that he couldn't tell me enough. He was well informed about professions like medicine and engineering. He had plenty of reading matter about these fields. Besides, he had friends in these professions. But his personal contact with artists was too infrequent. And like the librarian, he had no book to help him advise me.

My high school art teacher was eager to help. He was a good painter and knew his way around the art galleries. His illustrations had appeared in books and magazines, so he knew the publishing business. He told me all he could about these fields. But he added that there were many other art jobs he knew almost nothing about. He mentioned art careers I'd never even heard of, like industrial design. But he was quick to admit that he was short on details.

And so I went on buttonholing anyone who might have a few facts. I talked the ears off exasperated neighbors who happened to be Sunday painters. I went to the local art schools and gave patient teachers the third degree. And I hungrily combed art school catalogs and art textbooks for a few sentences of advice.

It was a slow, painful, haphazard search. Looking back on those discouraging days, I'm amazed that I didn't just give up. Somehow, I stumbled into the right school and the right profession. And by some miracle, I got a job, after a long, badly managed job hunt.

My days of painful groping were typical of art students then and *now*. Each year, I meet scores of art students and young job hunters who seem as ill-informed as I was. Our vocational guidance methods have improved enormously. There are whole libraries of "career books." But somehow the art profession has been left out. Maybe we have a romantic feeling that artists aren't guided by facts, but by the stars. Whatever the reason, facts about art careers are still hard to find.

The purpose of this book is to assemble these facts in one small package. Not *all* the facts, of course. No one knows all the facts, and no single book could hold them. But this brief handbook contains the basic facts I wish I had when I began my own art career.

A word to the student

This book is meant to guide you from your high school days, through your years of professional training in art school, to the time when you go out to find your first job.

The next chapter will help you decide whether a career in art is really for you. The following two chapters will tell you how to plan your high school program, then how to pick the right art school, college or university art department.

Then there's a series of chapters, each describing one of the major art fields you may enter. The eleven fields are: fine art, which includes painting, sculpture, and printmaking; illustration; graphic design, sometimes called advertising design; fabric design; interior design; architecture; industrial design; photography; art teaching; art museum jobs; and crafts. Within these chapters, you'll find facts about specialized offshoots of each field. For example, the fine art chapter discusses such specialties as portrait and mural painting. The chapter on illustration touches on book and fashion illustration. The graphic design chapter mentions such diverse careers as package and book design. I've tried to define each field-within-a-field. The section closes with a chapter on job prospects and artists' incomes.

The next four chapters tell you how to organize your job hunt. One chapter gives detailed instructions to help you write a resume of your qualifications. A second chapter suggests ways of planning your job campaign. The third chapter contains pointers on preparing a portfolio of your work. And the final chapter in this section discusses how to conduct yourself when you arrive at the big moment: the job interview.

The book concludes with a directory of art schools, colleges, and universities that offer professional courses in the eleven career fields. The schools are listed by state, to help you find the ones nearest your home.

Some advice to parents

This book was written to encourage you. These twenty-two brief chapters should reassure you that there's a place in the world for your youngster's talent *if* he or she has what it takes.

This book gives you a means of helping the student find that place. I suggest you read along with your young artist. Since you may carry the cost of four or five years in art school, it's natural for you to feel involved in the decisions the student makes about a career and a professional school.

These decisions demand a lot of self-knowledge, perhaps more self-knowledge than many students have. This book is meant to help young readers get to onow themselves. In the process, the student is going to do plenty of thinking out loud and ask a lot of difficult questions. None of you will know all the answers. You'll find many of the answers in this book, though not *all* of them. Too many questions are uniquely personal. They're questions that young readers must answer for themselves, with the help of a good sounding board: you. This book should help you become a better sounding board, the most vital role you can play in the life of a young artist struggling to find the route to a career.

The book should also help you perform other services. It may help you advise your teenager on a high school course schedule. If you visit art schools—and I think you *should* if you have the time—you'll be better prepared to ask the right questions there. You'll also be a more astute judge of the answers. The concluding chapters may even suggest ways of helping your young artist find a job.

You need no art training to read this book. The text contains very little shop talk. Whenever technical terms are used, for lack of simpler words, they're explained in the text.

Suggestions for teachers, guidance counselors, and librarians

This is both a reference book and an informal textbook. You can dip into it to find the answer to a specific question. Or you can read the text as a continuous "story."

A true reference book is organized in a way that makes facts easy to find when you want them. This volume tries to achieve this in two ways. First, the sequence of chapters and chapter subdivisions follows an obvious logic: the facts are where the reader expects to find them. Second, the format is designed to make facts accessible. Though the "story line" is continuous, there are a great many "heads" and "subheads" within each chapter.

On the other hand, I've said this is a textbook, though it's more informal than most textbooks. I do hope that these pages will make lively reading. I think you'll find the book useful as a classroom tool or for outside assignments. The contents and reading level are geared to the high school art major and the art school student. Probably the ideal time to assign the book would be the final year of high school or the freshman year of art school, when the student has to choose a major subject.

Individual chapters can be assigned when they relate to current class projects. Or the chapters can be read consecutively. I think it's best to read Part Two—the chapters that describe the major art fields—in quick succession. This helps the student to compare the various careers while they're all fresh in the reader's mind.

As a counseling tool, this book is something you can assign to parents as well as students. In my experience, one of the common counseling problems is that the student, though often ill-informed, still knows more about art careers than the family does. The parents feel helpless. They don't feel equipped to advise their youngster because they just don't have enough facts. They're intimidated by all the half truths and pseudo-professional lingo their teenager has begun to build up. For these parents, this book can be a short course to strengthen their confidence and bridge the gap that divides them from the son or daughter they want to help.

Help for mature job hunters

Though this book stresses the vocational problems of young people, the mature job hunter will also find help here. This is someone who's unhappy in one line of work and wants to try another. You may be working in one art field and want to switch to a different art career. Or you may not be an artist at all. An art career may be a totally new idea in your life.

Switches like these are common. My own circle of friends includes an engineer who became an architect, then turned to industrial design; an industrial designer who changed to graphic design and is now art director of a national magazine; a successful art director who quit his job to teach and paint; a painter who became a leading advertising photographer. And I know dozens of others.

If you're thinking of making such a change, but you're not sure which art field is the right one, this book may help. The chapters in Part Two will help you compare various art jobs with your present job. As you read these chapters, you may discover that you need more schooling. If so, you'll want to examine the school directory section and the chapter on picking an art school.

For someone who's already in an art job, the chapters on job hunting *may* seem unnecessary. Having interviewed hundreds of job hunting artists, designers, and architects, I've been astonished to see how badly most job campaigns are managed. Seasoned professionals often act like disorganized amateurs when the time comes to plan a job campaign. The final chapters of this book explain how to *program* your hunt, to find the right job in the shortest time.

A word to the maverick

When he heard that this book was under way, one noted art director asked: "What about the maverick, the off-beat character who doesn't fit anything you say, whom no book can help?"

Among thousands of artists and art students, there's always the rare bird. There's always the man or woman who has a unique contribution to make. We can make generalizations that fit most artists and art students, but these generalizations don't fit *this* case. Such an artist defies classification, and for just this reason, often has a long struggle to find the right route. I once knew a sculptor who spent years shaping statues, until one day he discovered that he really wanted to shape visionary wooden houses with his own hands. The maverick may waste years on the wrong track before getting on the right one.

Is it really true that no book can help such a reader? I think there *is* one basic service that this book may perform.

My daughter was once given a book about a little animal who awoke, one morning, from his long winter sleep and couldn't recall what kind of animal he was. He went through the forest asking other animals, "Can you tell me what I am?" None of them knew. Someone suggested he go to the zoo, which housed all the animals in the world. There he would surely find other animals like himself.

So he went to the zoo and patiently walked from cage to cage. He looked at lions, tigers, elephants, zebras, giraffes. But none of them looked like him. Finally, the wise owl looked at him carefully and said: "Why don't you go over and see the bears. You look to me like a kind of a bear." He went to the bears and they agreed. He was a kind of a bear. But what kind? He wasn't like the other bears. He was different. The oldest and wisest of the bears thought the problem over and solved it very simply. "You're not a kind of a bear," he said. "You're a Very Special Kind of a Bear." Our hero was satisfied. He returned to the forest and lived happily ever after, being just what he was: a Very Special Kind of a Bear.

The Very Special Kind of an Artist may find it worthwhile to tour this book as my daughter's bear toured the zoo. If the book does nothing else for you, it may tell you all the things you aren't. Knowing what you *aren't*, you may find it easier to decide what you *are*.

Future editions of this book

Like most books, this one probably contains its share of errors and omissions. Every word has been checked by experts: leading artists, educators, and professional organizations. But even this doesn't mean the book is without flaws. Every book can be improved and this one is no exception to the rule.

In future editions of *Art Career Guide*, I hope to make these improvements with your help. If you have suggestions to make about the next edition, though it may be a few years off, I hope you'll take the time to drop a note to the publisher, who'll forward your note to me.

2
Should you become an artist?

How do you know you're cut out to be an artist? For some readers, the answer is simple. They just *know*, that's all. They've *always* wanted to be artists. They've never even considered any other career. But for many readers, life isn't that simple.

There are so many things that may confuse the issue. What if your high school report card says you're good at several things? You get good grades in art, but you also get them in English, history, languages. Maybe you should be a journalist, teach history, enter the foreign service. Or your father's a doctor; you've always admired him and you wonder if you'd make a good doctor too. Perhaps you built your own hi-fi set last summer; it was so much fun, you wonder if you might enjoy being an engineer. And what if there's a profitable family business? Your family might be happy if you went to work for Uncle Pete.

Despite all these distracting possibilities, how can you tell you're really an artist at heart? Are there any special signs, any characteristics that artists have, even in their teens?

It's fair to say that most artists, designers, and architects have *certain* traits in common. In this chapter, I'll try to tell you what some of these traits are. But as you read, remember there's no law that says a successful artist *must* have all these qualities. No two artists are alike. This chapter isn't a "test" you must pass. I know several first rate artists, designers, and architects who might not pass. But if you *do* have many of the qualities described here, you should feel encouraged.

Is there an artistic temperament?

One popular idea about artists is that they have something called artistic temperament. Artists are said to be moody, unpredictable, hot-tempered. There are just enough legends to keep this idea alive. Michelangelo is said to have thrown a paint pot at the Pope. Leonardo da Vinci got bored with many of his greatest paintings and never finished them. Cézanne, we're told, tossed his masterpieces into the bushes and his wife went out to retrieve them. And it seems to be true that van Gogh sliced off an ear.

But despite these tales, some true, some false, artistic temperament is a poor test of talent. In fact, I doubt that artists are really more temperamental than other professional groups. The most erratic people *I've* met aren't artists at all. They're waiters. If you live in an apartment house, *your* candidate for the temperament prize is probably your building superintendent. And any business executive will tell you about all the moody salesmen and saleswomen.

In short, artists have no corner on temperament. It's just that nobody makes movies or writes magazine stories about hot-tempered cab drivers. The exploits of artists make more glamorous material.

There are other stereotypes about so-called artistic temperament that need puncturing. We're told that artists are impractical, that they're bad at business. We're told that they're bad organizers and bad administrators. Yet it's obvious that there are thousands of highly paid artists, designers, and architects who couldn't have succeeded if they weren't good at business, meeting deadlines, collecting their bills, organizing their own efforts, and directing the work of others.

We're told that artists are irresponsible dreamers who neglect their families and would rather paint than eat. Yet most artists are as happily married as other people, hold down good jobs, feed and clothe their children, and manage to send them through college. I know hundreds of artists and very few of them look underfed.

So forget about the myth of artistic temperament. You'll never spot a potential artist, designer or architect by an explosive personality or a far-away look. There are more concrete signs to watch for, more significant questions that you should ask yourself as a potential artist. Here are some questions you should think about.

How much do you see?

Old friends of Picasso say that when he looked at a painting, they were amazed to find any paint left on the canvas. He seemed to devour things with his eyes.

One striking thing about artists is that they literally *see more intensely* than other people. They watch everything, notice everything: how people dress, how they decorate their homes, how food is arranged on a plate. They often see things other people don't see at all. They discover rich colors in "gray" shadows and may find the subtle shape of a dusty pebble as beautiful as the shining facets of a diamond.

Artists *react strongly* to what they see. People are often baffled by the excitement an artist may find in the tilt of a tree or a slight color change in the sky. My designer friends are actually angry when they see an ugly piece of furniture or an ugly building going up.

You *can* learn to see as an artist sees. This eye can be cultivated, and a good artist's eye becomes sharper every year. No psychologist or geneticist has ever proven that babies are *born* with the artist's eye. In many people, however, the artist's eye seems to develop almost by itself when they're quite young. This can be an important sign of things to come.

What do you do with your hands?

Artists want to do more than just watch. They feel a powerful urge to do something about what they see, something with their hands.

To an artist, a memorable face is more than something to look at. It's something to draw, paint, sculpt, or photograph. When a designer is dissatisfied with a new chair, that's a good reason to haul out tools and rebuild it.

I know one designer who's forever rebuilding every stick of furniture in his home. Like most good designers, he's never satisfied. He always has a new idea for improving his surroundings. He's never forgotten the afternoon he brought his future wife home to meet his parents. She was a pianist. Naturally, she was asked to play. The unlucky girl selected a sonata that began with a thunderous series of chords. As her fingers struck the keyboard, the piano collapsed like a load of lumber falling off a truck. Her future husband had been experimenting with a new kind of piano leg. The experiment hadn't worked.

Looking back on high school, I recall many future artists, designers, and architects who had similar obsessions. My friends and I drew constantly, not only in art classes, but in every spare minute we had. The margins of our notebooks were crammed with little sketches of teachers, classmates, an idea for a painting or a school poster. Others among us always seemed to be building things. Their rooms at home bulged with ship and plane models, wood carvings, weird furniture, dioramas, kites, and unfinished constructions that nobody could identify.

Not every artist has this sort of one-track mind. You may have diverse interests like music, writing, sports, gardening. Nor do you always discover your vocation as early as high school. I know several outstanding artists, designers, and architects who were mature men and women—successful in jobs that had nothing to do with art—before they recognized their true vocation.

But whenever it comes, however it comes, the urge to be an artist implies an urge to work with your hands. You must *like* to work with your hands if you hope to be an artist.

Do you like hard work?

A well-known watercolorist was painting outdoors one day when he heard footsteps behind him. He was working in a cornfield near a major truck route. A huge tank truck had pulled up along the side of the road. The driver had climbed out of the cab and strolled over to watch the painter at work. The trucker had never seen this spectacle before. For ten minutes he stared silently over the artist's shoulder. At last, the trucker tapped him on the arm and asked wonderingly: "Tell me the truth. Would you rather do this than work?"

It comes as a surprise to many people that art *is* work, hard work. True, you become an artist because art is fun. But when you reach art school, you must be prepared to face four or five years of rigorous training. A good art, design, or architectural school is as tough as any engineering school. There will be times when you'll work far into the night to get passing grades.

And when you land your first job, you'll soon discover that art is more than the usual 9-to-5 routine. Art demands more of you than many other kinds of work. Your mind must be bubbling with fresh ideas throughout the work day. Your hands will work all day, perhaps into the night. For when ideas are surging in your head and your hands are racing to give these ideas tangible shape, you can't just turn off this process when the clock strikes. Even when your hands are idle—evenings, holidays, weekends— your work may still revolve in your mind because your work is something you love.

This means that a career in art will demand all the energy and dedication you can muster. You don't just *put in* your eight hours like a clerk-typist in the army. You must give all you have, all the time. To live the life of a successful artist, designer, or architect, you have to *relish* work and come back for more when someone else would be tempted to go home and lie down. Though *Sunday painting* may look easy, there's nothing soft about the life of the professional artist. The more you love what you do, the harder you're going to work.

Are you adventurous?

One of America's best graphic designers has a unique way of testing her students to separate the sheep from the goats. Each year, she takes her seniors to a fine, though inexpensive, little French restaurant to celebrate their graduation. Some students always try to order hamburgers. These, she says, are the ones who are doomed to be second-raters. Others stick their necks out and order the unfamilar dishes on the menu. Their teacher predicts: "These are the ones to watch."

This is hardly an infallible test, but it does spotlight an important characteristic that most good artists seem to have: they approach life with a spirit of adventure. They're never satisfied with the status quo. They're hungry for new, refreshing experiences.

Most of my friends are constantly combing art galleries, museums, books, magazines, movies, TV shows, the theater, trade exhibits, even department store counters, for new ideas. They're travel hungry. When they finally save up the money for a trip abroad, they don't stay at the fashionable hotel where the help speaks English. The artists pick the little hotel on a side street, where they'll be forced to learn a new language.

Artists are always experimenting. When a new plastic becomes available, industrial designers rush to try it. When a new type face is stocked by typographers and printers, graphic designers are impatient to use it in a layout. It's been said that a true architect might try building with old newspapers if they'd stand up when it rained.

Art is no place for the stick-in-the-mud. There's no room for the person who turns away from the unfamiliar and insists: "I like what I'm used to."

Do you like to work alone?

Working in the silence of an attic studio or in a bustling office, artists spend much of their professional life alone.

The painter, sculptor, and printmaker are almost always alone with their thoughts. Some sculptors and mural painters have assistants, and there are models, of course. But fine art is essentially a one-person job.

What about the graphic designer in an advertising agency, the illustrator in an art service, the draftsman in an architectural office, and all the other artists who work as members of a team? Even in a team job, you're on your own much of the time.

When client meetings and office bull sessions are over, when the work has been scheduled and each worker has been given part of the project, each member of the team returns to the drawing board. If you have a door, you close it. If your drawing board is in the bullpen with a dozen other boards, you put up imaginary walls and shut an imaginery door. You may open that door to ask a question, give an order or take one. But you're on your own till your part of the job is done.

To work on your own—whether in your own studio or "alone" among others—takes some rare qualities. You must have an unusual amount of self-discipline. You have no supervisor standing over you, directing you, making sure you keep at it. It's entirely up to you to get the job done. You must be able to organize your energies, pace yourself, and "keep your eye on the ball." Can you resist the temptation to dawdle, stare out the window, go out for a soda, or make just one more phone call? Can you work steadily, not in fits and starts, but with a smooth, controlled rhythm, like a good long distance runner?

Obviously, such self-discipline is impossible unless you have exceptional ability to concentrate. Artists are often accused of absent-mindedness. Their spouses complain, "You never heard the doorbell," or "You never look at your watch and that's why you don't get home on time." My particular vice is to nod when people talk to me, but never hear a word they say. This behavior may be irritating, but *absent-mindedness* is the wrong word. The artist's mind is very much there. But your mind is so intent on your work that you've closed the door to everything else.

An outstanding fabric designer put it this way: "A real artist has a kind of filter built into the brain. It filters out all distractions—voices, noises, invitations, TV—that might take you away from your work." Of course, this isn't *always* true. Though artists who work in offices must develop a knack for ignoring the chaos around them, there are others—many painters, sculptors, freelance illustrators—who can get nothing done unless they retreat to a lonely barn in the country. But one thing is true of *all* these artists. They know how to cut themselves off from the outside world. They're amazingly single-minded. When they have a job to do, they focus their minds on that job and nothing else.

All this suggests that artists must enjoy their own company. You may ask, "Don't we *all* enjoy our own company?" On the contrary, most people are bored stiff when they're by themselves. In fact, most people's free time is spent *avoiding aloneness.* It's spent getting together with other people or at least watching the TV set to give the illusion that other people are near.

Though artists are as sociable as most people, they really relish being by themselves. A solitary walk in the woods, along a deserted beach, or through the back streets of a strange city may sound depressing to many people, but this is an artist's idea of pleasure. Artists find it stimulating to be alone with their thoughts.

Self-discipline, concentration, and pleasure in your own company—you *can* manage to be an artist without these rare qualities. But there's not much chance that you'll be a *first-rate* artist without them.

Can you work with people?

Reading the last few paragraphs, you may have spotted a paradox. Artists must like to work by themselves, *but* many artists spend their lives working with people.

Painters, sculptors, or printmakers can spend their lives in an attic if they choose—though not many do—but what about architects, interior designers, fabric designers, illustrators, photographers, industrial designers, graphic designers, and all the other artists who have clients, bosses, and co-workers? What about all the painters, sculptors, and printmakers who *don't* live in attics, but make part of their living by teaching?

Most artists must not only like working alone, they must be able to work with people. Working with people *well* takes as many rare qualities as working alone. Most important is a spirit of give-and-take. Though you must have the courage to stick up for your convictions, "give-and-take" means having respect for other people's ideas too. It also means the ability to compromise, exchange ideas with others, and accept criticism gracefully. Whether you're an architect or designer working in an office, a painter or sculptor teaching in an art school, you must *enjoy* this give-and-take with your co-workers or students.

This really brings us back to the issue of artistic temperament. The spirit of give-and-take is the *opposite* of artistic temperament. At the beginning of this chapter, I said that having a stubborn, arrogant, fiery personality was no sign of talent. Now I'll go a step further: so-called artistic temperament is one of the biggest roadblocks you can erect in your own path.

How much do you care about money?

Contrary to legend, most good artists, designers, and architects earn a comfortable living.

With some notable exceptions—everyone seems to know the sad fate of van Gogh—most of the painters we remember as old masters and not-so-old masters *were* fairly well known in their own day. The architects we remember as great *did* get to put up important buildings. The sculptors we recall as great *did* manage to land commissions for important monuments. In fact, these names *couldn't* have come down to us if patrons hadn't recognized these artists, paid for their work, and preserved it for posterity.

Today, most art fields pay reasonably well. In architecture and industrial design, to cite two examples, beginning salaries compare quite well with the earnings of engineering and other technical school graduates. In fields like graphic and interior design, beginners often take a financial beating, but potential earnings are high. Teachers' salaries are nothing extraordinary, but they've gotten better. Unfortunately, it's the painters, sculptors, and printmakers—the group known as fine artists—who have a rough time.

Make no mistake: the art world is intensely competitive and can be cruel to the job hunter who doesn't make the grade. Avertising agencies have their share of disappointed pasteup artists who once aspired to be art directors. Architectural offices are full of middle-aged draftsmen who float from job to job, who'll never claim credit for designing a building. And no one can count the number of painters, sculptors, and printmakers who'll never have a one-artist show.

However, for the artist who has the necessary talent, training, and perseverance, the financial prospects are encouraging. There's not much chance of your getting rich, but neither are you likely to waste away in a garret. You *can* earn a comfortable living, doing the work you love.

But no one becomes an artist because of *money*! You choose the profession for its own sake. Ask a serious artist what he or she would do if there were no financial worries, if some forgotten uncle's will left a thousand acres of Texas real estate bristling with oil wells. The artist would think for a moment and then answer: "I guess I'd just go on being an artist."

If money is an important goal in your life, art is certainly *not* the way to make it. There are much better ways to make big money: become a stockbroker or a sales executive. Even if you achieve financial success on a big scale—which happens now and then—you succeed precisely because you place your art first and money second.

Aptitude tests

In recent years, psychologists have developed various tests designed to help people choose the right career. These are often called *aptitude tests* or *vocational tests*. But these terms are too narrow. They give no idea of the scope of a good battery of tests.

Psychologists speak of a *battery* of tests because they normally expect you to take a selected *group* of tests, not just one. A complete battery includes four kinds of tests. First, there are intelligence tests: how well does your mental equipment operate? Second, there are personality tests: what's your psychological makeup? Third, there are interest tests: are your interests, your attitudes, your personal philosophy more like those of artists or some other professional group? Finally, there are aptitude tests: what are your *native* abilities?

Why not just take a few art aptitude tests and skip the rest? Because these few tests can't tell you enough. Guidance specialists don't claim that talent can be tested. As one distinguished psychologist put it: "We have no workable definition of artistic talent. Thus, art aptitude tests have no predictive value, just comparative value." That is, they can't tell you if you'll be happy or successful in art. All they can tell is that you have more or less skill, knowledge, or "aesthetic judgment" than the others who've taken the test. This leaves out imagination, ambition, and all the other unknowns that determine an artist's future.

A good guidance agency usually recommends that you take many tests that seem to have nothing to do with art. The tester is interested in studying you from many angles. When the battery is completed and scored, the psychologist hopes to give you an objective picture of yourself, free of any preconceptions or illusions you may have. The tester won't write you a directive, telling you exactly what to do with your life. The idea is to help you take a fresh look at yourself, so you'll be better equipped to solve *your own* problems. The tester will tell you many things you may not know about yourself, then make some recommendations about types of work that will suit you, and characteristics you should look for in a job. Equally important, the tests may confirm some of your own opinions. But at this point, the problem is back in your lap. With the self-knowledge you've gained from the tests, you're better equipped to answer your own questions.

Who should take these tests? Not everyone needs them, of course. If you know you want to be an artist, but don't know which art field to pick, tests may not help. Your first year or two in art school will be more likely to solve this subtle problem. However, if you're trying to decide between two *totally different* fields, like art and engineering, then a battery of tests, administered by a reputable guidance agency, may be a worthwhile investment. If you're not sure whether a series of tests will help you, discuss your vocational problem with the people at the agency. They'll tell you whether they feel your questions can be answered by tests or simply by enrolling in art school.

Where can you find a reputable guidance agency? There's probably a college or university within driving distance of your home. Many of these now have their own guidance services. College and university guidance services are often open to the public. Charges are generally reasonable.

Many states and major cities have publicly supported guidance agencies. Your local YMCA or YMHA may have a guidance service. So may other public agencies. Many churches and synagogues now have guidance facilities. And many enterprising psychologists and educators have set up their own guidance offices.

When you choose a guidance agency, it's important to go on the recommendation of someone whose judgment you can trust. Your high school guidance counselor should know the reputable agencies in your area. If your nearby college or university has no guidance office open to the public, the psychology or education department should be able to make a recommendation.

How much do high school grades mean?

Obviously, the grades you get in high school are worth watching. If you get good grades in art, this should encourage you to consider art as a career. Your teacher has probably seen the work of hundreds of art students and knows many signs that distinguish a future artist from a hobbyist.

But having been a teacher, I know that no teacher is infallible. The intelligent teacher always has a secret fear of flunking a future Matisse or Frank Lloyd Wright. And sometimes it does happen. All of us can name distinguished artists, designers, and architects who did badly in school.

If you're that rare bird, you won't be tempted to give up because of low grades. Your urge to be an artist will be so strong that *nothing* can discourage you. Your teacher *could* be wrong, and will be the first to congratulate you when you prove it.

3
Planning your high school program

Many high schools have just one art teacher. If there's just a one-person department, the teacher's time is limited, which means that *you're* limited in the number of art classes you can take. Bigger high schools are often lucky enough to have several art teachers. This may mean that more art classes are open to you. In some large cities, there are high schools with art programs as ambitious as the programs of many art schools.

Whatever the size of your high school's art department, you probably have *some* choice when it comes to the amount and type of art you take. Generally, you also have some choices to make about other subjects, like languages, the sciences, and so-called industrial arts classes, such as wood working and mechanical drawing. In this chapter, I'll try to make some suggestions about how to plan your high school program. I'll also make some recommendations about extracurricular activities, as well as part-time and summer jobs that provide good experience to back up your high school art studies.

How much art should you take?

If you're absolutely sure you're going on to art school or to a college or university art department after high school, then the answer to this question is "All you can get!" If you're really set on an art career, it's important to sit down with your art teacher, or the head of your high school's art department, to plan a course schedule that will give you the most complete art training the school can provide. But bear in mind that you'll probably be expected to take a "college preparatory program," which means a limited amount of art and a lot of academic subjects (liberal arts, science, etc.).

In a small school, you may find yourself taking every art class available. In a bigger school with more art classes, there may be only a certain number of art classes you're *allowed* to take. The school will limit your number of art classes so you'll have time for history, science, mathematics, literature, languages, and other subjects necessary for a well-rounded education. Your art department will help you decide *which* art classes are best for you, within the limit set by the school.

However, if you're not certain that you want to be an artist, you can't load up just on art courses. You have to plan a program that lets you experiment with a variety of subjects.

For example, if you're weighing engineering against architecture, you can't expect your high school to have courses in bridge building or the design of small houses. But you *can* take math and physics, which are basic training for engineers as well as architects. You can also take some classes in drawing and painting, both fundamental to architecture. It may also be wise to take some classes in "shop" or mechanical drawing, which will help you in *either* field. Some schools even teach architectural drafting.

The trick is to find room in a crowded program to experiment with all these subjects. Keep in mind that the teachers in these various departments are there to help you. Don't hesitate to ask their aid in planning a complicated class schedule.

What art subjects are most important?

In a big high school lucky enough to have several art teachers, you may find that different subjects are taught in different art classes. One class may emphasize drawing and painting, while another may stress crafts like ceramics, metal and leatherwork.

Which class will be most valuable to a future artist, designer or architect?

Smaller schools rarely have specialized art classes, but one art class often manages to cram in an astonishing variety of subjects. You may get a taste of painting, drawing, sculpture, printmaking, illustration, fabric design, poster design, and art appreciation all in one class. If you have a choice of assignments, which should you pick?

Drawing is first on the list. An artist who can't draw is as unthinkable as an author who can't read and write. Whatever art field you finally choose, drawing is something you must learn at the very beginning.

As you might expect, next on the list comes painting. When you draw, you learn to think in terms of line, light, and shadow. Painting reveals the vast possibilities of color and texture. Wherever you go in the art world, you must carry with you the lessons that only painting can teach.

Third on the list is sculpture. When you draw and paint, you work in two dimensions. Sculpture introduces you to the third dimension. This is why many art schools call their sculpture courses *three-dimensional design*. Having explored the possibilities of line, light and shade, color and texture, you now face the challenge of building real forms in space.

Finally, nothing is more valuable than a good knowledge of the great art of past and present. Such courses usually go under the heading of *art appreciation* or *art history*.

Not a very long list. But if you've studied these four subjects thoroughly, you've had a taste of the fundamental problems you'll meet later in *any* art career. This short list of basic subjects should encourage you if your high school seems too small to offer a broad art program. Even if a school has just one art teacher, you can probably take these fundamental subjects. Most good art teachers recognize that these four subjects come first.

On the other hand, if your high school—like some big city schools—offers a confusing diversity of art subjects, it helps to keep in mind that just four subjects form the foundation of all art training.

What other art subjects are useful?

Today it's possible to find some high schools teaching interior design, architecture, industrial design, ceramics, photography, book and magazine illustration, printmaking (etching, woodcut, lithography), graphic design, fabric design, silversmithing, and still other subjects that come under such vague headings as *art appreciation* and *arts and crafts.* The list could go on for a page. If you have several of these subjects to choose among, which ones deserve your time?

The value of a subject depends in part on how well it's taught. I once watched a superb teacher of design devote a week to showing his class how to split, whittle, and chop shapes out of bamboo. If any other teacher had scheduled this classroom project, it would have seemed a waste of time. But *he* made "bamboo week" an unforgettable episode in the lives of thirty future designers.

Nevertheless, I think it's possible to make a few generalizations about the comparative value of some common art subjects.

For the purposes of this chapter, it may be helpful to divide high school art subjects into *general* and *pre-professional.* By general, I mean basic subjects that are useful background for any art profession you may finally choose. By pre-professional, I mean subjects that prepare you for later professional training in a specific art field, but may not be useful background for some *other* art career.

If you haven't set your mind on a particular art field, then it's best to stick to subjects in the general category. Beyond the four basics—drawing, painting, sculpture, and art history—there are a number that can be valuable training for any art career.

Printmaking tends to teach the same lessons as drawing and painting. Unhappily, too few schools have etching presses, lithographic presses, and the other necessary equipment. Ceramics can be almost as good training as sculpture, with the added advantage that ceramics will teach you a lot about color. Again there's the trouble that not all schools can afford kilns, potters' wheels, and other equipment. Though illustration might be put in the pre-professional category, it has general value too. After all, illustration is just drawing or painting under another name.

Often a subject is given some vague title like *design* or *visual techniques*. If this means experimentation with color, line, texture, form, and other basic design elements, then this qualifies as good general background.

Now, what's the value of pre-professional subjects like industrial design, fabric design, and the others mentioned at the beginning of this section? Certainly, if you're dead set on being an industrial designer, it pays to take the subject in high school, *if* you can get it. The same holds true for any art profession you're *sure* you want to enter. If you're lucky enough to attend a high school that teaches the subject, take it. It's no substitute for professional training in art school, college or university, but it will help you when you get there.

But let me add one note of caution: you *may* change your mind about the art field you want to enter. Art schools are full of students who have switched majors, even as late as their senior year. This could happen to *you*. If you do change your mind, you'll be grateful for all the general subjects you've taken. Everything you learned from your drawing, painting, sculpture, and art history assignments can be used in your new career field, just as it was in your previous field.

In short, if your high school *does* offer the right pre-professional subject, you should certainly take it. But don't load up on pre-professional classwork at the *expense* of general art subjects. You may regret it.

Are industrial arts subjects worth taking?

Many high schools offer a variety of subjects roughly classed as *industrial arts*. A few of these may be useful to future artists, though in a limited way.

Woodworking, metalworking, and other "shop" subjects can be good experience for the future industrial designer, architect, interior designer, furniture designer, sculptor, or any other artist who works in three dimensions. These classes can be a good introduction to the problems of structure and materials.

Drafting, often called *mechanical drawing* in high school, is a skill no architect, industrial designer, or interior designer can get along without. This is a skill that's worth developing early *if* you're sure you're heading for one of these fields. High school can be a good place to begin.

The point is simply this: take these industrial arts subjects *only* if you're certain you're going into an art field where you can use them. There's no sense in taking metalworking or woodworking, for instance, if you hope to be an illustrator. Above all, don't invest so much time in industrial arts subjects that you neglect your other art classes.

Why are academic subjects necessary?

Earlier in this chapter, I pointed out that most high schools insist that you take a great many classes outside the art department. Most of these are the so-called academic subjects, such as English composition and literature, history, social studies, languages, music appreciation, mathematics, and sciences, like biology, chemistry, and physics. Why are these so important?

You'll find the most obvious reason by scanning a few art school catalogs. It's difficult to get into most good art schools, colleges, and universities without a reasonable number of academic subjects on your high school record.

But this isn't the only reason. A noted consultant in the interiors field once put it this way: "Take two young designers of equal talent and equal art training. The one with the richer education in the liberal arts and the sciences will go ahead faster."

With a *liberal education*, you know more about more things. Your curiosity reaches out in more directions. You read more and get more out of what you read. You express yourself more effectively, in writing or in conversation. You're like an athlete who's built up *all* your muscles, not just a few. This is why a good high school expects you to be more than a good *art* student. The high school's job isn't to train artists, but rather to build a *whole person*.

What extracurricular activities are good experience?

High school is more than classwork. All sorts of extracurricular activities can be part of your high school art training. These are good experience and they're a good thing to have on your record when you apply for admission to art school.

For example, high schools need posters that advertise everything from a dance to fire drill instructions. A poster is a good basic graphic design problem. Doing the lettering may be your introduction to typography. If the poster carries a picture, this can be a stimulating job for a future illustrator or photographer.

School publications—newspapers, magazines, yearbooks—often need illustrations too. And with the exception of the newspaper, traditionally "made up" by the editors, some future graphic designer must lay out all these pages before they go to the printer.

Stage sets for school plays also demand the services of artists and designers. Backdrops are paintings on a vast scale. Designing a set that's practical, durable, handsome, and easy to build—something that actors can really live with while they're on stage—can be fine experience for a future architect, industrial designer, or interior designer. The same holds true for the many exhibits that are designed and built in high schools each semester, another opportunity for the future architect or designer.

Every high school presents different opportunities. Is there a dance for which you can paint, carve, or construct decorations? Does the school need murals, reliefs, banners, new stationery? Is there a parade for which you can design floats? This is a good job for a future sculptor. These are all opportunities you should watch for. And there are many more.

What if your high school art program is too limited?

Not all high schools have adequate art programs. *Some have no art teacher at all.* Others may share an art teacher with neighboring schools. Still others may have one or more art teachers, but have such crowded classes that you can't get enough personal attention. What can you do if you can't get enough art instruction in your high school?

If your high school doesn't have a full-time art teacher, ask your advisor or your principal if it's possible to transfer to a nearby school that has a more ambitious art program. You may have to get up early in the morning and do some heavy commuting, but it might be worth the trouble.

If your art classes are crowded and you can't get enough of your teacher's time, your fellow students and your overworked art teacher may be just as frustrated as you are. If there are *enough* art majors to back you up, you may be able to get the school to hire an additional art teacher. Your present teacher may be delighted to get some help. Discuss the idea with teachers, your principal, the Parent-Teachers Association, and the school board.

If these suggestions turn out to be impractical, you may have to go outside the school for supplementary art training. Is there an art school within commuting distance? Many art schools now offer evening and weekend classes. Is there a local artist who teaches a private class? Your high school art teacher might be able to recommend someone.

What if you can't afford outside art classes? What if there's no art school nearby? Many outstanding artists have been self-taught, at least in their early years. Buy whatever art materials you can afford and devote all the time you can spare to painting, drawing, and sculpture. You'll be amazed at how much you can learn on your own by hard, steady work. We're told that Giotto, the first great artist of the Renaissance, was a shepherd boy who taught himself to draw with a stick in the dirt.

Your local library or bookstore can be a fair substitute for an art school. An extraordinary number of good art textbooks are now available. Distinguished art teachers have put their knowledge into print. If you *must* work on your own, these books are the next best thing to having a teacher at your elbow.

Must you major in art?

It's not uncommon for a high school student to decide on an art career in the senior year or even after graduation. By then, it's too late to switch to an art major. How can you catch up with your fellow students who *were* art majors?

As I explained a moment ago, you can still take some courses in a nearby art school. Or you can work independently, with the aid of some good art instruction books. Even if you've already graduated, there may still be time to take a summer course in art school or spend the summer working on your own.

Since time is short, it's wisest to concentrate on drawing and painting. Sculpture is a slow process, too slow if you're embarking on a "crash program" to prepare for art school in the fall. Better put that off until you're in art school.

But what if you didn't major in art, and circumstances have prevented spare-time study? What are your odds of getting into a good art school? Don't be discouraged. Many of the best art schools, colleges, and universities will give you a chance to prove yourself. This is one good purpose of the foundation year that begins many art school programs.

4
Choosing an art school

The dean of a well-known art school was talking to a little boy enrolled in the Saturday morning classes for children. "What made you come here?" the dean asked. The little fellow pondered the question for a moment. At last, he seemed to hit on the reason: "It smells better than the zoo."

Many mature artists look back to find that they picked their schools for reasons that weren't much better. A famed advertising art director worked as a farm laborer in his teens, saved just enough money for a year in art school, then hitchhiked 2000 miles to an obscure school whose ad caught his eye in a magazine. A noted illustrator picked her college because "the girls seemed so well dressed." A successful interior designer picked the university with the most picturesque campus: "I was impressed by the groves of trees and the ivy on the walls."

Choosing your art school, college, or university isn't that simple. You're investing years of your life and thousands of dollars. This isn't all that's at stake. Your professional future depends, in part, on your professional training. The wrong school can do damage that takes years to repair, *if* the damage can be repaired.

There are more bad schools than good. How do you pick a *good* school out of the hundreds that advertise, get listed in school directories, and mail catalogs to all comers? How can teenagers and their families—whose only contact with the complex art world has been the local high school—hope to make the right choice?

Where to go for information

Don't rely on your hunches. Don't rely on the so-called reputation of a particular school: reputations are often undeserved. When you finally settle on a school, your decision should be based on thorough, hard-headed research. This research isn't hard to do. Here are some suggestions about where to go for facts and opinions.

A logical place to begin is your high school. Your art teachers are often familiar with the art schools, colleges, and universities nearby. They may not know all the schools, but they've probably had students who went on to these schools and reported back. Your teacher may be a graduate of a local school. Over the years, your teacher probably gathered plenty of pros and cons. If your teacher is willing to recommend a school, that judgment is worth noting.

You should also talk to your high school's guidance counselors, sometimes called college advisors. They won't claim to be art experts, but like your art teacher, they've probably heard the reports of students who've gone on to various art schools, colleges, and universities. It's also their job to know something about the admission requirements, programs, facilities, and costs of these schools. They usually have stacks of catalogs and reference books with this data. If they don't have *all* the facts on hand, they'll know where to find more.

You should certainly try to meet graduates of the schools you're investigating. Your high school teachers and guidance counselors may know some who live nearby. As a matter of fact, there may be many local artists, designers, and architects who are worth meeting, whatever school they attended. A mutual friend or your high school art teacher might arrange an introduction. If there's no mutual friend to introduce you, I see no harm in getting the names of some professionals in the neighborhood and writing them a note. Not all of them will have time to see you. But you may be surprised how many busy men and women are willing to spend a few minutes advising young people. Even if they can spare just fifteen minutes, that conversation can mean a lot.

Obviously, you should try to visit the schools themselves. There can be no substitute for a first-hand look at faculty, students, facilities, and student work. Write or phone ahead for an appointment. There may be special visitors' days. When you arrive, don't be shy about bombarding faculty members with questions.

School catalogs come *last* on my list of information sources. Write for the catalog of every school that interests you. It will usually be mailed to you without charge. Catalogs contain useful data about faculty, course lists, admission and graduation requirements, deadline dates and calendars of events, descriptions of facilities, plus a lot more.

But many catalogs are meant to do more than inform. Their job is to advertise, to *sell* you. The photos naturally show the well-equipped studios and ignore the badly equipped workrooms elsewhere in the school. When "typical student work" is illustrated, it's far from typical. The rare examples of outstanding student work are shown. The text spotlights famous faculty members, though there's no reason to believe that celebrities make better teachers than lesser known men and women.

I must emphasize that I see nothing wrong with a catalog that tries to sell you. A school has every right to put its best foot forward. Nobody expects a catalog to show dingy classrooms and crude student work. But as you read a catalog, you must do your best to separate facts from sales talk.

Actually, catalogs that avoid sales talk are often worse. Year after year, an appalling number of schools issue catalogs that neither advertise *nor* inform. Many excellent schools have catalogs that are tastelessly designed, shabbily printed, haphazardly organized, and ponderously written. Few readers can wade through this morass of bureaucratic gobbledygook. Facts may be even *less* accessible than the facts in the sales-talk catalog.

If some schools' catalogs are obviously designed to lure you, many others seem designed to drive you away. This simply proves that you can't take a catalog at face value. Handsome publications don't necessarily come from good schools. Nor do shoddy publications always represent bad schools. Get lots of catalogs and read them as carefully as your patience allows, but don't pick or reject a school on the basis of its printed matter. A catalog is just one more source of information. It can answer some questions, but not others.

A checklist of questions you should ask

You can talk to all the people I've listed and read catalogs from cover to cover, but still end up knowing very little. It's too easy for people to tell you about schools in general terms, exchange pleasantries, and get way off the subject, letting you go home wondering what the conversation was all about. Reading can be just as useless. After you've read a few catalogs, they all begin to sound alike. Your head bulges with facts, but they don't line up in any useful order. They're just one big blur.

This won't happen if you know what facts you're looking for. You must plan your conversations as carefully as a newspaper reporter plans an interview with a busy celebrity who can spare just fifteen minutes. Nobody will resent it if you write down your questions in advance and show up with a little book to take notes. People will probably be flattered. It may also be helpful to keep certain questions in mind and take notes as you read a catalog. Or you may find it simpler to mark up the catalog with a red pencil as you read.

It's best to start out with a basic list of questions you'd like answered. You won't ask everyone *all* the questions, just the questions you think they can answer. You'll also find that unexpected questions not on your list will pop up as the conversation moves along. However, there are fourteen questions I'd like to suggest as your basic list. Though you may want to add some questions of your own, these fourteen represent the essential facts you need to know about any art school or university art department.

(1) How long is the school's program?

Most art educators have found that it takes at least four years to train an artist, designer, or architect. A few top art schools manage to do a good job in three, but most leading schools have standardized on four. Colleges and universities almost always have four-year programs. Subjects like architecture and industrial design often take five. Steer clear of art schools that offer shortcuts and promise "quick results" like some patent medicine.

One of the first things you should check in a school catalog is the length of the program. Keep in mind that a four-year program usually leads to a degree or some sort of certificate. In some art fields, degrees are vital. Part Two of this book—the chapters that deal with the various art professions—will tell you the fields in which degrees count. Keep in mind, too, that many schools allow you to get a degree in three years, *if* you attend summer classes.

(2) What majors are offered?

Many leading schools offer a separate professional program in each art field. There may be a distinct program in any of the major fields dealt with in this book: painting, sculpture, printmaking, illustration, graphic design, fabric design, interior design, architecture, industrial design, photography, art teaching, museum work, or crafts.

Other schools offer just one program, usually called a *general art major*. This includes a bit of everything. You can often take one or two courses in *any* of the fields I've listed. In a few fields—particularly fine art subjects like painting and drawing—there may be several classes open.

A third type of art program is really a compromise between the general art major and the specialized professional program. This is called a general art major with *areas of concentration*. You still take a bit of everything, but you also pick one or two art fields in which you take all the courses you can get.

Finally, there are highly specialized schools that teach just one subject, such as painting or photography.

Which kind of school is best? I'd choose the school that offers a separate professional program in each art field. Or I'd pick the school that offers a general art major with areas of concentration, provided I could take *a lot* of courses in my special field. Unfortunately, many schools *claim* to offer areas of concentration within the general art major, but this often means nothing more than a couple of extra courses.

Without a real area of concentration—a solid block of specialized courses—the general art major just doesn't qualify as professional training. After four years, you may discover that you know a little about lots of things, but you're not really a professional in any single art field. When the time comes to land a job, you'll find it hard to compete with graduates who majored or concentrated in a specific art profession.

My objection to the one-subject school is quite different. Actually, a highly specialized school often does an excellent teaching job just because it concentrates on one subject. But you have to be mighty sure you want to be an interior designer, for example, before you enroll in a school that teaches nothing but interior design. Few students have picked their art field before they enter art school. They know they want to be some sort of artist, but they haven't settled on a particular art profession yet. It takes a year or two of experimentation, maybe more, to find out. Even when students feel sure at last, they often change their minds. In the one-subject school, you obviously can't experiment with several art fields. Nor can you switch your major or shift your area of concentration if your professional interests change.

What about teachers' colleges, where you can study only art teaching? Aren't *these* one-subject schools? As you'll find when you read Chapter 13 on art teaching, a good teachers' college actually offers the equivalent of a general art major. Furthermore, the best teacher's colleges encourage you to concentrate in one or more art fields.

A school's catalog will tell you what majors or areas of concentration are offered. It should also specify what courses are available in your area of concentration. If the catalog is unclear, ask when you visit the school.

(3) How flexible is the program?

Contact with many art fields is an essential part of your education. Though I've stressed the importance of specialization, you *should* have the freedom to take courses in many fields outside your major or your area of concentration. Good schools often insist that you *elect* several art classes from a list of subjects distantly related to your major.

Unhappily, there's one notable exception to this rule. Architectural programs are often rigidly separated from other art programs. In many universities, the architectural school is kept entirely divorced from the art or design school, and the two have amazingly little contact. I think architectural training has been severely damaged by the separation. The most you can do is pick an architectural school that will allow you some slight freedom to take courses in other art fields.

A school's catalog will probably list *electives* along with required courses. Again, if the catalog is unclear, you can check when you visit the school.

(4) Does the program begin with a foundation year?

Most good art programs begin with what educators call a *foundation year*, a year of basic training. This includes fundamentals like drawing, painting, sculpture, printmaking, design in two and three dimensions, and art history. You have no major subject this first year. Or if you do have a major in a specific art field, you take only a few classes in this field. Most foundation year courses are required: they're the same whatever your major or your area of concentration.

This year of basic training has two purposes: it builds up your muscles for the more advanced courses you'll face in the years ahead. And, equally important, this exploratory year helps you get to know yourself better in preparation for choosing a major or an area of concentration.

The school catalog will tell you whether there's a foundation year. Remember that it doesn't *have* to be called the *foundation year*. It might be called the *orientation year* or have no name at all. The thing to look for is a list of first year required courses: basic subjects which all students must take.

When you visit the school, you can get more details about the first year course list. Alumni of the school can also supply you with details.

(5) How much emphasis is placed on fine art?

Just as your year of basic training emphasizes the fine art subjects on which all art is based—drawing, painting, sculpture, printmaking—your advanced years should include some of these too. If you major in a fine art field, of course, you'll be able to take a great many. But you should continue to absorb these fundamentals no matter what your major.

After the foundation year, many schools continue to *require* fine art courses in succeeding years. If not, the school may arrange your program with gaps for *elective* fine art courses. In the latter case, the choice is left up to you. Either way is good.

Check the course lists in the catalog for fine art requirements and electives. You might also discuss this with faculty members and alumni.

(6) Are the advanced courses really professional?

Beyond basic fine art subjects, a school's program must include many specialized, practical, professional courses. These courses must really duplicate—as far as any class can—what you'll be doing for a living when you graduate. Industrial designers should develop and build products that really work, that could be made on a real production line and sold. Graphic designers should create pages that could be sent right down to the printer, ads that could sell real products. Painters, sculptors, and printmakers should be expected to turn out work that is of exhibition caliber.

These seem like obvious requirements. They're certainly obvious to your future employer, client, agent, or dealer. Yet a surprising number of schools make no attempt to duplicate professional working conditions. Design students, for example, are often starved for practical problems while they mark time in fine art classes and classes in design theory. These fundamental subjects *are* vital. But devoting *too* much time to such courses is a common dodge: this can be a school's way of covering up its inability to teach *professional* design subjects.

Fine art programs are often *frankly* non-professional. Many painting, drawing, and sculpture classes—particularly in colleges and universities—are given as a form of recreation, like sports or "social dancing." Amateurs and future professionals may work side by side in the same classroom. Hobbyists almost always outnumber professionals in these classes, and the instructors are *forced* to devote most of their time to the amateurs.

How can you find out whether a school's program is *really* professional? The catalog won't tell you. Nor will the faculty. You have to ask local artists, designers, and architects who've hired graduates and tested their professional skill. Above all, talk to alumni. After a few years on the job, they'll know how well, or how badly, the school prepared them for a career in the competitive art world.

(7) Are liberal arts and science courses included?

In the previous chapter, I stressed the importance of academic (or liberal arts) subjects in high school—pointing out that the function of high school isn't to train professional artists, but to develop well rounded young men and women. Colleges, universities, and most of our art schools will also expect you to take a fair number of liberal arts and science courses—essential if you want a degree—on the assumption that broadly educated people make the most successful artists, designers, and architects.

Frankly, I think this is a *debatable* assumption. When I was an art school administrator, I believed in the gospel of the *well-rounded man or woman* (I was paid to believe in it), but now I have my doubts. Among the hundreds of successful people I've met in the art world, there are plenty who do owe their success to a well-rounded education, but there are also many who went to the top because they had one-track minds, with room in their heads for nothing but art. You may be the sort of artist whose creative powers are enriched and invigorated by studying the liberal arts and the sciences; or you may be so absorbed in your art that courses in anything else seem irrelevant and distracting. Whether you have a one-track mind or the multi-track mind of the well-rounded person, there's room for you in the art world either way.

Unfortunately for the one-track mind, our educational system is rigged in favor of the well-rounded student. Our college and university programs are dedicated to the concept of a *liberal education* leading to a degree, which means plenty of liberal arts and sciences. And many of our art schools are now patterned after liberal arts colleges.

If you lean toward a broad education—and if you definitely want a degree—one advantage of a college or university is that you can take so many more courses in the liberal arts and sciences. Colleges and universities usually teach these subjects better than art schools. An art school often recognizes this and arranges for students to take their academic courses at a nearby college or university. However, some of the bigger art schools now have their own courses in the liberal arts and sciences, taught by full-time faculty members or by teachers borrowed from other institutions.

The subjects are similar to the academic courses taught in high school, though on a more advanced level, of course. You'll be required to take a selection of the following: English composition and speech; literature; history and social sciences; philosophy; mathematics; psychology; sciences like chemistry, physics, geology, biology, astronomy, and others; perhaps a modern foreign language like French, German, Spanish, Italian, Russian. You'll also be expected to take subjects like physical education and hygiene. Depending upon the size of the school, there may be other subjects like political science, American civilization, anthropology, and still more. Check a school's catalog to find out what academics are offered and which are required.

If you dread the idea of taking lots of liberal arts and science courses, you'll face less of this in an art school than in a college or university. In fact, some art schools will let you skip the academic subjects entirely if you wish. You get a degree if you take the academics along with the art; you get a certificate or diploma (but not a degree) if you skip the academics and take *only* art. But let me repeat that most good art schools do offer degrees, for which you *must* take a certain minimum number of academics.

If you're headed for a degree, be sure you pick a school that gives you a rich selection of academic subjects, provided that your art courses don't play second fiddle. Even if you're taking a degree program under protest—because you must have it for professional reasons—it makes sense to get the most stimulating academic program you can find. You might enjoy it more than you think.

(8) How stiff are the school's standards?

When I asked a friend why he left his teaching job at a large state university, he explained: "Anybody can get into this place and anybody can get a diploma." This, in a nutshell, is what educators mean when they say a school has low standards.

Good schools have stiff admission requirements. They ask for a transcript of your high school record and hope to see good grades on the sheet. They check on your extracurricular activities. They want letters of reference from your teachers and from intelligent people who've known you for years. If you don't measure up, the school sends you a polite rejection note.

Good schools may not be easy to get into, but they're even harder to stay in. They expect you to work hard to maintain passing grades. If you don't, out you go. Nor are good schools satisfied with grades that are *merely* passing. The school may not be able to toss you out, but your faculty advisor may encourage you to drop out or try a new field.

Rugged graduation standards are a moral obligation. A British designer once defined a good art school as "a place that throws you out *for your own good* if your teachers don't think you can earn a living when you graduate." A responsible art teacher knows that he can't honestly accept tuition money from a student who'll never be a professional. The school is cheating such students if they let them stay.

Will a school let you spend four or five years there if you're unfit for an art career? Or will the faculty be honest enough to forget your tuition money and tell you to move on, even if your grades are barely passing? These are painful questions, but you *must* ask them. Ask your high school art teachers. They know which art schools took the least promising students and which took only the best ones. Alumni will recall whether passing grades were too easy to get. Other local artists, designers, and architects have probably seen recent graduates on job hunts. Ask these professionals whether non-professionals are allowed to graduate and embark on hopeless job campaigns.

(9) How good are the instructors?

Schools like to boast that faculty members are professional artists, designers, and architects, not just teachers. This isn't the only test of a teacher's qualifications, but it's a good one. Art, design, and architecture—like other professions—are hard to teach well unless the instructors spend part of their lives *doing* what they teach. Good schools hire seasoned professionals and give them free time to continue outside work.

But the old "practicing-artists-make-the-best-teachers" line mustn't be taken *too* seriously. Many fine teachers devote very little time to their art. The best painting teacher I've ever known was a mediocre weekend painter. It was his *students* who became good painters. His art wasn't painting, but teaching. He gave his energy and inspiration to his students and saved very little for his paintings.

By the same logic, first-rate professionals may be second-rate teachers. They may give all their energy and inspiration to their own work and save none for their students.

Beware of big names. Art schools, colleges, and universities like to list famous people as faculty members or under such vague titles as coordinators, visiting critics, or consultants. Though many of these people do make an important contribution to the school's program, plenty of others just lend their names on the condition that no work is required. If they do show up, it's once a year to give a brief talk or to criticize student portfolios. It's important to find out whether celebrities really turn up in the classroom or if they just appear in the catalog as window dressing.

Catalogs sometimes carry brief biographies of faculty members. Read these but keep in mind that this is all part of the catalog's sales talk. Alumni and other professionals are the best people to ask about a school's faculty.

(10) Are the school's facilities adequate?

One important reason to visit a school is to see the campus and walk through the classrooms. Arrange your visit well in advance so there's time to schedule a tour, not just a brief chat.

Examine the classrooms just as you would your future home. Are studios well lit? Plenty of daylight? Plenty of artificial light for dim days? Is there enough room so students aren't jammed together, too close to the model, unable to see over all the shoulders? Is there plenty of air? A stuffy room reeking of turpentine, rubber cement, and fixative is a tough place to work.

Equipment is just as important as surroundings. Do easels and drawing boards look sturdy and professional, not flimsy and makeshift? Do the industrial designers have shops with well-kept machinery to build things? Do the graphic designers have real metal type to set, plus a printing press or two? Do photography students have a spacious studio, lots of lights, and a thoroughly equipped darkroom?

What other facilities are there? A large, well-stocked library? An art materials store that sells supplies at cut rates? An exhibition gallery where student *and* professional work is shown? An art collection? An audio-visual department, with motion picture, video, and slide projection equipment? A collection of movies, videotapes, film strips, and slides?

I won't try to give you a complete checklist of the faciities an ideal school should have. But these few paragraphs should suggest the *sort* of things to watch for.

However, don't expect things to look neat and new. School equipment takes incredible punishment. An easel is covered with dried paint and a book with thumbprints after a few months' use. Much equipment comes second-hand and is reconditioned and kept in working order for generations of students.

The same holds true for the campus. Don't expect every good school to have bright, new, steel-and-glass buildings or ivy-covered collegiate gothic. Many great schools are in dingy, tumbledown architectural monstrosities. It's what goes on *inside* the buildings that counts.

After you've toured a school, compare impressions with other people. Talk to alumni. They've *lived* in the school. Talk to your high school art teacher and guidance counselor. They may have toured the school recently on a special visitors' day for educators. If not, you might be able to arrange your own visitors' day for a group of students and teachers from your high school. Your teachers' practiced eyes will spot a lot that you might miss.

(11) What extracurricular activities are there?

A good school regards extracurricular activities as part of your training. These activities are carefully planned and encouraged by faculty members, often specially appointed for the purpose.

Professionally, the *least* important extracurricular affairs are dances, alumni reunions, and sports, which *most* schools have. But what are the activities that relate directly to your professional training? Are there student clubs that hold exhibitions and invite distinguished speakers from various professional fields? Are student committees responsible for school events like forums, film programs, competitions, exhibitions? Do these clubs or committees arrange student tours of artists' studios, designers' and architects' offices? Is there a school magazine or newspaper for which students write and illustrate articles on professional subjects?

Catalogs often list extracurricular activities. Faculty members and alumni can give you details.

(12) Does the school have a placement service?

The climax of your years in school isn't the moment you get your diploma. It's the moment you get your first paycheck. If you can't find work when you graduate, your professional training has been wasted. Recognizing this fact, many leading art schools, colleges, and universities have set up special offices to find work for graduates.

A school's placement service functions something like an employment agency, though, of course, the service is free. The placement office gets to know potential employers in the community and other parts of the country. At the same time, the office gets to know the students by studying their records, talking to instructors, and interviewing the students themselves. When they have openings to fill, employers call the placement office. The placement director knows where to find the right person for the job. Often it works the other way. After spotting a particularly good student, the placement director may phone an employer out of the blue: "I think you should meet a student who's graduating this year. Just the right type for your office."

Frequently a school's placement method is more informal, though it may be just as good. Individual faculty members are expected to keep in touch with potential employers. When employers have an opening, they call the instructors, who select candidates from their classes. Even schools that *have* formal placement procedures often rely on these informal methods. It's important for a school to have a placement service of *some* sort, formal or informal, so that students aren't just handed a diploma and flung out into the world.

A good placement office may also get part-time and summer jobs for students. A few visionary schools (*too* few) have so-called *cooperative programs*—alternating periods of study and on-the-job training—and such a program is also the responsibility of the placement office.

If a school has a placement office, the catalog usually says so. But it won't say how active or effective the service is. Nor will the catalog say how much informal placement is done through the faculty. Ask about placement when you visit the school. It's even more revealing to ask alumni who may or *may not* have gotten jobs through the school. You might also talk to local artists, designers, and architects who may recruit talent from the school. They'll know how well the service works for the *employer*.

(13) Where do graduates find work?

Where do graduates find their first jobs and where do they go from there? This double-barreled question is the ultimate test of a school.

Every school, even the worst, can point to a few alumni who've made their mark in the world. I know one mediocre art school that continues to boast about a world-famous painter who spent a few weeks there thirty years ago. A few famous names mean nothing. Where do the *bulk* of the students go from school? Can the school honestly say that graduates in the top half of their class can expect *good* jobs? Can the faculty honestly claim that the others—except for the *just passing* students who weren't wise enough to drop out—get *decent* jobs? How many students don't find jobs at all?

No school catalog dares to answer these questions unless the placement record is unusually good. Nor can you count on faculty members for a straight answer unless the record is really impressive. You must ask the alumni and the local artists, designers, and architects who employ them.

(14) Is the school accredited?

In each part of the country, educators have set up accrediting groups that rate local colleges and universities. When a school asks to be accredited, the group sends in a team of investigators to examine the faculty, courses, facilities, and standards. If the school passes this rigorous examination, the catalog proudly announces accreditation. Most good colleges and universities are accredited by these regional groups.

Many art schools now grant degrees and aspire to the status of colleges; a number of these have won accreditation from groups that accredit colleges and universities. Most—but not *all*—good art schools are accredited by the National Association of Schools of Art and Design. In choosing an architectural school, be sure to look for the stamp of approval of the National Architectural Accrediting Board.

For an *art school*, how important is accreditation really? If an art school meets the requirements listed in this chapter, don't turn up your nose because its catalog doesn't carry the stamp of the regional accrediting body. On the other hand, if an art school *is* accredited, this is one more argument in the school's favor.

When picking a *college* or *university*, on the other hand, accreditation really counts. But remember that accreditation is no *guarantee* that a college or university can turn out a professional artist. The school may still do an inferior job in the complex field of art. When the time comes to select a school, you must do *your own* accrediting. That's what this chapter is for.

An exception: fine art

Having argued so fiercely for a formal, well-planned art education, I think it's important to name one artist who's an exception: the fine artist. Many of our best painters, sculptors, and printmakers have had the most *informal* sort of training or no training at all.

Though architects and designers normally spend four or five years in one school, fine artists often wander from one school to another, from one private teacher to another, or simply work on their own. They follow their instincts and work out their own curriculum as they go along. Then discipline isn't imposed by a school, but comes from within.

For many noted painters, sculptors, and printmakers, this informal kind of education has worked well. If you choose your teachers wisely, you can tailor your education to fit you as precisely as a custom-made suit. But you're taking a chance. If you make the wrong choices, you can do yourself real harm. If you lack self-discipline, there's no school program to impose discipline. Like too many art students, you can waste years coasting through various schools and private classes without ever being nailed down to serious work.

So then, there *are* some valid reasons for formal training even in fine art. By long trial-and-error, a good school has developed a program that fits most students reasonably well. The school knows that this program won't fit every student perfectly, so your course schedule is usually flexible enough to let you experiment with various instructors and subjects. With the advice of your teachers, you *are* encouraged to make many of your own decisions. For every successful fine artist who followed his or her hunches and wandered from school to school, there's another who voted for formal training and spent years in just *one* school.

And don't overlook one other argument, and a powerful one, for formal training. The next chapter will tell you that few fine artists make a living at painting, sculpture, or printmaking. For many of them, teaching jobs are the main source of income. And many of the best teaching jobs demand a degree, which means at least four years of formal training.

A word about small colleges

The fourteen-point checklist you've just read eliminates many small colleges. Often the best liberal arts and teachers' colleges are just too small to have the full-scale, professional program advocated in this chapter. Does this mean that a future artist, designer, or architect should steer away from small colleges?

On the contrary, a good, small college is a splendid choice *if* you recognize the purpose of such a school. Liberal arts colleges—plus the many teachers' colleges now set up on similar lines—educate the whole person. Their purpose is to provide a broad education in the liberal arts and the sciences, the kind of education that builds a solid intellectual foundation for any profession you may choose.

Many talented artists, designers, and architects go to a small college first, take all the art they can, along with all their other courses, *then* go to art school for real professional training. Several top art schools have special two-year programs for college graduates. Other art schools will arrange special programs on request. This combination of college and art school takes time, but I'm tempted to say that this is the ideal training for a future artist *if* you can afford it.

The role of the small art school

My fourteen-point checklist also seems to eliminate the small art school and the private class. Yet it's certainly true that many of our leading fine artists have gone to schools with just two or three faculty members working in a loft on some side street. Other have studied with an artist in a studio and never gone to school at all. Just what can the small school or private class contribute?

I've already pointed out that *fine art* training can be quite informal. Some of the greatest names in painting, sculpture, and printmaking conduct private classes or teach in schools that don't have a formal program or grant a degree.

A small school may also be particularly good if the teachers stick to just one subject like photography or fashion illustration. This sort of school might also be useful for a limited, rather technical subject like drafting or photo-retouching.

A private class or a small school may also be an exciting *supplement* to the program of a bigger school. If you're majoring in fabric design at a big, four-year school, you may still want the inspiration of working Saturdays or summers in the private class of a noted weaver.

If your formal training is behind you and you want to switch fields, a few courses in a small, specialized school may be all you need to add the necessary background. For example, if you're an illustrator who wants to move into the related field of graphic design, all you may need are some classes in layout and typography. A small school or private class may also be an ideal place for a refresher course in some half-forgotten subject.

What most small school are *not* good for is the comprehensive professional program on which most art careers are built. Such schools have neither the staff nor the facilities to do a job this big.

Evening and Saturday classes

Many art schools and university art departments offer professional programs in the evening or on Saturdays. Such part-time programs are planned for students who work during the day. These courses may lead to some sort of certificate or even to a degree.

Part-time training has some obvious drawbacks, but it also has some advantages that are often overlooked. The most conspicious drawback is simply that part-time education takes so terribly long. If full-time training takes four years, equivalent work in evening and Saturday classes may take twice that long. A school's usual solution is to offer a stripped-down version of the daytime program. At its best, this is a really concentrated series of courses, an intensive professional program for people who are willing to work *harder* than day students. At its worst, this often turns out to be a superficial program, covering less territory in less detail.

But there are also real advantages in evening and Saturday classes. If you're working at an art job of some kind during the day, and attending art school at night, your lessons may seem far more real than they do to the full-time student who's never really worked at art professionally. You apply by day what you learn at night. Another advantage of evening and Saturday classes is that you sometimes get better teachers than during the day. Many top professionals can't spare the time to teach during the day, but they *can* teach after hours.

Should you work during the day and go to school part-time? Yes, but only if you *must*. If you can afford four or five years of full-time training, you'll have more fun, be less exhausted, and probably get a more complete education. But if you have to earn money during the day, part-time training is your only way of becoming an artist. Pick your part-time school as carefully as you'd pick a full-time school. The same fourteen questions apply.

A final warning about choosing a school

Art is a profession and, like all professions, demands long, hard, and well-organized training. But few art schools or university art departments can meet the professional standards set forth in these pages.

Unlucky students pay the price. Each year, thousands of would-be artists finish school and begin pounding the pavements looking for jobs, freelance assignments, and one-artist shows. They've been led to believe that they're professionals, destined to move ahead in a glamorous and rewarding field. But too few really have the talent or training to survive in the fierce competition of the art world. For each graduate of professional caliber, there are others who'll take dead-end jobs if they can get them, stay there, or drop out of the field altogether.

Week after week, employers see the crude portfolios and hopeful faces of the beginners who won't make the grade.

There are the students who've spent a year or two in some fly-by-night school, taking a few painting and drawing classes, plus a few courses in some vague subject called *commercial art*. All they have to show for their money are some battered oil paintings, some crudely lettered posters and book jackets, a few dog-eared charcoal sketches, and some examples of photo-retouching.

There are also graduates of bigger, better known art schools who should never have gotten a diploma. Maybe the school couldn't afford to refuse their tuition money. Maybe the instructors never had the courage to flunk them out or advise them to leave. Whatever the reason, these unlucky students are in the wrong field and no one has had the guts to tell them.

Then there are college and university graduates who took an art major without realizing that they weren't really enrolled in a professional program. Their teachers had never really decided whether the program was meant to train real artists or simply "raise the cultural level of the students." There were many courses that were *almost* professional, but not quite, a lot of classes in a lot of subjects, but not enough in *any single* subject. Misguided graduates walk the streets with their portfolios and are stunned to discover that they're not equipped to hold down a job in *any* art field. They're not even sure which art field they want.

Most painful are the job hunters who have obvious talent but chose the wrong school. Too often the wrong school is a large, widely publicized art school, college, or university that fails to live up to its reputation. In the *right* school, these students would have blossomed. but they chose the school by its *name*, not by its performance, and their talent has been allowed to stagnate. After four years, they're still amateurs and may remain amateurs for life. They *know* they're good—or could be—and wonder why no one offers them a job.

These young people have been cheated. Their teachers have permitted them to invest money, time, and hope in a worthless education. It takes a long, depressing job hunt to reveal the grim truth. Some of the talented ones will make it in spite of their inadequate training. They'll teach *themselves* or go back to school, a good school this time. But others, perhaps just as talented, will be permanently maimed. And God knows what happens to all those whose barely passing grades encouraged them to stay in a profession where they don't belong!

Choosing the right school is far from easy. Few art schools or university art departments can give satisfactory answers to all fourteen questions in the checklist you've just read. But you must insist that a school give *reasonable* answers to *most* of them. Your professional future depends on these answers.

Choosing your major subject in art school

Having picked your school, your next problem is to pick the art subject you plan to major in, or the subject you'll choose for your area of concentration if you're taking a general art major.

For most students, this is a difficult choice. There's so much you need to know about each field before you can decide. What sort of work do you actually do in a particular art field? What must you study to prepare for the job? What's a typical first job like? What will later jobs be like?

As I've already pointed out, your first year of training, the *foundation year*, is planned to give you a taste of many kinds of work. However, the foundation year can't answer *all* your questions. Its main purpose is to help you get to know yourself—your skills and your leanings—so that you can answer *your own* questions. Just as you did when you picked a school, you have to do some research. Talk to students in advanced classes—they've already picked their majors—and ask what their classes are like. Attend lectures by visiting professionals and fire questions at them. Talk to your teachers and to every professional who's willing to share his or her knowledge with you.

The chapters that follow are meant to help you in your fact-finding. Each of these chapters presents a thumbnail sketch of a professional art field. For each field, I'll try to answer the basic questions most students have on their minds. As you read these chapters, compare one art career with another and measure yourself against all of them. Just where do your personality, your interests, and your abilities seem to fit?

PART TWO
Choosing a Career

5
Fine art

The Mexican muralist, Diego Rivera, rarely worked outdoors. But one afternoon, a peasant discovered Rivera in a field, working on an immense canvas. The canvas was covered with daubs of color. Even more color was piled on the small wooden palette in the artist's hand. For ten minutes, the peasant watched Rivera's brush flash from palette to canvas, then from canvas back to palette. The artist turned and asked, "What do you think?" The peasant replied solemnly, "It is very beautiful. But tell me, do you take the colors from the piece of wood and put them on the canvas, or do you take them from the canvas and put them on the piece of wood?"

The story contains a lesson. If you plan to devote your life to fine art—painting, drawing, sculpture, printmaking—be prepared for lots of public curiosity, but not much understanding. It takes real courage to become a fine artist. This is the toughest of all art careers.

What is fine art?

Most teenagers begin as would-be fine artists. They draw, paint, carve wood, model clay. They do this for no "practical" purpose, just for the joy of expressing themselves. Perhaps this is the simplest way to explain the phrase *fine art*, in contrast with what's sometimes called *useful* or *applied* art. Fine art—a drawing, painting, sculpture, or print—is an end in itself. You hang it on a wall or set it on a pedestal and there it stands. Unlike applied art—a building, a fabric, or a piece of furniture—fine art has no job to do. Its only function is to be looked at and enjoyed.

By the time they reach art school, many teenage artists decide to channel their skills into the applied arts. The young painter may become an illustrator or graphic designer. The young sculptor may turn to architecture or industrial design. But despite parents' and teachers' warnings to "be practical," a surprising number of young people make the courageous decision to stay in a fine art career.

Can a fine artist earn a living?

If you plan to devote your life to painting, drawing, sculpture, or printmaking, there's one unpleasant fact you *must* face. You can't count on earning a living by the sale of your work.

Many surveys have been conducted among the nation's fine artists to find out how they make a living. Inevitably, the researchers find that most artists depend on sales for only a small part of their income. As a painter friend of mine put it, "When you sell a picture, it's like finding money in the street: great when it happens, but you can never count on it."

Most fine artists rely on some other source for the bulk of their income. For many artists, this source is a teaching job. Painters and printmakers often do freelance illustration or graphic design; or they hold down steady jobs in these fields. There are sculptors who design furniture and painters who design fabrics. And there are many fine artists who make their living at something totally unrelated to art. Among the best artists I know are an engineer, a lawyer, a dentist, a writer, two actors, and a beautician.

You may ask: "What about the really big name artists, the ones who exhibit at the big New York galleries, get into museum collections, and get written up in art magazines? Don't *they* live by selling their work?"

The unhappy truth is that even well established artists usually teach or do something else outside their studios. Even among artists with international reputations, only a handful can afford to spend *all* their time in the studio. These are the few "greats" whose names are almost household words; leaders of some style momentarily in vogue, like the "abstract expressionists" who dominated the 1950s, the "pop" and "op" artists who leapt to fame in the 1960s, or the photo-realists of the 1980s; a small circle of society portraitists; plus a few lucky mavericks who fit no current vogue, but whose style has somehow caught on. But most good painters, sculptors, and printmakers quietly accept fate and take some sort of outside job.

Why is it so hard for fine artists to live on the sale of their work? Artists advance all sorts of reasons. Some say there can't be enough customers to buy all the art that's produced. The supply is said to exceed the demand. Others blame art dealers' business methods: high prices; inadequate publicity; too much emphasis on a small, upper class buying public; too little interest in selling art to the public at large. Still others point out that contemporary art is too complex to have widespread public appeal. And artists currently riding high emphasize that the art world is fickle: "Though you may be selling like mad, you can't be sure your luck will last. At any moment, the wind can shift. Then you're glad to have a steady job and a weekly paycheck."

Whatever the reasons, you just can't count on being one of the lucky few who live on fine art. You *must* expect to earn your living some other way, perhaps teaching, perhaps in another art field, or even *outside* the art world. Fine artists accept this situation grudgingly. But they refuse to be discouraged. If this prospect *does* discourage you, fine art is no place for you.

Jobs for fine artists

Though fine art may be your first love, you must be realistic and plan ahead for the job that's going to earn you the income you can't get from your paintings, drawings, prints, or sculpture. There *are* jobs in other art fields, where you can make a decent living and still devote time to fine art.

Teaching seems to be the most common job among fine artists. Art schools and university art departments have expanded rapidly. Elementary, junior, and senior high schools employ more art teachers than ever before. Although the highly-publicized job boom for teachers ended in the 1970s as school enrollments tapered off, there's still the usual job turnover at art schools, colleges, universities, elementary and high schools as teachers retire or switch jobs. As in all art and design fields, competition for such jobs is keen—keener than it's been in years. And don't forget that there are art teachers in many museums, YMCA's, YMHA's, and community centers.

Though teachers are modestly paid in comparison with many other professions, artists feel that teaching is the one job that allows enough time for studio work. You *don't* teach forty hours a week. You *may* not teach every day. And you get vacations that make nonteachers green with envy *if* you don't have to work summers to pick up extra money.

As I've said, many fine artists hold down 9-to-5 jobs in the applied arts. Others feelance from their own studios. Fine artists who work in the applied arts claim two advantages over teachers. If you're good, you can make more money. And many fine artists feel they'd rather spend 9-to-5 producing *some* sort of art, architecture, or design, even if it's not fine art. But in holding down a 9-to-5 job or maintaining an active freelance practice, many artists complain that they spend all their creative energy. "When I get home at night," says one art director, "I've got nothing left for my painting. I just can't pick up a brush."

Short of inheriting a fortune, there's no ideal solution. There are pros and cons to *any* job a fine artist takes to earn a living. But you have to decide. You must pick a job that gives you reasonable satisfaction and a comfortable, if not luxurious, income. Having made your choice, you must then have the self-discipline to live a double life successfully. You're a teacher or an applied artist during "working hours," a fine artist whenever your time is free. You have to measure out your time and energy to handle both careers. You're like a runner who has two races to run in a single day: you must budget your strength to win both.

What does a fine artist study?

It's vital to pick your future job early, so you can plan a double education to fit your double life. In the right art school, college, or university, you can set up a program that will train you simultaneously for a career in fine art and a career in teaching or applied art. This is one more reason for choosing your school with care. Not all schools have a wide enough range of courses to perform this dual function.

If you're considering a career in fine art, you should still read the chapters that follow, each dealing with an applied art career that *might* be your job, even if your first love is painting, sculpture, or printmaking. Each chapter describes the job in some detail and tells you what applied art courses you should expect to take along with your fine-art subjects. Certainly, if you expect to pair fine art with a teaching career, you should read Chapter 13 for a realistic view of the teaching profession and the training required.

Now, what fine art subjects can you expect to take? Though the professionals often disagree violently on what kind of training makes a good painter, sculptor, or printmaker, there *are* certain subjects you're likely to find in most fine art programs.

Painters, sculptors, and printmakers are all required to take lots of drawing. Classes normally draw the nude and clothed figure, plaster casts of sculpture, plus various other still life objects from bottles to bananas. When the weather is decent, you'll probably go outdoors to sketch the landscape, architecture, passers-by, and even the animals in the local zoo. You'll also be asked to draw from your imagination and try abstract experiments with line, tone, and texture. Instruction in the principles of perspective is standard. And you'll get a chance to try out a variety of drawing media: pencil, charcoal, pen-and-ink, brush-and-ink, wash (usually black or brown watercolor), chalk, or even something exotic like silverpoint.

One brief word about drawing the nude. Life classes, as they're called in the trade, aren't an educational burlesque show invented by professional Peeping Toms. Artists' models aren't movie stars; most are far from glamorous. Life classes are important simply because drawing the nude figure teaches you more about the craft of drawing than you'll learn from still life, landscape, or any other subject.

Few schools permit you to *major* in drawing, by the way, just as few professional artists devote their full time to drawing. In school, as in your professional life, you'll probably concentrate on painting, sculpture, or printmaking, with plenty of drawing courses thrown in. Of course, you may be one of those rare birds who wants to do nothing but draw. In that case, you may still be obligated to choose painting, sculpture, or printmaking as your *theoretical* area of concentration, but a sympathetic school should be willing to arrange your program to include more drawing than usual.

Painters are obviously expected to take a lot of painting courses, exploring such media as oil, watercolor, acrylic, tempera, casein, and pastel. Early classes usually emphasize still life. You then move on to landscape, the nude and clothed figure, portraiture, and abstraction. Painters rarely take sculpture classes, except during the foundation year, when most schools require some basic training in three dimensions. Printmaking, however, is often part of the painter's program.

But what *is* a print? Instead of painting a picture on a canvas or drawing it on a sheet of paper, the printmaker incises it on a copper plate, cuts it into a block of wood, or draws it on a slab of limestone with a grease pencil. The plate, block, or stone can be inked, covered with a sheet of paper, then run through a press. When the sheet of paper—the print—is peeled off, it carries the image that was on the copper, wood, or limestone. Thus, the print is an original work of art that comes from the artist's own hand. A great advantage of printmaking is that the artist can produce dozens of identical originals and sell them at a modest price.

The printmaking media are sometimes called the "graphic arts" or just plain "graphics." I've avoided these terms here to prevent confusion with the very different profession of graphic design, which will be discussed in a later chapter.

There are many ways to make prints, all more complicated than I've made them sound, of course, and the student printmaker tries various methods before settling on one or more favorite techniques. You may try half a dozen ways of making prints from copper plates, like etching, aquatint, engraving, and others. You'll probably try doing woodcuts and wood engravings. You may do lithographs on zinc plates as well as stone. Most often, you begin by working in black and white, then move into color printmaking when you've developed enough skill. You also have to accumulate *far* more purely technical information than the painter: about chemicals used to process plates and stones; about the mechanics of etching and lithographic presses; plus a thousand details about papers, inks, and other materials of the trade.

The painter-printmaker is a frequent combination. Just as painters generally take some printmaking classes, printmakers normally take painting. Sculpture also attracts some printmakers. Though few schools require printmakers to take sculpture beyond the foundation year, you should be able to elect advanced courses in this subject.

Though the painter and printmaker share many classes, the sculptor's training follows a very different road after the foundation year. You're most likely to begin by exploring a variety of materials and techniques. You may model clay figures; carve wood and stone; construct abstract forms in wood, plaster, metal, wire, paper. As you advance, you'll probably channel your energies into a specific medium: you may find you're most comfortable carving, rather than modeling; or you may discover that you do your best work in welded metal. Naturally, your subject matter tends to be limited to the human figure, animals, and abstract shapes. Still life and landscape are more the territory of the painter and printmaker.

Sculpture, like printmaking, demands a lot of technical knowhow. If you model in clay, you must learn to make plaster or metal casts of your clay originals. Building armatures—wood and metal skeletons inside clay figures—is a craft in itself. So is the manufacture of sculptors' tools. You may be expected to make your own chisels, hammers, and modeling implements. Of course, carving demands intimate knowledge of the quirks of each kind of wood or stone. And welded sculpture demands technical knowledge of metals. One well-known sculptor says, "I'm not just a sculptor. I'm a carpenter, a plumber, and I could double as an auto worker."

Few sculptors paint, and their training rarely includes much painting beyond the required courses. On the other hand, many sculptors are active printmakers in school and afterward.

Art history forms an essential part of any artist's training. Knowing the work of the great artists of the past, you're better able to judge your own. You can also learn valuable lessons by studying their working methods. And one distinguished museum curator adds that studying art history is a kind of insurance: "Knowing what's been done before, you won't slave to come up with something that seems tremendously original, and then discover it's old hat."

Instructors

There are often big philosophical differences between schools and even between instructors in a single school. One school may be dominated by abstract artists who just want to train other abstract artists. Another may be run by realistic landscape and figure painters who have no patience with abstract art.

Before you enroll, try to learn something about a school's bias, if there *is* a bias. Better still, try to pick a school where the instructors don't all work in the same style. It's healthy to have a wild-and-woolly member of the avant garde and a traditionalist teaching in adjacent classrooms. Each artist has something to offer you. When you've had a taste of both far-out and traditional modes, you'll feel freer to develop a style of your own. Far from forcing you into a mold, a good art school, college or univerity art department hopes you'll profit by the differences among your teachers.

Does a fine artist need a degree?

No art dealer will ask if you have a degree before the gallery exhibits your work. Nor will any purchaser. What matters is the quality of your work, not whether you can write B.A. or M.F.A. after your name.

However, if you plan to earn your living as a teacher, it's wise to pick a school that grants a degree. One noted painter comments bitterly: "If Rembrandt wanted to teach in one of our colleges, he wouldn't have much chance without a degree." A famous artist *can* sometimes land a top teaching position without a degree. But you can't be sure you're destined for fame. The chapter on teaching goes into degree requirements in greater detail. Here I'll simply point out that a bachelor's degree is a minimum requirement for most teaching jobs, and your bargaining power is even greater with a master's degree or a Ph.D. If you're interested in public-school teaching, you should pick an art school, college, or university with a special teacher training program that leads to a degree in *art education*.

How art galleries operate

The usual way artists sell their work is through a gallery. Though most galleries pride themselves on looking non-commercial, art dealers are essentially agents who accept goods on consignment. If they like your work and think it will sell, they agree to display what you produce. The dealer pays the rent, but you owe each other nothing until the gallery makes a sale. When the dealer does sell something for you, the gallery gets a percentage of the sale price. The average is in the 40%–50% range.

American galleries rarely *buy* the work of living artists unless the artist is really a big name. Before investing money in a work of art, dealers must be *sure* they can resell it at a profit. For this reason, most dealers play it safe. They pay you nothing and make no promises. All they ask is that you make no deals with competing galleries in the same city. They may have no objection to your having another dealer in a different city too far away to compete. Nor can a dealer object when you switch to another gallery if your work isn't selling. The dealer may be just as pleased to sever the agreement.

Business arrangements between artists and galleries have tended to be informal, but artists have learned (the hard way) that verbal agreements are hard to enforce in court. So artists are gradually learning to be more businesslike. This means drafting written agreements for gallery representation, getting receipts for work that you leave with a dealer, and putting on paper the arrangements for a show. Artists and dealers sometimes agree to share expenses like framing, shipping, exhibition catalogs, and advertising. Of course, when a gallery is lucky enough to land a well-known artist whose work really sells, the dealer may be willing to absorb all costs. At the end of this chapter, I'll recommend some books to read on the business aspects of fine art.

A gallery will exhibit your work in two ways: group shows with other artists handled by the gallery, and ultimately a one-artist show devoted entirely to your work.

Though dealers' business methods differ in detail, this description fits most reputable galleries in the United States. However, rental galleries, sometimes called *vanity galleries*, are a different story. Though these galleries *look* like others, they're really nothing more than exhibition spaces for rent. You may hire the whole gallery or pay for each picture they hang in a group show. Any artist—good, bad, or indifferent—can arrange a one-artist show if he or she can pay the rental fee. If you can afford the additional expense, the vanity gallery may buy advertising space in newspapers and art magazines, make some attempt to get publicity, and arrange a cocktail party the day your show opens.

The big trouble with the vanity gallery is that you get so little for your money. As the words *vanity gallery* imply, you're buying nothing more than a boost for your ego. The gallery has no steady public. Collectors, critics, and museum people have all learned to stay away because they've seen so many second-rate shows there. The only visitors likely to show up are your family, friends, and a few curious passers-by. Nor can you expect the owner to take any real interest in building your reputation for the future. The gallery's goals are strictly short range. The dealer does no more than you pay for, like a motel-keeper renting you a room for the night.

Finding a dealer

The best-known art galleries are in larger cities, such as New York, Los Angeles, Washington, Boston, Philadelphia, Chicago, San Francisco, and their suburbs. But more and more galleries have opened in smaller cities and even in out-of-the-way spots like an island off the Maine coast or a California seaside town. So you no longer have to go to a sizable city to find a dealer.

But don't just walk into the first gallery you see and try to strike a bargain. First you have to do some research.

Galleries tend to specialize. One may handle nothing but contemporary American artists, while another handles only French art. Some dealers show nothing but paintings, while others are known for prints and drawings. A gallery may become known for a particular style: abstract, minimal, realistic, or whatever. Some dealers never show the work of beginners, but stick to artists with reputations. Others like to give young artists a start.

Before you begin your dealer hunt, you must get to know the galleries. Visit all you can and study each gallery's group of artists, sometimes referred to as the gallery's *stable*. A group show is a particularly good time to survey the entire stable at one crack.

You can also learn a lot about the galleries by reading exhibition reviews in magazines like *Arts* and *Art News*. Most big city newspapers have art critics who cover the local galleries. Since you can't possibly pay regular visits to the hundreds of galleries in New York, it's worthwhile to follow the *New York Times* art pages.

Having settled on a handful of galleries where your work might fit, you can start making contacts. Again, don't walk in without warning and expect the dealer to drop everything and spend an hour looking at your samples. Write or phone ahead for an appointment. If you can get an introduction from a teacher, collector, or established artist who knows the dealer, so much the better. Don't be surprised if the dealer asks you to send photos of your work before agreeing to see you. You might save the dealer the trouble of asking: send some black and white photos or color slides with your first letter.

A dozen photos are enough to send, just to give the dealer a preliminary idea of your work. You'll probably want your photos back, so be sure to enclose a postpaid, self-addressed envelope. If you live far away and you're planning a special trip, be sure to say when you're coming to town.

Though not every dealer will read it, some recommend that you include a short biographical sheet with your letter. I don't think such a sheet means much if you're just out of school. If you're a beginner, it's probably simplest to include a few facts in your letter to the dealer: age, place of birth, academic honors, and any well-known teachers. If you're a seasoned artist, *then* you might put these facts on a separate sheet, along with a list of one-artist shows, with dates and places; juried shows (more about these in a moment); museums and well-known private collectors who own your work. Try to hold yourself down to a page.

Don't expect everyone to write you an enthusiastic invitation. Some will turn you down flatly. Others will see you out of curiosity or because you've come through a mutual friend whose request they can't turn down. A few dealers may be genuinely interested.

When you do land an appointment with a dealer, you may be asked to come in on a special day reserved for young hopefuls. Tuesdays, Wednesdays, and Thursdays are usually the quietest days in a gallery. One of these will probably be the day you're invited. Remember this if you're planning a trip from out of town.

When you select samples to show, remember these suggestions made by a New York dealer. Show examples of your dominant style. Though you may have been through several styles, just show the one style you want the dealer to remember. Equally important, show your dominant medium. Don't haul in work in every medium you've tried in art school. If your main interest is etching, just bring etchings. Don't confuse the dealer by bringing in a few wooden figures you carved one summer for a change of pace.

How many samples should you take to your first interview? If you're carrying prints or drawings, you can easily handle a dozen, unless they're unusually big. You'll probably have trouble carrying that many paintings, unless they're small watercolors. Half a dozen or even four will do. Sculpture is often impossible to carry around for interviews. Photos will have to suffice, plus a couple of small pieces *if* you do small things.

If dealers are impressed, they'll come to the studio to see the things you couldn't carry. Or if you're too far away, you'll be asked to get hold of a truck and make that big second expedition. If the expedition is a success, you'll go home in an empty truck. Your work will go into the dealer's active stock.

When you're ready to do serious business with a gallery, do some checking behind the scenes. Talk to some artists who've been handled by the dealer to make sure that the gallery staff is hardworking, businesslike, honest—and pays its bills promptly. Too many galleries are hobbies for rich amateurs, or simply marginal operations run by people who have highbrow pretensions, but not much business sense. Do your homework. Be sure the gallery has a track record, and won't be here today, gone tomorrow.

The one-artist show

Though it's your dealer's responsibility to promote your work year after year, the gallery's most important single job is to give you a one-artist show. The dealer hopes to schedule such a show every two or three years, though this will depend on how much you produce. Some artists work so quickly that they have a show almost every year. Others work so slowly that five or six years elapse between shows.

What *is* a one-artist show? Your dealer turns over the whole gallery—or a large part—to you alone. Each piece in the show is numbered. The numbers reappear in a small catalog, with the name of the piece. Visitors can usually take catalogs free of charge. Prices are rarely listed in the catalog, but they're often posted with the pictures or on a price list at a desk. When a piece is sold, a red star is pasted onto the frame or pedestal. A one-artist show usually runs three or four weeks.

It's customary to take a small boxed ad in the art magazines and the art pages of local papers announcing your show. Artists and dealers may agree in advance to share this expense, plus framing and catalog printing costs. More often, the *artist* absorbs these expenses. If the artist has to invest a lot of money in frames, the dealer *may* share this too or perhaps advance some money against future sales. Instead of taking money from the artist, some dealers may accept a work of art.

Announcements, catalogs, and sometimes personal notes are mailed to the gallery's clients. A news release may be mailed to the press and a few photos of your work may be shot for local art critics, whom your dealer will try to bring in to review the exhibition.

Keep in mind that your dealer may not be able to give you a show immediately. Most galleries schedule exhibitions six months or a year ahead. The so-called *art season* runs from early fall through late spring. Don't be surprised if your show can't be scheduled until the following season.

Above all, don't feel that you must rush into a show as soon as you're out of school. An intelligent dealer may say, "Your stuff looks promising. Come back and see me in two or three years. Maybe *then* you'll be ready for a show." This is no brushoff. A one-artist show means you've achieved a certain maturity of style. Until you've reached this stage in your development, you can afford to wait. Many outstanding artists have worked quietly for a decade or more before they felt ready for their first show.

How important is a New York show?

Because New York is the nation's art capital, young artists often make great sacrifices to arrange an exhibition there. Many go into debt to pay their fare and freight costs for their work. And some go further into the red to hire a vanity gallery if they can't land a dealer.

Is a New York show worth all this? Does your future reputation really hinge on this one city?

Hundreds of one-artist shows open in New York every month. Critics race around town and review as many as they can, but bypass most for lack of time and newspaper space. Few shows sell enough to break even. Most get scant attention from the art public and are forgotten the day they close. Only a handful of shows cause any stir and most of these are forgotten too.

A New York show is worth striving for if you're realistic and recognize that you're betting on a long shot. Don't imagine that a New York show automatically means you've hit the top and all museums and collectors will open their doors to your work. A one-artist exhibition at a reputable New York gallery—not a vanity gallery—is worth a reasonable investment in time and money, on the *slim* chance that the art world's spotlight will swing your way for a moment. But it doesn't justify wiping out your bank account.

Across America, there are thousands of good artists who enjoy local reputations. Many of them have never had a New York show. They exhibit in local galleries and their work seems to sell as well—or as badly—as it might in New York. One museum curator explains: "If you're good, you'll create your own audience sooner or later, wherever you live."

Juried exhibitions

Another way of showing your work is in juried exhibitions sponsored by museums and local or national art organizations. The juried show is a free-for-all. Artists for miles around submit their work to a jury of well-known artists, critics, museum people, or other authorities. The jury decides what to exhibit and what to reject. This same jury, or a separate group, may award cash prizes, medals, or certificates to entries judged outstanding.

Some juried shows are strictly regional: open to artists in a given city, county, state, or group of states. Others are national, and a few are international. The artist usually absorbs the cost of packing, insurance, and shipping round trip. There may also be an entry fee.

The best way to keep track of forthcoming juried shows is to read the art magazines regularly and watch bulletin boards in museums and art schools.

There's great debate about the value of juried exhibitions. Those in favor feel that juried shows are a good testing ground for an aspiring artist. If your work is accepted, you can see how it stacks up when it's hung beside the work of your contemporaries. If you're turned down, you know that you have a way to go before becoming a real professional. Advocates of the jury system also point out that it weeds out second-raters who don't really belong in the field anyhow.

Another theoretical advantage of the jury show is that it spreads the word about up-and-coming artists. Museum curators, collectors, and dealers *may* discover you. You *might* win a prize and get some publicity. And if you have no dealer, the jury show may be your only way to exhibit and perhaps make a sale.

However, there are also very damaging arguments against the jury system. Attackers say that no juror can avoid bias. Jurors can't help favoring friends and students—the art world is small—and liking styles similar to their own. Jurors *try* to be fair, but it's charged that personal differences in taste always lead to log-rolling deals: "I'll vote for the picture you like if you'll vote for the one I like."

Not only are individual jurors said to be biased, but whole juries often lean toward a particular kind of art. Bring together three abstract painters and they may automatically turn down all traditional work. Conversely, a traditional jury may toss out anything abstract. Many annual jury shows pick the same kind of jury each year. The word soon gets around that only a certain style is likely to be accepted.

What this means, say attackers of the jury system, is that such shows are *not* good testing grounds for young artists. A turndown doesn't necessarily mean you don't measure up. It may just mean you don't fit the jury's bias or you were squeezed out in a log-rolling deal. Acceptance may be just as meaningless for exactly the same reasons. To make things *more* confusing, a picture is often rejected by one jury and accepted by another. It might even be argued that the best artists don't get into juried exhibitions because they don't conform to the tastes of any current clique.

Opponents of juried shows go on to point out that attendance is usually scant and sales are few. Although critics *may* write up big juried shows, only a few artists are ever singled out in the reviews. Few museum people see these shows, and many dealers frankly admit that they don't go and aren't impressed by an artist's long list of jury acceptances.

Another argument against juried shows is simply a matter of expense. You can spend an awful lot of time and money crating, insuring, and shipping things back and forth. For each piece accepted, some artists warn, you may have several turned down. It's common for a jury to receive 2000 submissions when there's gallery space for just 200. This means 1800 pictures *must* be turned down. This seems a very costly way to get your work shown. One artist observes wryly: "If you took the money you spent on jury shows and used it to rent an empty store for a month, you'd probably sell more stuff."

There's also a *moral* argument against the jury system. When a juried show charges you an entry fee to finance the expenses of the exhibition—and then turns you down—you're actually paying for a show that doesn't even include your work! The large number of artists who get turned down are paying the bills for the much smaller number who get into the show. Unfair? Of course. Many noted artists now boycott juried shows. And artists' groups are lobbying—with limited success—for the elimination of entry fees.

Whether submitting work to juried exhibitions is worthwhile, no one can say for certain. Though many good artists have given up sending things, the juried show remains an established exhibition method. If you do decide to invest in juried shows, be sure to investigate each jury and each show's history to see whether your work will fit in. Though you can never be *sure*, you can often predict which juries will be sympathetic to your style.

The role of museums

Beside backing juried exhibitions, museums often support contemporary artists in two other ways. Many museums arrange shows of contemporary work *without* a jury or a fee. And many buy the work of living artists.

Like juried exhibitions, museum shows may be regional, national, or international. But artists don't necessarily submit their work to a jury for acceptance or rejection. Instead, the museum staff invites a limited number of artists to exhibit one or more things, which the staff may actually select from the artist's studio or gallery. Some museums actually try to sell things in the show. Others just refer customers to the artist or the dealer.

How do you get invited? Curators rely on their knowledge of the field, gained from visiting galleries, other musuems, and juried exhibitions. If you have no dealer and don't participate in jury shows, you might send along a short note with some photos, requesting that the museum consider you. Some enlightened museums even have special days when they look at the work of newcomers.

Museums occasionally give some artist a show. This isn't for beginners. Nor can you *ask* to be given such a show. The museum reserves this honor for important artists with established reputations.

Museums purchase the work of living artists in very much the same way. They watch your development and buy something when they feel you're mature and important enough to be in the collection. They rarely take a flyer on an unknown artist. You can't just walk in and try to make a sale. The museum will come to *you* when they're ready. However, there's nothing wrong with you or your dealer sending over some photos and tactfully inviting a curator to visit your show or your studio.

No artist expects to live on sales to museums. There aren't enough museums and they often get a hefty discount from dealers. Artists and dealers are eager to sell to museums purely for the prestige. When an important museum makes a purchase, collectors often follow suit.

Portrait, mural, and monument commissions

Though most portraits are now done by photographers, there's still a certain amount of work for portrait painters and sculptors. Your gallery may find customers among its clients. Good dealers spend leisure hours broadening their social contacts and may turn up portrait commissions in the process of circulating. Naturally, the dealer collects the usual percentage of the sale price. Many leading portrait painters have no dealer, but ride the cocktail party circuit themselves.

Another source of portrait commissions is the satisfied customer. If sitters are proud of the portrait you've done, they make a point of showing it off to friends. If friends like what they see, they may be your next sitters.

Contacts are also the key to landing mural commissions, architectural sculpture, and civic monuments. *Social* contacts mean less than knowing local architects, interior designers, city planners, and members of the city fine-arts commission, if such an agency exists. The Federal government—as well as many states, cities, and counties—now requires that the budget for every new public building must include a percentage for art.

There was a time when painters and sculptors were invited to submit models and sketches in competition for a big job. Though such competitions are still held here and there, especially for public buildings, most private commissions are now awarded on the recommendation of the architect or designer doing the building. Art for public buildings and monuments may be commissioned directly from the artist by civic agencies, subject to approval by various boards or committees. Again, one commission can lead to another. One successful mural or sculpture in a prominent location can set off a chain reaction.

Muralists and architectural sculptors must learn to be precise and hard-headed about business dealings. Too often, a half completed project is suddenly canceled because of budget troubles, or a dissatisfied or indecisive client. To guard against losing a major investment in time and money, the experienced muralist or sculptor often insists on being paid in three stages: one third of the price when the job is begun, one third when it's finished, and one third when it's installed. The artist also expects to be paid for preliminary sketches or models, even if the job stops right there. All these arrangements must be spelled out in written agreements.

Other methods of selling fine art

There are many other places where you might exhibit and sell your work, particularly if you live where galleries are scarce.

Bookstores, furniture stores, and interior designers' shops often exhibit and sell paintings, drawings, prints, and small sculptures. There are even restaurants and coffee shops whose owners are delighted to liven up the walls with works of art *and* collect a percentage if a sale is made. Corporate office buildings often provide wall space for exhibitions, both in the public spaces and in the offices themselves.

Some enterprising artists have saved their money and actually rented a store for a few weeks. In smaller cities, where everybody notices a new store and news spreads quickly, this has sometimes turned out to be a simple and profitable way of arranging a one-artist show. Even in a city as big as New York, I've seen this bold approach tried successfully.

A logical extension of this idea is the *cooperative gallery.* Instead of hunting for a dealer, a group of artists rent a store or a gallery where they can show their work throughout the year and share all expenses. Enterprising art groups and entrepreneurs are turning old warehouses, unused theaters, abandoned skating rinks, empty stores, and other big shelters into so-called "artists' spaces" with lots of square footage for exhibitions.

Not all successful artists exhbit their work publicly. I know quite a few who have sufficient reputation to sell directly from their studios. They rely on purchasers to send up *future* purchasers. Artists may have special visiting days or show their work by appointment so people won't just barge in. Though this system works best for well-known artists, there also are some little-known artists who sell this way and manage to build a small but faithful following. One popular idea is to buy a big, old house and convert a floor, a wing, or perhaps the barn into your own gallery.

Still other artists are experimenting with direct mail selling—particularly for prints and other "multiples"—as well as direct sales to corporate art collections, hotel and motel chains, and other large-scale clients in the business world.

The best-known method of selling art without a gallery is the traditional sidewalk exhibition. How much work is *really* sold this way is anybody's guess. But I've met old timers who say it works.

Where can you get more information?

Though there's no nationwide art press in the United States, there are monthly art magazines worth following. *Art News* and *Arts* are useful for art reviews, critical articles on art history, current trends, and the work of major figures, past and present. *American Artist* is particularly valuable for articles that analyze the working methods of contemporary artists. Our one national newspaper, *The New York Times*, also attempts to cover art news across the country.

By far the most useful book on finding a gallery, exhibiting, promoting, and selling your work is *The Artist's Guide to the Art Market* by Betty Chamberlain. The best book on the business aspects of fine art is Diane Cochrane's *This Business of Art*. Kenneth Harris's *How to Make a Living as a Painter* takes a fresh and witty look at the artist's business problems and suggests a practical program for selling your work without relying on "name" art galleries in major art centers. Also worth reading is *The Artist's Guide to Sidewalk Exhibiting* by Claire V. Dorst.

Another good way to keep up with the art world is to attend your local museum regularly. Most population centers now have art museums that show their own collections as well as traveling exhibitions and art films. Museums also have lectures, forums, and guided tours of the exhibitions. Many museums now have extensive art libraries.

To get the most out of your museum, it's worthwhile to pay the modest price of an annual membership. For a small annual charge, you'll be kept informed about all museum events and you'll be invited to many that aren't open to the general public. You may get free admission to movies, lectures, and special exhibitions for which other visitors have to pay. You may get special publications—pamphlets, exhibition catalogs, books, even a museum magazine—prepared by the museum staff. The art library will be open to you. You may also get discounts on art books, reproductions, and magazines.

Finally, you should do your best to see all the important gallery shows and juried exhibitions that come your way.

6
Illustration

Of all the applied arts, the profession closest to fine art is illustration. You might say an illustration is simply a drawing or painting created for some practical purpose. Most often, the practical purpose of an illustration is to adorn or explain the printed word: a story, an article, an advertisement, or a book. Like the writer, the illustrator normally creates material for the printed page.

What does an illustrator do?

Illustration is a highly specialized profession. Your style, your interests, and "the breaks" will determine what field of illustration you choose.

Most familiar, I suppose, are magazine illustrators, who create the drawings and paintings that appear inside our weekly and monthly periodicals. But there are even specialties within the magazine field. One artist's style lends itself to women's magazines. Another's style makes the artist a specialist in sports magazines.

This is equally true in book illustration. One artist's style is just right for children's books. Another's style proves best for technical books and textbooks. And paperback covers are an important and specialized field.

Advertising is a fertile field for the illustrator, but the

enormous diversity of clients and products again encourages specialization.

Fashion advertisers—and the fashion magazines—have created their own special breed of illustrators. Fashion illustrators have a style quite unlike any other kind of illustrator. They devote their lives almost entirely to fashion ads and fashion magazines. Fashion illustrators have just one subject: clothes.

Particularly in advertising—though also in magazine and book illustration—subject matter is often a specialty. Some illustrators are so good at rendering cars that they devote their lives to automotive advertising. And an illustrator who becomes known for drawings or paintings of pretty girls, children, animals, food, or famous personalities may soon be doing practically nothing else.

A medium may also turn into a specialty. Many illustrators work only in black and white. An artist may be best known for pencil sketches or pen-and-ink drawings. Someone else may make a reputation for a special way with watercolor.

Though cartooning seems a narrow specialty at first glance, even here you find a surprising number of fields. One cartoonist specializes in witty drawings for ads, stories, and articles with the light touch. Another's bold style leads into adventure comic strips. A totally different craft, demanding special training or experience, is the animated cartoon for TV or the movies.

Where else might an illustrator's work appear? Pamphlets, posters, film strips, manufacturers' catalogs, scientific and technical publications, record album covers, greeting cards, political cartoons, packaging. These are just a few of the possibilities.

How much specialization is necessary? Must you be backed into a tight corner and stay there? This depends on your own abilities. If you're versatile enough, you can cut across several fields, like many magazine and book illustrators who also do advertising work.

But the fact is that every artist is strong in some areas and weak in others. Besides, advertisers and publishers need *so* many different kinds of artwork. No one artist can do them all. Even the most versatile illustrator soon develops a few areas of specialization. These turn out to be convenient and profitable because many clients remember you for your specialties.

ILLUSTRATION 93

There *are* situations, of course, in which an illustrator is hired for sheer versatility. If you work in a small organization, you may be expected to draw fashions one day and machinery the next. You may have to be equally skilled in color and black and white. You may do lettering, photo-retouching, and even photography in a pinch. But if you're like most aspiring illustrators, your goal is freelancing, which almost always means some degree of specialization.

Let me add an important footnote about the profession of illustration. When I was an art student three decades ago, illustration seemed the most glamorous of all the art fields. Illustrations dominated our national magazines; many illustrators were virtually household names and earned enormous incomes. Today, photographers get many of the assignments that used to go to illustrators. For example, fashions were once illustrated almost entirely by drawings; today's fashion magazines depend substantially on photographs, while fashion drawings are still used extensively in newspapers. Although there's still a reasonable amount of work for a good illustrator, it's no exaggeration to say that photography now dominates advertising and editorial art. But there are cycles in such things and some magazines are turning to illustration again.

It's also fair to point out that the illustrator is at the mercy of rapid changes in taste. At one moment, the taste may be for realism; at the next moment, the trend may shift to a more decorative or design-oriented style. Thus, the illustrator must not only face the powerful competition of the photographer, but must be resourceful and flexible enough to change with the times—or be out of work.

Where does an illustrator find work?

As the last sentence implies, a large number of successful illustrators are self-employed. They earn their living by freelancing. This means that they have their own studios (or share space with some other artists) and take on assignments from many clients.

The main sources of freelance work are advertising agencies, magazine and book publishers, printers, public relations firms, plus the advertising, public relations, and sales promotion departments of stores and manufacturing companies. Some of these organizations have their own art departments, but even these departments often call for freelance help.

Don't take this to mean that an illustrator *must* freelance. Obviously, there are good 9-to-5 jobs—staff jobs, they're called—in the organizations I've just mentioned. The difference is that staff artists are often used at the idea stage, not for the finished artwork. Most big advertising agencies, for instance, use their art departments primarily to hatch ideas and visualize them for the client in sketch form. When the client gives the go-ahead, a freelance is usually called in to do the finished artwork. Magazine and book publishers tend to work the same way.

Staffers *do* get to create finished artwork, but these are usually the smaller assignments. These might be black and white drawings for small ads and pamphlets, technical manuals, or posters used in the plant. Bigger, more ambitious illustrations tend to be given to freelance artists who are specialists in the subject or the style needed.

Because of this division of labor between staff and freelance artists, young illustrators are often advised to *start* in a staff job to learn the ropes. But the goal is freelancing.

However, not all staffers hope to freelance. Many illustrators take jobs in art services or art studios and stay there. An art service is a *firm* of artists—salaried employees, partners, or even shareholders in a small corporation—who turn out artwork for a variety of clients. Many art services—art studio is just another term for the same thing—pay substantial earnings to top artists who have no intention of freelancing.

In the field of fashion illustration, top people often hold down well-paid 9-to-5 jobs with department stores or manufacturers. This becomes particularly vital when an artist's style becomes identified with a store's name or a manufacturer's product.

Many staff illustrators decide not to freelance because they *like* to concentrate on ideas and leave finished artwork to someone else. These artists become art directors: planners and idea creators with executive responsibilities in an agency, magazine, book

ILLUSTRATION 95

publishing house, store, or manufacturing firm. At this point, the illustrator begins to fuse with the graphic designer—the organizer of the printed page—whose job I'll discuss in the next chapter.

What about geography? Most illustrators—staff or freelance—find work in big advertising and publishing centers like New York, Philadelphia, Chicago, and Los Angeles. However, the so-called communications business is becoming more and more decentralized. Every city big enough to have one or two daily papers and a TV station is likely to have an advertising agency. The nation's big industries, with their art and advertising departments, are scattered from coast to coast. In scores of cities, department stores hire staff artists and freelance artists too.

What does an illustrator study?

Above all, illustrators are acute observers of the life around them. Thus, the foundation of your training is drawing. You spend a great deal of time drawing the nude and clothed figure. Rapid sketches of the passing scene and precise renderings of still-life objects are equally important.

Painting classes are also vital and these too emphasize observation. The illustrator paints a wide range of subjects: still lifes, landscapes, abstractions perhaps, and especially the human face and figure. You explore many media: oil, watercolor, gouache, acrylic, and pastel—any medium you may use in your future profession.

Printmaking courses are often included for experience. Though books are sometimes illustrated with prints, the printmaking media are rarely used in advertising or publishing.

Note that all these fine art courses are *beyond* what the illustrator gets in the foundation year. Though every student gets a sampling of drawing, painting, and printmaking in the first year, the illustrator is likely to take these subjects throughout the school years.

There are also specialized courses in the illustrator's craft. These may be called "Illustration: Elementary, Intermediate, and Advanced." Or they may be divided into subjects like book, magazine, advertising, technical, and fashion illustration. In these classes, you get assignments that are meant to duplicate assignments you can expect on the job. The top schools make photography classes available to illustration students.

Other specialized classes often include layout—the planning of the printed page—typography, and lettering. It's also essential for an illustrator to learn the mechanics of the printing industry: how type is set, how drawings and paintings are made into plates for reproduction, and how pages are printed.

Some schools offer a major in illustration: a program that prepares you for any area of illustration you may decide to enter. Other schools may offer a major in some specialized field of illustration, like fashion drawing. This often includes courses in fashion design and the fashion industry. Many schools offer a broad major under the heading of *commercial art*, combining illustration and graphic design.

Does an illustrator need a degree?

All a client or a boss wants to see is your portfolio, not your diploma. If you have a degree, this *may* impress an employer who recognizes the value of a broad education. But few employers and *no client* will even ask.

What part-time and summer jobs are good experience?

While you're in school, the best summer or part-time job is obviously *anything* that gives you a peek into the workings of an ad agency, magazine or book publishing house, printing plant, or the art staff of a store or manufacturing firm. The job doesn't even have to be in the art department. You might learn valuable lessons in an agency's production department, where printing is ordered and followed through.

If you're especially good, you might even be able to pick up

ILLUSTRATION   97

some freelance work from these sources while you're still in school. Even the smallest assignments make good portfolio pieces to prove you've had *some* experience when you go job hunting.

What is a typical first job?

In an agency, studio, or publishing house, you might be assigned to act as "Man Friday" or "Gal Friday" to an art director or a more experienced illustrator. You'll probably run errands, paste type and photostats together for client presentations or the printer, mount drawings, fuss with files, and retouch photos. When you've won your employer's confidence, you'll be asked to sketch out some of your boss' ideas, do some routine lettering, and draw small black-and-whites called *spots*.

In a store, these chores might be mixed with some display work and sign painting. A manufacturing company might add some technical illustration to the blend. A printing plant might also train you to handle production.

As you prove yourself, you'll get bigger and bigger drawings to do. You may move from black and white into color, from spots to more ambitious artwork. You'll begin to hatch your own ideas and do the finished art yourself or assign this to a freelance.

But if your *goal* is freelancing, why not just start freelancing as soon as you finish school? Top students often succeed in developing a salable style by the time they graduate. With a few summer or part-time jobs behind them, they may know enough of the ropes to start a modest freelance practice. They begin with small drawings and slowly work up to bigger assignments.

However, you have to be exceptionally good to start out on your own. Unless your teachers, friends in the field, and potential clients encourage you to freelance right away, it's best to begin by taking a 9-to-5 job. After a few years, when you've built up professional knowledge and contacts, you may feel ready to freelance. By then, of course, you may have risen so high in your job that you prefer to stay there.

What are later jobs like?

Successful free lance illustrators normally have their own studios, perhaps an assistant, and a variety of clients coming and going with all sorts of assignments. If you're lucky, you may have a few steady clients who virtually regard you as a member of their staff and feed you a stream of work throughout the year. As a freelance, you may act as your own salesperson, carrying your portfolio of samples from one prospective client to another. Or you may have an agent who carries the portfolio and collects a percentage of each check.

With deadlines every few days and a variety of clients to serve, the freelance illustrator is usually under pressure. Life is fast-paced and hours are irregular. To enjoy this existence, you have to be tough, adventurous, well-organized, and brimming with energy.

Though many freelance illustrators prefer to remain a one-artist operation, others build up a staff as business increases. This is how art services and art studios are born.

For the illustrator who prefers a somewhat steadier life—though *any* illustrator's life is fairly hectic—there are rewarding high-level staff jobs. Magazine illustrators often become magazine art directors, who plan pictorial content and page layout. In the advertising business, a staff illustrator also tends to move up into art direction. A staffer in a store or manufacturing company may become head of the art department. All these artists tend to move away from the drawing board as they take on executive responsibility. They hatch ideas and pass them on to other artists—staffers or freelances—who execute the finished artwork.

The successful staff illustrator soon reaches a crossroads. Either you become a planner, a decision maker, an organizer of other artist's efforts, or you decide to *stay* with the drawing board and quit your job to freelance or join an art service that will pay you a top salary to produce finished artwork. At some point, the freelance may make the opposite move, of course. You may take a staff job as an art director.

ILLUSTRATION 99

Where can you get more information?

Illustration and graphic design are covered jointly in several good magazines and annuals. *Art Direction*, *Print*, and *Communication Arts* are magazines worth following. *American Artist* covers the work of leading illustrators as well as fine artists. *Graphis* is published abroad, but its available here with English text and it's widely read by American illustrators.

The *Art Directors Annual*, the *Illustrators Annual*, and AIGA *Graphic Design USA* carry the work of top illustrators. (These are published, respectively, by the Art Directors Club of New York, the Society of Illustrators, and the American Institute of Graphic Arts.) The Swiss *Graphis Annual*, with English text, is also sold in the United States.

An excellent book about the practical aspects of the illustrator's profession is *The Graphic Artists Guild Handbook: Pricing and Ethical Guidelines*, published by the Graphic Artists Guild, whose address you'll find in the list of professional organizations at the back of *Art Career Guide*.

Many large cities now have local Art Directors Clubs; these local groups often hold exhibitions which you should attend. If you get to New York or live there, you'll also find lively exhibitions at the Society of Illustrators.

And it hardly seems necessary to say that you should watch the books, magazines, newspapers, and other printed matter where the work of outstanding illustrators appears regularly. The periodicals room of your local library is a place you should get to know.

7
Graphic design

The graphic designer and the illustrator dominate the field sometimes called *commercial art*. Both professions are concerned primarily with the printed page. While the illustrator creates paintings and drawings for reproduction, the graphic designer has been described as the *architect of the printed page*.

What does a graphic designer do?

As a graphic designer, your job is to create a plan for the printed page—this plan is called a layout—then select type, hand lettering, drawings, paintings, and photos. You may go even further and specify papers, inks, printing processes, and binding materials. Your job is to organize all these elements into a harmonious and effective design.

This design may be an advertisement in a magazine or newspaper. It might be the magazine itself, a pamphlet, or a book, planned page by page on the graphic designer's drawing board. But the design may not always be a printed page. It might also be a poster, a record jacket, a television commercial, a film strip, a package, or even a display unit in a store.

A graphic designer is sometimes a specialist, sometimes not. There *are* freelance graphic designers who'll design anything a client may ask for, from a trademark the size of your fingernail to a trade exhibit 100 feet square. On the other hand, many graphic designers do specialize. Advertising and magazine art directors rarely design books, while book designers rarely do anything else. Some graphic designers concentrate on television. Package design has become an important specialty. Many graphic designers specialize in exhibits and mass-produced display units, which brings them closer to industrial design, the subject of a later chapter.

A graphic designer may become so fascinated with typography that he or she becomes known as a designer of type faces or a hand-lettering expert.

The designer may or may not create the finished artwork for the layout. In a large organization, you're likely to call on other staffers or freelances for illustrations, photographs, and lettering. In a small organization, operating on a low budget, you may act as your own illustrator and lettering artist at least some of the time. A handful of unusually versatile designers manage to divide their time between layout and illustration, but the tendency is to specialize in one field or the other.

Where does a graphic designer find work?

Probably the best known graphic designer is the art director who works for a magazine or an advertising agency. Art studios and art services also employ graphic designers, as do the advertising and art departments of stores and manufacturing companies. Book publishers and printers often have a graphic design department, while typographers sometimes hire a graphic designer who has a special interest in type. Display houses hire graphic designers who want to specialize in three dimensional advertising. Industrial design offices use graphic designers for packaging jobs.

These are all 9-to-5 staff jobs, but every one of these organizations also uses freelance talent. Even an art studio with a large, versatile staff may use a freelance when no member of the firm has exactly the right style or experience.

In illustration, the juiciest assignments go to the freelance, but this isn't true in graphic design. A graphic designer may do very ambitious work on a 9-to-5 job. It's hard to name a famous illustrator who isn't a freelance, but I can name scores of leading graphic designers who have 9-to-5 staff jobs. The choice between staff work and freelancing is a matter of temperament. Opportunities are equally good on both sides of the fence.

Should you start freelancing right after school? Some illustrators try this successfully as I've said, but few graphic designers can manage it. Graphic design is more technical than illustration. There's much more to absorb about the mechanics of printing, advertising, and publishing. It's far easier to learn the tricks of the trade in a staff job than on your own. A beginning freelance can feel terribly lost without the prior experience of a good nuts-and-bolts staff job. It usually makes sense to start out in a staff job and *then* try freelancing when you know your way around.

The geography of the graphic design profession is something like illustration. The big advertising and publishing centers—the big cities like New York, Chicago, Los Angeles, and Detroit—are the main job markets. But there are now many good jobs in ad agencies, studios, stores, and manufacturing companies in smaller cities. The book and magazine publishing business is still centered in places like New York and Chicago, but many smaller publishing organizations are springing up in unexpected places and creating job opportunities. Many universities, for example, have set up publishing operations in out-of-the-way spots. The traditional pilgrimage to Madison Avenue no longer seems quite so necessary.

What does a graphic designer study?

The graphic design student may find the subject called many different things, depending on the school. Instead of graphic design, it may be called advertising design, commercial art, advertising and editorial art, communication design, or even something as baffling as commercial design.

Beyond the basic fine art and elementary design classes of the foundation year, you can expect various classes in layout, with practical assignments in the design of ads, mailing pieces, pamphlets, magazine pages, posters, and packages. There may be special classes dealing with production: the mechanics of typesetting, engraving, printing, and binding. Typography and lettering are common subjects. Some schools have special courses in package design, television design, and display work.

Most graphic design programs include a fair amount of illustration. The mixture may be half-and-half if graphic design and illustration are grouped together and given under the heading of commercial art.

Photography now appears in many graphic design programs. A handful of schools are lucky enough to have facilities for typesetting and printing, so students can actually turn out small pieces of printed matter. One well-known school *requires* each graphic design major to design and print a small book.

Does a graphic designer need a degree?

In graphic design, as in illustration, a degree means less than your portfolio. Since graphic design requires a good deal of technical know-how, *some* employers may take your degree as evidence that you've had the necessary courses. But a degree is hardly a requirement of the profession, as it's become in fields like industrial design and architecture.

What part-time and summer jobs are good experience?

You can learn *something* valuable from any low-level job you might be able to land in an advertising agency, publishing firm, printing house, or the art department of a store or manufacturer. Even if your job has nothing to do with art—you're more likely to run errands and do chores around the office—you can learn a lot just by being around artists, copywriters, and production people.

Jobs in such places may not be so easy to get, particularly if your home or school is in an out-of-the-way place. What other summer or part-time jobs might contribute to your professional background? I'd recommend *anything* related to the printing business, even if it's running errands in a small town printing shop or working in the stock room of a paper house or a bindery.

Or I'd try for any job that allows you to use a pencil or a brush. Even as a sign painter or a sign painter's helper, for instance, you may learn important secrets about lettering.

If you hope to be an advertising agency art director, you might find that a selling job in a store teaches you a lot about the consumer for whom your ads will someday be designed.

What is a typical first job?

An advertising agency often assigns a beginner to assist a seasoned art director. As a beginner, you get your on-the-job training by looking over the art director's shoulder and doing routine chores. The newcomer runs the boss' errands; mounts layouts and artwork; pastes type, photostats, and artwork together for the printer; retouches photos; may do some small drawings; and eventually does small layouts under the boss' supervision. When you've proven yourself, you're allowed to develop small layouts on your own, then more ambitious ones as you gain experience.

A magazine's art department may follow a similar procedure or you may be given some specialized job to do. You might be assigned to assist a photo editor for a while. Or you might work on just one section of the magazine, which you and your boss lay out each week or each month.

In a printing house, you'll also start out assisting someone and eventually get a chance to do small layouts, lettering jobs, and perhaps minor illustrations for small clients who don't have their own art department or can't afford a freelance.

The pattern is more or less the same in a book publishing house, store, manufacturing firm or art studio. You start out as someone's "Man Friday" or "Gal Friday," then slowly win greater freedom as you prove yourself.

What are later jobs like?

As a senior art director in an agency, you may be assigned to one or more clients. You may design all of the client's advertising, from newspaper ads to TV commercials. Or you may share the account with other art directors in the office, each of whom handles a different phase of the advertising campaign. You work closely with the clients, as well as with the agency's own copywriters and researchers. You often have a beginner assisting you. And you constantly interview freelance designers, illustrators, photographers, and lettering artists.

As an agency art director, you're expected to know more than graphic design. You're an expert on selling products.

As a magazine art director, you're also more than an artist. You're a journalist. You know how to pick the right picture or series of pictures to tell a dramatic story. You know how to lay out a page that will intensify that story by the intelligent use of type, color, and other design elements. You may design the publication from cover to cover—except for the ads, which agency people design—or you may divide various articles and sections with other art directors. Like the advertising art director, you interview freelance talent. You also work closely with the editors and writers whose pages you must plan, and you sometimes go on location to direct photographers.

If you're a book designer in a publishing house, you not only design the book page by page, but you're often deeply involved in book manufacturing. Design and production are often handled in the same department or in overlapping departments. The situation is similar in many printing plants, where the designer may be concerned with production.

If you're a graphic designer in an art service, you function very much as you would in an agency. Agencies themselves may be among your clients. So may the other organizations I've just mentioned. For illustrations and finished art, you may turn to other staff members or call in a freelance.

As a freelance graphic designer, you may get assignments from any of the staff designers I've listed. Sometimes you carry your own portfolio and act as your own salesperson. Or you engage an agent to drum up clients and collect a percentage of sales. You may be just a one-artist organization and prefer it that way. Or you may find yourself building up a staff, really your own art service, if business really booms. You probably have a few steady clients, plus many others that give you scattered jobs. The freelance designer may call in other freelances—illustrators, photographers, lettering artists—and deal directly with type-setters, engravers, printers, and binders. In short, you may supervise the whole job for your client. Or you may just be paid to create layouts which your clients put into production.

Whether you work 9-to-5 or maintain the erratic hours of a freelance—some designers manage *both*—the graphic designer usually works under the same pressure as the illustrator. In the field of advertising and editorial art, there are always publication deadlines to meet, unpredictable clients to satisfy, and jobs to be done at desperate speed.

Where can you get more information?

Graphic designers read the same magazines as illustrators. *Art Direction, Communication Arts*, and *Print* are the leading American magazines in the field. *Graphis*, a Swiss publication, has English text.

The *Art Directors Annual* (published by the Art Directors Club of New York), *AIGA Graphic Design USA* (the annual of the American Institute of Graphic Arts), and *Typography* (the annual of the Type Directors Club) are the leading American publications of their kind. The *Graphis Annual* is available in the United States.

AIGA (the American Institute of Graphic Arts) also publishes the *AIGA Education Directory*, a list of schools that teach graphic design. And the Graphic Artists Guild publishes the *Graphic Artists Guild Handbook: Pricing and Ethical Guidelines*. Both these organizations' addresses appear in the list of professional organizations at the end of *Art Career Guide*.

Like the illustrator, you should certainly see the annual exhibitions of the local art directors clubs in various major cities. The traveling exhibitions of the AIGA are always worth seeing if they come your way. And you should train yourself to examine every handsome piece of printed matter you come across.

8
Fabric design

Fabric design, like illustration and graphic design, is too often regarded as an extension of painting. This is partly true of *printed* fabrics. But most fabric designs are *woven*, and the construction of a woven fabric is really a form of three-dimensional design.

What does a fabric designer do?

The name *fabric design* hardly describes this complex profession, which embraces many specialties and reaches into several big industries.

The fabric designers who spring to mind first are the ones who create the printed patterns that appear on dress fabrics, blouses, scarves, upholstery, curtains, and dozens of other things we wear or buy for our homes.

But *weavers* are also fabric designers. Designers of printed fabrics create patterns to be stamped onto the surface of a piece of cloth. Weavers, on the other hand, literally construct the cloth, interlocking fibers to form a built-in design. Weavers may really be hand weavers, actually turning out fabrics on their own looms. More likely, they're designers of woven fabrics turned out by machines for a mass market. One designer *may* master both techniques, printed *and* woven fabrics, but most designers specialize in one or the other.

However, fabric designers don't necessarily design fabrics. A designer of printed fabrics may also create wallpapers or even *specialize* in this field. The decorative patterns on wall and floor tiles may be developed by fabric designers. So may decorative plastics for upholstery, wall covering, table tops, and other interior items.

Fabric designers may also design rugs, knitted and embroidered fabrics, shower curtains, lampshades, towels, linens for the bedroom and dining room, wrapping paper, decorative screens and wall hangings, wallboard, and *any* surface that might be enriched by design.

You may concentrate on one field or cut across *several* during your professional life. Either way, you must get to know the industry you enter. If you design dress fabrics, it's helpful to have a thorough knowledge of the fashion industry. If you design upholstery fabrics, floor and wall coverings, it's extremely useful to know the home furnishings industry.

Where does a fabric designer find work?

The greatest number of fabric designers have 9-to-5 staff jobs. They're employed by manufacturers of printed and woven fabrics, wallpaper, floor tiles, carpeting, and all the other products I've mentioned. A handful work in design studios similar to art studios in the commercial art field. But there are very few of these and only a limited number of jobs.

The would-be freelance designer—the person selling work to a string of clients—floods the fabric design field and has a terribly tough time surviving. Here and there, weavers have set up their own shops, producing cloth by hand and selling directly to the public. Like freelancing, this handcraft approach is a difficult way to earn a living (see Chapter 15).

The best opportunities are staff jobs with manufacturers, most of them in the eastern half of the country. The nerve center of the textile industry is New York, where most design studios are located and where many manufacturers and converters have their design departments. There are also many jobs in the plants themselves, scattered along the east coast from New England to the southern states. Manufacturers of other products, like plastics and floor tile, may be scattered as far as the midwest.

A surprising number of fabric designers divide their time between New York, the capital of the fashion and home furnishing industries, and the far-flung towns where plants are located.

What does a fabric designer study?

Courses in two- and three-dimensional design are basic. Painting and printmaking also appear on many programs. The purpose of all these is to develop your fundamental design sense. Though these subjects appear in the foundation year, they're often carried right through your senior year.

Practical courses normally include assignments in many fields: fabrics for fashion and home furnishings; wallpapers; accessories like scarves and placemats; decorative patterns for plastics and other synthetic materials. You're taught how to print fabrics with silk screens, stencils, and wood or linoleum blocks.

Weaving may be a required subject, available as an elective, or even a major in itself. Most art schools and university art departments emphasize *hand* weaving. This has brought criticism from professional designers and manufacturers, who point out that hand weaving bears little resemblance to the enormously complex operations of a textile mill. They charge that hand-weaving classes aren't adequate training for a future designer of mass produced woven fabrics, who must really combine the skills of the artist with the technical knowledge of a textile engineer. One well known designer says: "If I could re-live my school days, I'd spend four years in a good art school and then switch to a textile engineering school."

A few schools have profited by these criticisms and begun to broaden the technical training of fabric design majors. Because fabric design is so strongly linked to fashions and home furnishings, many schools offer special courses introducing you to these industries. In general, a greater effort is being made to make the training of fabric designers more professional.

In some schools, fabric design may be called textile design or pattern design. The subject may also be offered as part of a general major in fashion, since the largest number of fabric designers go into the clothing industry.

Does a fabric designer need a degree?

A degree isn't a requirement, but if you do have a degree from a school that offers extensive *technical* training, an employer is likely to be impressed. As in other design fields, the number of fabric designers with degrees is on the rise.

What part-time and summer jobs are good experience?

The logical summer or part-time job would be something in a manufacturer's design department, no matter how low level your duties. You might find such a job in the textile industry or in some other industry that uses fabric designers. There's also a slight chance that you might find a job in a design studio, perhaps as a replacement for a junior designer who's on vacation.

There are many jobs outside industry that might be good experience. Selling fabrics, wallpapers, floor coverings, and similar products in a department store will teach you a lot. In fact, any store job in fashion or decorating will add to your background. You might also look for a job in the fashion industry itself.

What is a typical first job?

As in most art fields, a beginner usually starts out assisting an experienced designer. You'll make color sketches of senior designers' ideas and perhaps try color variations of your own. You may weave samples of new design ideas if weaving is your specialty. For presentation to management or clients, you may create precise renderings of your bosses' design ideas in paint or in woven samples.

Later, when you've won your employers' confidence and absorbed the necessary technical knowledge, you may be turned loose to work out your own designs. But this day may be far off if you hope to design woven fabrics and you lack the technical background. One noted designer-manufacturer says frankly, "I have to start most beginners from scratch, just as if they never went to school."

Though this description fits most beginners in the textile industry or a wallpaper manufacturing firm, a newcomer's life in most other industries follows the same lines. In any industry, there's a lot of technical detail to absorb before you really begin designing. In the plastics industry, for example, the designer must be educated in the properties and manufacturing problems of a material that may be totally unfamiliar.

What are later jobs like?

Senior designers in a manufacturing firm are responsible for creating their own design ideas and following them through from sketches to the stage when they're ready to be produced. This means that you do more than sit at a drawing table. You work closely with the engineers—textile engineers, chemists, plastics experts—who supervise production. You may work with the researchers who study what the public will buy and with the marketing staff that sells your designs. With these co-workers, you plan new product lines. You may design these products yourself or, if you're the top designer with the title, "design director," you may sketch out your ideas and pass these on to your staff.

In the textile industry itself, senior design jobs may be broken down into specialties. A colorist, as the title implies, concentrates just on colors: predicting and promoting color trends, determining the most salable color combinations, and coordinating the colors of product lines. A stylist, on the other hand, may do no actual designing; the job is to organize product lines, selecting and orchestrating various products, much as a graphic designer organizes the elements on a printed page.

A few designers have succeeded in establishing studios, with a staff serving a variety of clients. The number of these studios remains small. A fair number of designers have expanded into manufacturing, producing the fabrics they design.

Since most successful fabric designers hold staff jobs, they aren't subjected to the same kind of pressure as artists in free-lance fields, like illustration. There aren't quite as many rush jobs or dry spells when you wonder where your next assignment will come from. But the fashion and home furnishings industries are among the most unpredictable in our fast-paced economy. The textile industry itself has had violent ups and downs in recent years. Keeping up with the rapid shifts of public taste and trends in the industry itself—in fashions, these shifts take place several times each year—takes a quick mind and involves as much pressure as any job I know. Many fabric designers say that theirs is the most volatile of all the art professions.

Where can you get more information?

The leading magazine is *American Fabrics*—rather expensive for a student, but usually available in a good library.

Aside from this one, there are no magazines published just for fabric designers, but you can learn a lot from publications in related fields. The fashion magazines, with their rich pictorial content, are a splendid source of information. The best known are *Vogue* and *Harper's Bazaar*. The daily newspaper of the fashion industry is *Women's Wear Daily*. The home furnishings press also devotes a lot of space to fabrics, as well as to wallpapers and floor coverings. *Interiors, Interior Design,* and *Contract* are the leading magazines. *Home Furnishings Daily* is the newspaper.

It also pays to dip into magazines like *Architectural Record, Progressive Architecture,* and *Industrial Design* for information about new flooring materials, decorative plastics, tiles, and other products developed by fabric designers working *outside* the textile industry. *American Craft* usually has important articles about hand-weaving.

The *Graphic Artists Guild Handbook: Pricing and Ethical Guidelines,* contains practical information about the fabric designer's professional problems. You can order this book from the Guild, whose address is listed among the professional organizations at the back of *Art Career Guide*.

Though there's plenty to read, the most valuable information is always gathered first-hand. You have to haunt the stores where fine fabrics, wallpapers, fashions, and furniture are sold. You have to attend fashion shows and go to see new public buildings where fabrics, floor coverings, and wall coverings are intelligently used. Wherever you go, you must be a constant observer. Everyone's clothes, everyone's home may contribute something to your education if you're always on the alert for a fresh idea.

9
Interior design

The term *interior designer* may be new to you. Interior designers used to be called *interior decorators*. But the profession is rapidly abandoning the word *decorator*. As you'll soon see, decoration is just one of the designer's responsibilities. The interior designer does far more.

What does an interior designer do?

Interior designers select and organize the furnishings of homes and offices, as well as hotels, banks, restaurants, hospitals, schools, and other public places. They determine what furnishings are needed, then decide where these will be located. They determine color schemes and choose furniture, fabrics, carpeting, wallpaper, lighting fixtures, and other items to fit into the plan. Designers prepare plans like those drawn by an architect, make sketches in color, and may even build scale models of fully furnished interiors to explain ideas to the client.

This is more than a *decorative* arrangement. In defining the role of the interior designer, the American Society of Interior Designers explains that the professional must have "specialized knowledge of interior construction, building codes, equipment, materials and furnishings" and consider "the health, safety, and welfare of the public" an essential part of the job.

As an interior designer you must often work within functional limitations, like walls you can't move and built-in lighting. You must study the tastes and living habits of your clients. The interior must reflect their personalities and meet important functional requirements. The arrangement of furnishings must be convenient. The furniture itself must be comfortable and durable. The room must be easy to clean and *keep* clean. The lighting and color scheme must relax the eyes.

Like the architect, the interior designer plans the environment in which people must live and work. In Scandinavia, the profession is called *interior architecture.*

Beyond the job of *designing* or *redesigning* an interior, there are all sorts of practical problems that the interior designer must consider. If there's any construction to be done, any furniture or fixtures to be built in, you must supervise the work. You must be on hand to make sure that furnishings are properly placed, that paint matches the color scheme, and that wallpaper goes on the right walls. This means dealing with contractors and overseeing the work of carpenters, electricians, painters, paper hangers, and other craftworkers. Naturally the designer is expected to prepare cost estimates for clients and make sure that these estimates turn out to be accurate.

The ASID also points out that the designer must be prepared to "cope with a mass of paperwork, such as writing specifications and placing orders, figuring estimates, and keeping track of all the administrative details necessary in dealing with hundreds of items of merchandise."

The interior designer is often brought in to work with the architect when a new building is in the formative stage. Many enlightened architects and their clients now insist on this, so that interiors will harmonize with the total concept of the building and not look like an afterthought.

Beyond residential and commercial interiors, the interior designer may plan the passenger accommodations of ships, trains, buses, and airplanes; room settings for motion pictures, television shows, and stage plays; model rooms to display products on sale in stores; experimental interiors for magazines; window displays, exhibitions, and trade fairs.

In fact, interior designers may work on more than interiors. They often develop custom made furniture for clients. Many designers create lines of mass produced furniture, manufactured for sale in department stores and furniture stores. Others are drawn into some specialty like the design of lighting fixtures, which brings them close to the field of industrial design, the subject of a later chapter.

Designers may also specialize in some important area like supermarket planning, hotel work, offices, or residential interiors. Some interior design firms have built national reputations on such specialties. However, many designers move freely from one specialty to another or work in all these areas at once.

Where does an interior designer find work?

Many interior designers are really in the furniture business. They're employed in furniture stores or in the home furnishings sections of department stores. Others have their own shops, selling furniture, fabrics, lamps, and various accessories. These professionals plan an interior without charge on the condition that the client buys the furnishings from the designer. The designer's income is the profit on the sale of the furniture.

Interior designers may also work in design offices or may open design offices of their own. These design consultants have no stock of furniture, fabrics or any other products to sell. They're more like an architectural office or an art studio: a group of designers selling a service. Many operate simply on a fee basis or on a percentage of the total cost of the interior. Other design offices, particularly small ones, may make their money as stores do, by selling furnishings. Still others combine these methods of payment: they collect fees for their services *and* commissions on sales.

Interior designers are also drawn into manufacturing. Some design for furniture manufacturers, on a full-time or freelance basis. Makers of automobiles, airplanes, buses, and trains hire interior designers for full-time staff jobs or freelance work. A handful of designers manufacture their own furniture.

There are often jobs for interior designers in other kinds of design offices. Many architectural offices and industrial design firms now have interiors departments.

Other employers include hotel chains, which are constantly putting up new hotels and refurbishing old ones; store planning departments of supermarket chains; builders and contractors who find it useful to offer interior design services as an inducement to clients; even women's magazines, which hire designers to create interiors for how-to-do-it articles. Many designers teach and still others specialize in design journalism, writing for magazines and newspapers.

The *ASID Report*—the newsletter of the American Society of Interior Designers—published some interesting figures on designers' specialties. According to this 1982 survey, the "average" ASID member spent about 45% of the time working on residential projects, roughly 45% on so-called contract work (offices, banks, hotels, restaurants, etc.), and about 10% on specialties like furniture design. Some of the small but interesting specialties included the adaptation and reuse of old structures (2.5%), preservation of historic interiors (1.5%), and church interiors (.9%).

Interior designers are scattered across every state in the country. There are jobs and freelance work for interior designers in every population center big enough to have department stores, growing suburbs, and an expanding business district. This description fits *hundreds* of cities, large and small, where there are homes, offices, stores, and public buildings to design, furnish, and redesign. Interior design, unlike some other design fields, is a highly decentralized profession.

What does an interior designer study?

The Interior Design Educators Council says that the ideal interior design curriculum "should offer specialized courses in principles of design, history of art, architecture and interiors, freehand and mechanical drawing or architectural drafting, visual presentation techniques, space planning, residential and contract design, interior materials and systems, product design and construction, human factors and business practices and principles." What does this mean in more concrete terms?

After the introductory fine art and design courses of the foundation year, you soon find yourself planning actual rooms. This means more than selecting and arranging furnishings. You make sketches of interiors in pencil, watercolor, pastel, and other media. You build small, precise models of rooms, including tiny reproductions of furniture, lamps, drapes, rugs, and wall coverings. You draft plans and elevations of interiors, similar to architects' blueprints, showing how the space and furnishings are organized.

There are often separate courses in model building, drafting, sketching, and rendering. These are all "visual presentation techniques" that you'll use to explain your ideas to clients and contractors when you're on the job.

You may also take courses in color; fundamentals of archtectural construction; window and store display; graphic design for signs and displays in public places. Another *must* is usually a class in the history of art and architecture, with special emphasis on the great interior styles of the past.

Furniture design may be a special course or even a major subject within the interior design curriculum. Again, this means building models, not just tiny scale models, but full-size furniture. A course in furniture design almost always means a good deal of time in the woodworking shop. You'll not only learn the principles of good furniture design, but manufacturing methods and the structural properties of materials like wood, metals, and plastics.

Beyond the required program, you may be able to choose several elective courses such as fabric design, ceramics, and even industrial design, to which furniture design is closely related.

Does an interior designer need a degree?

Though many good interior designers never got a degree, it *is* significant that the most influential professional association in the field recommends a four- or five-year degree course or a three-year diploma. I doubt that many ASID members would consider a degree *indispensable* when they hire a new staff member, but the ASID's stand indicates that a degree has strong selling power. In most leading art and design schools, the three-year diploma simply means that you've taken all the *professional* courses for the degree, but you've skipped the *academic* courses.

However, there's another important hurdle. In 1974, the National Council for Interior Design Qualification was formed to develop a qualifying examination that would set a minimum standard of professional competence in the field. To join the leading professional organizations—such as the ASID or the IBD (the Institute of Business Designers)—you have to pass this exam. Some employers will ask you if you've passed the NCIDQ exam and some won't; but passing the exam does look good on your resume and may give you an edge in the stiff competition for jobs. For more information about the exam, write the NCIDQ, whose address appears on the list of professional organizations later in the book.

What part-time and summer jobs are good experience?

Though it may be hard to find, the best summer or part-time job is an apprentice spot in a design office, designer's shop, or the interior design staff of a department store or furniture store.

A selling job may also be excellent experience and might be easier to get. You can learn a lot about home furnishings by selling furniture, fabrics, lamps and lighting fixtures, wallpaper, and similar products in a department store or furniture shop.

Skilled trades like carpentry or upholstering can teach you a lot. It's worthwhile to try for a part-time or summer job in a cabinet-maker's or upholsterer's shop.

Another excellent spot might be a drafting job in an architectural, engineering, construction or manufacturing firm *if* your drafting is sufficiently advanced. Speaking of manufacturing, you might also try for a job in a plant that makes home furnishings. Even a production line job in a furniture factory would be valuable experience for a future furniture designer.

What is a typical first job?

The ASID points out that the beginning "designer must be prepared at first to do all kinds of routine work such as record-keeping, typing, filing, cataloging samples, and the constant study of old and new sources. After becoming thoroughly familiar with the firm's operation, he may, under supervision, draw floor plans, color schemes, and sit in on client consultations and installations."

Like most apprenticeships in the art field, your first job in interior design will probably be a motley assortment of low-level chores that teach you more than you realize. For instance, you may take care of filing furniture catalogs and photos, and samples of fabric, wallpaper, wood and paint. This will teach you the materials of the trade, as well as *sources*, the hundreds of places where you can find the furnishings and accessories that fill an interior.

Beginners are often used as shoppers, another good way to learn about products and their sources. On instructions from senior designers in your office, you visit showrooms to select samples and photos of furnishings that might be suitable for a current design project. You check prices, delivery schedules, and the merits of competing products, slowly building your own mental file of essential data.

At first, you may not get a chance to design any interiors on your own, but you'll sketch, draft, render, and perhaps build models of other designers' ideas. You may compile presentation folders of fabric, wallpaper, paint, and wood finish samples for clients. You may also assemble books of photos or sketches for client presentations.

In a store or shop, you may sell and advise customers on their choice of furnishings. This experience will give you insight into public taste and buying habits. It will also develop the poise and verbal skill needed to deal with clients.

What are later jobs like?

As you prove your ability, you're given projects of your own. You develop interiors with less and less supervision. You draft and sketch *your own* ideas. You begin to deal directly with clients, examining their needs and making recommendations. And you oversee the work of contractors who build, supply, and install the furnishings you order.

Now you're involved in the big decisions about space planning, the layout of the total interior, and the total design concept—which means specifying all the components of the interior, estimating the cost of the furnishings and the labor, creating client presentations (plans, color charts, models, photos, samples), and picking contractors.

Climbing toward the top of the ladder, you must ultimately face the choice of continuing to work for someone else or having your own business. You may become a key executive in a design office or head of the interior design department in a store or architectural office. You may decide to open your own shop or design office. If you end up in manufacturing, you may become design director of a furniture company, for example, or you may even decide to design and manufacture your own furniture.

In a top job in a larger organization—whether you're self-employed or on someone's payroll—your time at the drawing board will be limited. Your main functions will be to supervise your staff and deal with clients and management—if you're in manufacturing—and make decisons. You may develop design solutions in broad terms, then hand the details over to staff members down the line. If you're in manufacturing, you'll also spend a lot of time thinking about marketing problems and planning new product lines.

Your own small design office or shop may also limit your time at the drawing board, if only because you have to be a Jack-of-all-trades. You and one or two assistants may do everything: dealing with clients, designing, shopping, working with contractors, and keeping up the files. As one designer put it: "In the morning I roll up my sleeves and work at my board. At lunchtime, I put on my jacket and spruce up for lunch with a client. For the rest of the afternoon, I'm not a designer, but a businessman calling on prospects. Then I rush back to the office before dinner to write a few letters, clean up the office, and empty the waste baskets."

Your relationship with your clients depends on the nature of your business. If you concentrate on residential interiors, steady clients are rare. Since it's obvious that few home owners redecorate year after year, most of your work boils down to one-shot jobs, though many clients may buy new items of furniture from time to time. Designing commerical interiors may mean lots of one-shot clients who want a store or office done. But chains of stores, hotels, banks, restaurants, and other firms with many branches may provide a steady stream of assignments over the years. The same may be true of shipbuilders and manufacturers of automobiles and airplanes, who constantly develop new products that need interiors.

Where can you get more information?

The leading magazines for interior designers are *Interiors, Interior Design,* and *Contract.* The trade newspaper is *Home Furnishings Daily.* There are also mass magazines, influential and richly illustrated, such as *House Beautiful, House and Garden,* and *Better Homes and Gardens.* Nearly all the women's magazines and the women's pages of the daily newspapers devote extensive space to interior design.

The architectural magazines carry lots of material valuable to interior designers. The leading architectural monthlies are *Architectural Record, Progressive Architecture,* and the *AIA Journal.*

Both the American Society of Interior Designers (ASID) and the Interior Design Educators Council (IDEC) publish career pamphlets—quoted in this chapter. The Foundation for Interior Design Education Research (FIDER) publishes a list of accredited programs in art schools, colleges, and universities—though it's only a *partial* list because a number of the best schools haven't applied for accreditation. And the National Council for

Interior Design Qualification (NCIDQ) publishes a study guide that you'll need to pass their exam. All these addresses are at the back of *Art Career Guide*.

Certainly the best way to learn more about the field of interior design is just to keep your eyes open. Visit new—and old—public buildings that have notable interiors. Browse in furniture stores and in the home furnishings sections of department stores. Above all, develop the habit of looking carefully at every room you enter. In the years to come, you may design and redesign many such rooms.

10
Architecture

It used to be easy to describe what architects did for a living: they designed buildings. But this description is now hopelessly inadequate. Lots of architects *do* concentrate mainly on the design and construction of buildings, but they're also concerned with our total environment. Architects are becoming far more involved in the design of the town or city itself—so-called urban design—and in the preservation and shaping of our natural surroundings. Today's architect is interested in what professionals call the *built* environment and the *natural* environment—in buildings and their context, whether that context is made by man or nature. In this new concept of the design process, landscape architects loom larger than ever, so they also deserve an important place in this chapter.

What does an architect do?

For a great many architects, the original job description is still fairly accurate. Their job is to create buildings. But creating a building means solving problems for *people*. Before touching pencil to paper, the architect must study the living habits of the people who expect to live or work in the building. It's also important to analyze the client's finances to determine cost limitations. (Obviously, the architect needs a good head for figures.) The professional must also know how to research zoning laws, legal regulations, and other aspects that come under the heading of real estate.

Drawing plans for a building means more than creating a handsome exterior. The building's location on its site must reflect the architect's knowledge of traffic conditions, energy problems, weather, and the terrain. In a large building, there must be adequate corridors, stairways, elevators, entrances, and exits for normal traffic and for any emergency. The plan for the building itself must make proper provisions for plumbing, wiring, heating, and air conditioning. Above all, the architect's plan must make logical use of space and not waste an inch. One critic has said, "Architecture is the art of space."

But the architect's plan must do even more. Elaborate drawings must show how the building is put together. Pages and pages of diagrams explain details like window construction; the design of stairways; the anatomy of walls, floors, and ceilings. These drawings must indicate the location of such mechanical elements as heating and air conditioning units; elevator and escalator machinery; lighting equipment and plumbing. The architect must then select all the materials that go into the building, from bricks to light switches. Specifications must be put in writing to determine materials, quantities, and the kind of workmanship that will be needed.

From this mass of detail must emerge not only a safe, convenient, efficient environment, but an object of beauty, showing the sculptor's sense of form and the painter's ability to handle color, texture, light and shade.

The architect is expected to work closely with the general contractor and with consulting engineers—structural, mechanical, heating, and electrical experts—when the building is complex enough to require such a team. When the structure is ready to go up, the architect watches like a hawk to be sure that plans and specifications are followed accurately.

Though many architectural offices will design *any* kind of building, from a tiny beach house to a multi-story office building, others specialize. Some architects concentrate on houses. Others are best known for schools, hospitals, churches, or other public buildings. Office buildings have become a specialty because of their enormous complexity. Stores and shopping centers have emerged as a specialty. And many architects have become fascinated with the restoration and adaptation of old buildings for contemporary use—a specialty for the professional who enjoys historical research.

But many architects no longer just conceive a building, supervise its construction, and walk away. They know that buildings (and the needs of the people who live or work inside buildings) are inseparable from our man-made and natural surroundings, which means *other* buildings, of course, as well as streets, highways, bridges, parks, squares, shopping and business centers, housing developments, parking lots, land, trees and other growing things, bodies of water, the very air we breathe. All these things are the territory of urban design, which is now a major concern of architects.

In practical terms, architects become urban designers when they begin to design "systems": not an office building or a parking lot, but groups of buildings and interlocking patterns of streets, tunnels, bridges, parking lots, and other elements that comprise the built environment as a whole. To do these jobs effectively, the architect is not only a skilled designer, but must know how to ask the right questions about population trends, mass transportation, race relations, water supply, air pollution, zoning laws, taxes, local politics, and a huge list of other factors that influence the daily lives of masses of people who live in urban settings.

The specialist in the *natural* environment, of course, is the landscape architect. The American Society of Landscape Architects defines itself as "the design profession concerned with planning of outdoor areas." Just as many architects are concerned primarily with buildings, many landscape architects are still concerned mainly with natural surroundings. Using trees, shrubs, grass, stones, bodies of water, and the shape of the terrain itself as "building materials," such landscape architects literally shape (or reshape) our natural environment. They're called upon to design parks, the outdoor areas of campuses and shopping centers, gardens, sports facilities and country clubs, and the "landscaping" that surrounds buildings, highways, monuments, industrial complexes, and housing projects.

But just as the old definition of architecture no longer works for many professionals, the territory of the landscape architect has also broadened greatly. In the realm of urban design, the American Society of Landscape Architects points out that the profession now "participates in the development of neighborhoods, towns, and cities by preparing site plans for civic and community centers, housing projects, shopping centers, school and recreational facilities . . . collaborates in the planning of highways and parkways," and still more. So landscape architects no longer see themselves simply as specialists in shaping natural surroundings, but as planners of *many* aspects of the human environment.

Perhaps the best way to summarize the services of the landscape architect is to quote the ASLA's own career pamphlet, which I'll abbreviate slightly. "The landscape architect gives professional advice on land planning problems; selects suitable sites for definite uses; makes preliminary studies, sketches, models, and reports; prepares working drawings, cost estimates, and specifications for contractors' bids; supervises construction; approves materials and workmanship; prepares, reviews, or formulates plans for public land development; and administers public or private land planning and construction programs."

No picture of the architectural profession would be complete without mentioning that many architects specialize in interior design, while architectural training often leads to a career in industrial design. Roughly 3000 architects teach at accredited architectural schools. Still other professionals become architectural journalists, photographers, and executives in business and government.

Where does an architect find work?

Most architects are hired by architectural firms. These are essentially consulting organizations. That is, they accept work from a variety of clients: corporations putting up new buildings; real estate firms and builders planning housing developments; families who want to build new homes.

Some architects get staff jobs in industry. Corporations with long range building programs—supermarket chains, hotels, manufacturers with far-flung plants and office buildings—often have an architectural department. There are also jobs with builders and real estate firms. Other kinds of consulting organizations—engineers, industrial and interior designers, for example—frequently have architects on the staff. Federal, state, and local governments employ a number of architects full-time, usually on the basis of civil service examinations.

The best-known architectural firms are the big ones, of course. These can have hundreds of employees occupying whole floors of big office buildings in major metropolitan areas. But a 1981 study by the American Institute of Architects reveals a growing trend to smaller offices: at that time, 80% of AIA member firms had less than 10 employees. There are also more "nontraditional" practices: the architect-builder, the architect-developer, the "storefront architect" who opens up on the main street of a small town.

Geographically, architecture is quite decentralized. There's work for architects wherever people are putting up new buildings or revamping old ones. Logically, most architects are located in or near metropolitan areas, simply because that's where they find the most people and the greatest building activity. But there are successful architects in every city of reasonable size, as well as in many small towns.

Many landscape architects are self-employed—running their own offices and selling their services to corporate clients, government agencies, and homeowners—or they work for other landscape architects in offices similar to architectural firms. Some work for architectural, engineering, and urban planning firms. A surprisingly high number (about one third of all landscape architects) work for government agencies that deal with urban planning, highways, recreational areas, national parks, forests, and other types of land use. The profession is decentralized—there are opportunities throughout the country—although the growing emphasis on urban design means that many landscape architects must work in metropolitan areas, rather than out in the wide open spaces.

What does an architect study?

Because an architect's work involves public health and safety, all states require a license for the practice of architecture. A standard licensing requirement is usually graduation from an accredited professional school, usually a five- or six-year program, plus three years of experience in an office headed by a licensed architect. The licensing exam is basically the same in every state. When you pass the exam and get your license in one state, some additional paperwork will get you a license in another state.

Are all licensed architects graduates of architectural schools? Most states recognize that years of work experience, usually twelve, are equivalent to a formal education. However, architectural school graduates *can* get a license sooner.

Are *all* practicing architects licensed? Actually, there *are* professionals who work for years without a license and who may never get one at all. However, they must work *under* a licensed architect. Although unlicensed architects can get jobs, they can't rise very high or start their own firms.

Now let's look more closely at architectural school. The quickest route is five years in school, combining undergraduate pre-architecture and professional courses for a bachelor's degree. You can also do it in six years: four years as an undergraduate with an architecture major for a bachelor's degree, and then two years of graduate work for a master's. And if you spent four undergraduate years earning a bachelor's degree in some other field, you'll need three to four years of graduate architectural study to get a master's before you enter the profession—a total of seven or eight years.

Your first year in architectural school may be planned as a foundation year, but it won't be the same as an art school's foundation year. There are usually basic courses in two- and three-dimensional design, freehand drawing and drafting, perspective, plus introductory courses in architectural design and construction. Mathematics, with strong emphasis on geometry, is likely to be important. And since the five year program leads to a degree, you'll take your series of academic courses in the liberal arts and sciences, particularly psychology and sociology.

In succeeding years, you'll plunge more deeply into the principles of design and construction. You'll design small structures, then bigger ones, from the sketch stage to drawings that contractors could actually work from. You'll cover acres of paper with your drafting. You'll build models and learn to render buildings in pencil, pen, and watercolor for presentation to clients.

There will be courses in site planning, landscape design, urban design, and the history of art and architecture. There will be technical subjects such as structural systems, construction materials, specification writing, real estate, and professional practice, which means the way an architectural office functions.

Although urban design is likely to be included in any up-to-date architectural program, this specialty may also be a separate program, leading to an advanced degree after you get your bachelor's degree in architecture.

If this heavy program of architectural subjects leaves you any free time, you may get a chance to take a few classes in painting or sculpture, perhaps the greatest lack in the programs of our architectural schools.

Although landscape architects study many of the same art and design subjects as architects—basic design, architectural design, sketching, drafting, model making—they must also learn specialized subjects like surveying, landscape design, landscape construction, plant materials and design, and the behavior of climate and terrain. Landscape architects also take their share of urban planning courses, as well as the same business subjects required in architectural school: contracts, specifications, cost estimating, and office practice.

In twenty states, encompassing 80% of the nation's population, landscape architects must be licensed. To take the licensing examination, you need a degree, plus two to four years of job experience. Without a degree, you can generally take the exam if you've had six to eight years experience.

It's worth mentioning that many two-year colleges—often called community colleges—offer architectural courses that provide a good introduction to the field. With this two-year degree behind you, you can often transfer to architectural school to complete your training.

Does an architect need a degree?

Though it's possible, as I've said, to get a job and even a license without graduating from an architectural school, there's no question that a degree from an accredited school is a great advantage in job hunting. It's possible to take some short courses in drafting and elementary architecture, start at the bottom in an architectural office, and work your way up. But advancement is easier and faster for the graduate who has a degree. Noting that 85% of license applicants do have degrees, the American Institute of Architects strongly recommends enrolling in a degree program.

The same holds true for landscape architects. The degree does make a difference. And in both fields, the degree makes a license easier to get—and quicker.

Having emphasized that the degree is the quickest route to a license, I should certainly add that many excellent, highly successful architects have come up through the ranks and gotten their licenses without degrees. To clients and employers, what matters most is *experience*.

What part-time and summer jobs are good experience?

A good student in a respected school can often get a summer or part-time job in an architectural office. More quickly than other art professions, architects have recognized the value of such jobs, particularly summer jobs, as ways to spot potential talent.

If you can't get a summer or part-time job in an architectural office—which usually means routine drafting—*any* drafting job will be useful experience. Local construction firms, manufacturers, or engineering firms may have a temporary spot for you at a drawing board.

It's also worthwhile to investigate fields *related* to architecture. What about a job with an electrical, plumbing, or heating contractor; a supplier of building materials; a real estate firm? Any organization linked to the construction business provides an opportunity to build up experience while you're still in school. And doing *physical* work on a construction site—working with tools and watching how a building gets put together—is a fine way to learn about the practical realities of the profession.

For the student of landscape architecture, a job in an architectural or landscape architecture firm is the ideal answer. A job with a landscape contractor is another possibility. Nor should you overlook the chance of getting a job in a tree nursery, on a forestry or conservation project, or in one of the many areas of urban planning.

What is a typical first job?

A beginning job usually means drafting. Working at the drawing board, you'll explore design ideas suggested by your bosses and you'll visualize alternative solutions. You may do research on building types and materials. You may do photography or build models. And you'll do all sorts of routine office chores. As you begin to prove your skill and judgment on such lower-level assignments, your bosses will be watching and trying to decide what you're especially good at. As Stephen A. Kliment points out in the AIA publication, *Architecture: Professional Options*, "Architecture is not one narrow career, but a combination of many areas of knowledge ... separate and distinct career possibilities." When they know you better, your bosses will decide where you can be most useful in the office—which architectural "career possibility" is right for you.

In a big office, you're likely to find yourself assigned to one department, doing a rather specialized job for quite some time. If you're being groomed to be a designer, you'll move to the design department. Bear in mind that only a small percentage of architects or landscape architects actually do design work in a big organization. Some of the other specialties—which I'll tell you more about in a moment, when I talk about later jobs—include programming, project management, practice management, marketing, marketing communications, specification writing, estimating and cost control, and construction contract administration.

A small office is more likely to make you a Jack-of-all-trades from the very beginning. In addition to routine drafting, you may do some renderings, build some models, and even get a chance to watch construction and deal with contractors. Does this mean a smaller office is a better place for a beginner? It's true that a smaller architectural firm may give you more diversified experience. On the other hand, you may never work on the big projects that land in bigger offices. There's also the factor of temperament. Some beginners enjoy the often hectic pace of a small office, where everybody does everything. Others like the feeling of bigness and the knowledge that you have just one job to do well. Experienced architects often recommend that you start in a small office and then move to a big one to see how the other half lives.

What are later jobs like?

As you climb the ladder in a big office, you'll almost certainly move into a specialty. Young architects tend to feel that design is the most glamorous specialty. But Stephen Kliment lists many other rewarding specialties. Programming is the job of analyzing the client's requirements and defining the design problems that need to be solved. Project management means supervising the team that must deliver the project—on time, within a budget, and within definite quality standards. Practice management is the job of running the business side of the office. Marketing means selling the services of the office to potential clients, while marketing communications means explaining and promoting those services via written proposals, brochures, audiovisual media, and other types of publicity.

Analytical minds may lend themselves to specification writing, which means analyzing the items and materials that go into a building's construction. If you have a head for figures, estimating and cost control may be your specialty. And if you like being out there on the construction site, you'll enjoy construction contract administration, which means working with the contractors to make sure that the details of the job—as defined in the construction contracts—are properly executed.

The odds in favor of your doing *some* real design, after three or four years, seem to be better in a small office. This doesn't mean you'll design a building from top to bottom, but you may get a chance to contribute ideas and solve certain design problems. Having started as a Jack-of-all-trades, you can expect more of the same as you climb the ladder. Design, drawings, specifications, and client contact all become interwoven. There may be *some* specialization at the top—one partner may be particularly good at working with clients, while another is best at design—but you must all be prepared to handle *any* aspect of a job.

When you've risen to a key position in an architectural office, large or small, you may become an associate, roughly equivalent to a junior partner in a law firm. Later you may become a full partner. Partners and associates get a share of the profits in addition to their salaries. And they obviously have some say in how the business is run.

For most architects, the long range goal is to set up one's own practice. If you become an associate or a partner in an existing firm, of course, then you *have* your own business without going out and opening your own office. But you may not wait that long. You may be a one-person office, hiring junior personnel when you have a big push. Or you may share responsibilities with a partner or two, adding temporary or permanent staff as business expands. Ultimately, you hope, you'll have an organization of your own.

Architecture and landscape architecture are no more stable than any other freelance business. The ebb and flow of clients remains a problem. Workers are hired for a project and must be released when the job is finished, unless there's a new client to keep them busy for a while longer. The dividing line between permanent and temporary jobs is indistinct. Job hunters get used to being told, "The job's permanent as long as the work holds out."

Where can you get more information?

The leading American architectural magazines are *Progressive Architecture, Architectural Record*, and the *AIA Journal*. Architects also follow the rest of the design press. *Interiors, Interior Design*, and *Contract* are important reading for architects. *Industrial Design* covers a field that now attracts many young architects. The American Society of Landscape Architects publishes *Landscape Architecture*.

Architectural exhibitions are few and far between, but there are important ones circulated from time to time by New York's Museum of Modern Art and the American Federation of Arts. Watch the calendar of your local museum for such shows. The local chapters of the American Institute of Architects also hold exhibitions that you should attend.

The American Institute of Architects and the American Society of Landscape Architects both publish career pamphlets. The AIA also publishes Stephen A. Kliment's *Architecture: Professional Options*, by far the best survey of the many career possibilities in the field. The National Architectural Accrediting Board publishes a list of accredited schools. The Association of Collegiate Schools of Architecture has its own school list. And the National Council of Architectural Registration Boards publishes literature on the licensing exam. You'll find all these addresses at the back of *Art Career Guide*.

The way to learn most about the professions of architecture and landscape architecture is to look at buildings, landscaping, and urban design projects first-hand. Try to get around and see the best work in your area. Go inside buildings if they're open to the public. Visit parts of your town that are being "redeveloped" by the city planning commission. Architecture is all around you, waiting to be looked at.

11
Industrial design

Comparable to architecture in technical complexity is the profession of industrial design. Since the first appearance, in the late 1920s, of men who called themselves industrial designers, the field has grown so rapidly and in so many directions that no one has come up with an adequate definition for the profession. One spokesman says simply: "The industrial designer is a kind of modern Leonardo da Vinci. He must be prepared to design anything from a spoon to a city."

What does an industrial designer do?

To the public, the industrial designer first became known as a designer of so-called hard goods: cars, refrigerators, TV sets, stoves, air conditioners, and scores of other household devices from can openers to electric mixers.

But this is only one of the spheres in which industrial designers operate. They create many other household objects: furniture, lighting fixtures, tableware, the toys in the nursery, the tools in your tool box, the plumbing fixtures in your kitchen and bathroom, even your door knobs.

Industrial designers work on industrial products as well: products manufactured for use by industry itself. Among these are machine tools, trucks, farm machinery, and office equipment.

The armed forces have used industrial designers to work on

weapons, tanks and troop carriers, aircraft, and atomic subma-
rines. The transportation industries—builders of planes, trains,
buses, and ships—have used industrial designers to plan passenger accommodations. Industrial designers have been drawn into
architecture and interiors, particularly stores, banks, service sta-
tions, and other commercial buildings. A related field is exhibition design and display work. Though packaging might be called
a form of graphic design, since packages come off the printing
press, many industrial designers are active in this field.

In recent years, the greatest new opportunities for industrial
designers have opened up in the industries that specialize in applied technology. Designers are making important contributions
in consumer electronics, medical instruments, and the sophisticated office equipment of the electronic age.

Because the industrial designer does such diverse things, few
outsiders can figure out just what the designer does to all these
products. Certainly, the designer's most obvious job is to make a
product good-looking. The designer's job is to boost sales, and
one way is to design a handsome product.

But most good industrial designers also say their job is to
make a *better* product. Just as the architect must design a building
in which life runs smoothly, the industrial designer must create a
product that is safe, comfortable, and convenient to use. This is
why the armed forces have used industrial design consultants:
military men don't much care how a tank turrent looks, but they
want to be sure that the gunner is comfortably seated, that his
weapons are convenient to handle, and that he doesn't whack his
head when he swings around. Industrial designers apply this
same sort of thinking to non-military products. Designers are experts on the way people and products work together.

Thus, today's designers must be especially concerned with the
study of *human factors*: our physical dimensions; how we move,
see, and hear; how our bodies are "engineered"; and how all this
information must be put to use in creating industrial products
that match human needs.

Designers must also have a basic knowledge of engineering,
since they work closely with engineers in developing a product

and planning its manufacture. It's the engineers who create the mechanical part of the product, while the designers work on the parts we see and touch. Thus, industrial designers needn't be trained engineers, but they must know enough about fundamental principles to talk the engineer's language.

One leading designer has summed up the profession in words that may seem discouraging to some readers, inspiring to others: "The industrial designer is an almost impossible combination, blending certain qualities of the painter, sculptor, architect, engineer, graphic designer, doctor, and sales executive. No one can be all these things, really, but the industrial designer has to try."

Industrial designers combine all these skills because they're responsible for the *working relationship* between human beings and the manufactured objects we live with. This responsibility demands that the industrial designer, like the architect, be *more* than an artist.

Depending on the individual's background and the nature of the job, an industrial designer may do highly diversified work or may choose a specialty. In some consulting design offices, you might get a chance to work in all the fields I've mentioned. But you might also specialize in some particular family of products, like electronic equipment, appliances, cars, or packaging. A material may become a specialty: some designers work just for the aluminum or plastics industry. A handful of professionals design no products at all, but become experts on lighting or color.

By the way, it's interesting to note that the industrial design profession has long since given up the stereotype of "a man's business." Today, 50 percent of industrial design undergraduates are women.

Where does an industrial designer find work?

The nation's industrial designers are divided between consulting offices and the design staffs of manufacturing corporations. The design consulting firm, like an architectural office, has a variety of clients, usually in non-competing fields. For this reason, a consulting office usually has many kinds of products on its drawing boards. A job on the design staff of a manufacturing company normally means that you work on a more limited range of products. If you work for a manufacturer of medical equipment, for instance, you'll obviously concentrate on just that, perhaps with some packaging and display work thrown in. Of course, some manufacturers *do* make a diversified product line, which may mean more diversified work for the design staff.

Even with a full design staff, a manufacturing corporation may still retain a consulting design office. Just as a designer might find a 9-to-5 job in any of the industries I've mentioned, the consulting office finds its clients in these same industries. Many designers move back and forth from jobs in industry to jobs in consulting firms.

Most consulting offices are located in large cities centered in the nation's industrial regions. Wherever manufacturers are clustered, there are job opportunities for industrial design consultants.

Staff jobs are scattered completely across the map, wherever a manufacturing plant might be located. A factory can be in a major city, a small town, or a rural area. Though consulting is a fairly centralized business, a corporate staff job might take you anywhere in the country.

What does an industrial designer study?

After taking the foundation year courses that you share with other art students, you'll move into more advanced courses in two- and three-dimensional design. Quite soon, you'll be introduced to basic engineering, materials, and manufacturing methods. You'll learn drafting and model-making. You'll explore various sketching and rendering techniques.

But learning these techniques will mean far less than learning to solve *practical design problems.* Most important of all, you'll take courses in which you design actual products, just as you would in a design office. At first, you'll probably start with small products like hand tools or kitchen utensils. By your final year, you may have tried anything from computers to railroad cars. You may find your design courses divided into categories like product design, which usually means hard goods; transportation design; exhibits and displays; packaging, and so on. Or these subjects may be mingled in a series of classes labeled industrial design: elementary, intermediate, and advanced.

Supplementing these professional courses may be related subjects like graphic design, architecture, interior design, and even photography, a valuable tool in design research. None of these will be advanced courses, but they're useful additions to your background. You can also expect introductory classes in business and marketing methods. And if there's any time left, you may be encouraged to take a bit more painting, perhaps some sculpture or ceramics to strengthen your sense of three-dimensional form.

Verbal communication skills are essential in this profession. Thus, many schools emphasize courses, or at least assignments, in research and report writing. Psychology and the social sciences are often stressed. Courses in *human factors* are important. The computer has become an important design tool—as well as an essential tool in running a design office—so many schools now place special emphasis on courses that train you how to use and program computers.

Does an industrial designer need a degree?

There are many first-rate designers without degrees, particularly among older professionals who entered the field before schools had industrial design programs. But among younger designers, a degree is an essential qualification in most employers' eyes. This is particularly true in manufacturing companies. All leading industrial design schools, like architectural schools, offer degrees. A degree has come to stand for the most complete professional education.

What part-time and summer jobs are good experience?

The first place to look for a summer or part-time job is a consulting design office or the design department of a manufacturing company. Like architects, industrial designers often use summer jobs to test and train future employees. A few design offices have found a way of combining summer *and* part-time work: you're tried out for a summer, then kept on for one day each week during the school year if you make the grade. Many good design schools are willing to plan your schedule so you can work in a design office one day and attend classes four days.

However, if such a job can't be found, there are other fields where you can pile up some good experience. Any kind of drafting job—in an engineering or construction firm, for example—is valuable background. Many manufacturing corporations need drafting help too. You can also learn a great deal from a job in which you work with your hands or with machinery: a carpenter's shop or a machine shop can be a good place to learn about how things are put together and how they work.

Since the industrial designer is supposed to be the closest thing to the *universal designer*—the professional who can do anything—almost *any* art job might be valuable experience. Look back at the chapters that precede this one. Any part-time or summer job I've suggested for a graphic designer, interior designer, or architect might be a good suggestion for an industrial designer.

Perhaps the easiest summer or part-time job to get is a selling job in a store. This may seem far from industrial design, but an understanding of consumer psychology, what sells and why, is essential for a designer. Such a job can be extremely valuable.

What is a typical first job?

A beginner's main job, as in most other art professions, is to put your bosses' ideas on paper. You spend a lot of time drafting the designs of senior employees. Your ability to sketch and render will also be put to work. A design often goes through hundreds of sketches—just for study purposes, not for the client—before it reaches final form. If your renderings are really first rate, you may be asked to create finished presentation drawings.

In the same way, you may build models based on the drawings and suggestions of more experienced designers. These models may be clay, plaster, wood, metal, plastic, cardboard, even paper. Some will be just study models, sketches in three dimensions. Others will be presentation models, built to explain an idea to the client or to your co-workers in other departments of the corporation.

If you join a large design office or corporate design staff, you may find that the work is departmentalized. You may be assigned to the product design group, packaging, interiors and display, the model shop, or some other subdivision. A small consulting office or corporate staff is less likely to be specialized in its organization: here the Jack-of-all-trades is wanted. A few manufacturers employ hundreds of designers, divided among many departments. At the opposite extreme, some consulting design offices contain just a boss and an assistant.

Whenever you find work, you discover instantly that the industrial designer isn't a solitary visionary, but a member of a team. The designer is a member of a product development group and consists of specialists in engineering, marketing, manufacturing, and other areas of business and technology. These specialists may be your co-workers, members of the client's own crew, or other consultants.

What are later jobs like?

As you advance in the industrial design profession, you may become a senior designer or perhaps a department head in a consulting office or corporate design staff. Ultimately, you may become design director of a corporation. You may become an associate—a sort of junior partner—or even a partner in a consulting design office. You may finally decide to launch your own consulting organization.

In a manufacturing company or a large design office, the senior designer concentrates on contact work and developing ideas. As a senior designer, you create design concepts and supervise junior designers who put these concepts in the form of drawings and models. You do a good deal of sketching yourself, plus a certain amount of drafting, while you're exploring design ideas. But you leave model-making, rendering, and more routine drafting to younger staff members.

If you work in a consulting office, you must work closely with your clients' engineers and marketing executives to make sure that the design is practical and salable. Keeping the client sold is a major job in itself. If you're on a corporate staff, of course, these engineers and marketing people are your colleagues. But you must work closely with them and *sell* your ideas just as if these co-workers are clients.

However, if you start your own one- or two-person consulting firm, then you may have to be junior designer and senior designer all at once. You do your own drafting, model-making, rendering, research, client contact, and above all, selling future clients.

Where can you get more information?

The best-known American magazine devoted specifically to the industrial design field is called *Industrial Design*, as you might expect.

However, the industrial designer's interests embrace the entire world of design, so the magazine rack of a design office often includes the leading architectural magazines, *Architectural Record*, *Progressive Architecture*, and the *AIA Journal*; the top home furnishings magazines, *Interiors*, *Interior Design* and *Contract*; graphic design magazines such as *Art Direction*, *Print*, *Communications Arts*, and the Swiss *Graphis*, which includes English text.

The Industrial Designers Society of America publishes a journal called *Innovation* (three times a year), a list of schools that meet the IDSA's educational standards, and a career pamphlet on the industrial design profession. You'll find the IDSA's address at the back of *Art Career Guide*.

Exhibitions of industrial design are rare in the United States, but most designers would say that the real exhibition centers for design, both good and bad, are your local department store and the many trade shows that take place around the country. A tour of any large department store or trade show will tell you more about contemporary design (good and bad) than you can learn any other way.

12
Photography

Photography is an art so new that artists still argue about whether photographs *are* really art. This debate will probably go on for years. But for the purpose of this book, I think we can accept the photographer's conviction that a camera, like a brush or a pencil, is just one more tool for creating pictures.

What does a photographer do?

Though photography is barely a century old, the camera already performs an amazing variety of services and the field has become quite specialized.

The portrait photographer is probably most familiar. According to one professional association, this specialty attracts a greater number of budding professionals than any other kind of photography.

The phrase, *commercial photography*, like the equally vague phrase *commercial art,* covers a number of specialities. These include many kinds of advertising photography—from fashions to food—any one of which can be a specialty in itself. Publicity pictures—anything from theatrical personalities to a new office building—also come under this heading. The magazine photographer may be asked to illustrate articles on a *variety* of subjects. A so-called commercial photographer may work in *all* these fields at once. But there's an increasing tendency to specialize in one or a few of these areas.

Particularly in advertising, publicity, and magazine work, subject matter is likely to become a specialty. Many photographers are known entirely for their fashion pictures. Architectural and interior photography is an important specialty. Some professionals are best known for travel pictures, theatrical portraits, automobiles, food, or industrial subjects.

Photo-journalism has become a field in itself. The best-known photo-journalist is the newspaper photographer, who covers the news with a camera as the reporter does with a notebook. Magazines have developed their own kind of photo-journalist, who specializes in *picture stories* or illustrations for articles on personalities and events.

Industrial photography is another vague term that covers many different activities. Industrial photographers may call themselves that because they do advertising and editorial pictures for business magazines. Or they may actually work in the plant, photographing stages in the development or manufacture of a new product; recording the results of tests made by the research department; shooting pictures for advertising, publicity, or company magazines; making film strips to train new employees; illustrating catalogs of the company's products.

Scientific photography may range from photomicrography, which means shooting through a microscope, to astronomical pictures.

Motion picture and television photography are complex fields that are often subdivided into specialties. Some motion picture photographers are known for big Hollywood productions. Others concentrate on intimate, informal documentary work, the motion picture equivalent of photo-journalism. And the video technology that emerged in the 1980s has opened such opportunities as videotape production to the photographer—who may tape anything from weddings to elaborate audiovisual productions for clients in business, education, and entertainment. In fact, the whole field of audiovisual production—film strips, slide presentations, video tapes, and movies—has become an important and lucrative field for photographers.

I might go on for several pages, naming other specialties

within the expanding world of photography. Some professionals work almost entirely in color. There are legal photographers who use the camera to assemble evidence for the courtroom. There are medical photographers, police photographers, baby photographers, and even livestock photographers. An interesting specialty is photographic inventorying, which means shooting photographic records for insurance and protection. And wedding photography is a popular launching pad for budding professionals.

Where does a photographer find work?

Like illustrators and graphic designers, photographers can choose between freelance work and a staff job. Many regard freelancing as their goal, even if they start in a staff job. However, there are also staff jobs that offer a good future to the photographer who prefers a less hectic life.

Magazines—which means not only consumer magazines, but business magazines, trade publications, company magazines—may have staff photographers or use freelance talent. Many publications rely on both. Book publishers rarely hire staff photographers, but often use freelances. Newspapers and news services, on the other hand, rely mainly on staffers, but there may be opportunities for freelances too, particularly in the pages of Sunday magazine sections of big city papers.

Advertising agencies and public relations firms are unlikely to hire staff photographers, but use freelance talent on a large scale. Department stores sometimes have staff photographers, but more often use freelances, especially for large advertising campaigns. Manufacturing companies often have large photographic staffs and even small companies may have one or two photographers. In addition to staffers, many manufacturers use freelances.

Motion pictures are essentially a freelance business. The cinematographer is usually hired by the producer to shoot a particular movie, TV commercial, or perhaps a series of short films. A few motion picture companies have staff photographers, who may be supplemented by freelances when a big production comes along. Motion picture news services—they make news films for television—usually hire staffers. So do television studios, which frequently have cameras working around the clock.

When your freelance business expands rapidly, you may begin to take on a staff, unless you prefer to remain a one-person business. When you take on a staff, your organization is called a studio, and there are opportunities in such organizations for 9-to-5 jobs. The studio may even hire freelance talent when there's an overflow of work. Many large commercial studios have a handful of freelances on call.

Other clients for the freelance are practically unlimited. Just about everyone has a portrait photo made at some time. Nearly every business needs advertising and publicity photos of new products, personalities, and facilities. Most public institutions must document their activities: museums, for instance, normally use a staff or freelance photographer to record every object added to the collection. It's no exaggeration to say that nearly every individual, corporation, and institution employs a photographer for *some* reason, sooner or later.

Though many photographers prefer to work alone, I might add that nearly every successful photographer may be a potential employer. Sooner or later, there's a chance that a successful professional will need an assistant.

What does a photographer study?

There's not much agreement among photographers about the ideal training for a career in photography. What confuses the issue is that a number of talented professionals have become successful photographers *without* any real training. Among the most famous photographers is a former button salesman who just taught himself to take pictures in his spare time. There are just enough self-taught geniuses to perpetuate the legend that photographers need no training, just experience. Unhappily, for every successful, self-taught photographer, there are dozens who try to teach themselves and fail.

Most photographers agree that professional training is needed, but many question whether training in *photography* is vital. They point out that many of our best photographers attribute their success to fine art training. Some of these top professionals took a few photography courses. Others took none at all. But all of them had substantial training in drawing, painting, and design.

Another faction admits that while many of our best photographers started out as fine artists, illustrators, and designers, they were trained *before* most schools had photography programs. There was no choice but to take *other* art subjects and do spare-time work in photography. Now that it's possible to take extensive courses in photography—this faction argues—training in other art subjects seems less vital.

What this means is that the experts seem to approve two kinds of training for professional photographers. One kind emphasizes fine art and design courses *as well* as photography courses. The other program sticks to photography.

Let's look first at the fine-art-plus-photography program. Here you'll probably start with the same foundation year as other art students: basic courses in drawing, painting, and design. *After* the foundation year, you're introduced to photography. First, you work in black and white with one simple camera. You learn to process your film and make prints in the darkroom. You learn basic principles of optics and photographic chemistry. Later, you're introduced to other cameras, large and small; color photography; motion pictures; and specialized subjects like fashion, photo-journalism, portraiture, architecture, and product photography. You spend lots of time learning the subtleties of lighting and how to direct models. Throughout these years, you continue to draw, paint, make prints, perhaps sculpt, and you'll certainly take advanced classes in experimental design.

In the program that concentrates entirely on photography, you'll probably plunge directly into camera work, without any introductory art courses. At the outset, you're likely to get a lot of technical training in photographic chemistry, optics, sensitometry, mathematics, and a subject sometimes broadly titled photographic science. At the same time, you get your first camera assignments. You learn to process film and make prints. You're introduced to lighting, composition, black and white and color photography.

You then move into advanced subjects like advertising, fashion, architectural, and portrait photography. There are often specialized courses in photo-journalism and photo-illustration. You'll spend many hours on experimental darkroom techniques. You'll explore the special technical problems of motion pictures. All in all, your training will be far more technical than it would be in the program that blends fine art and photography.

Any good school—whether an art school or a photography school—will recognize the importance of training in the business aspects of photography. You must learn how to run your business efficiently, manage your money, market your work, and come out with a profit.

Which program makes a better photographer? Advocates of straight photography programs—no fine art—say their students have much greater technical skill and spend more class hours actually taking pictures. Those who argue for a blend of photography and fine art say their students think more creatively. Both arguments are convincing: leading photographers have been trained by both methods.

Does a photographer need a degree?

Though a degree adds a bit to your ammunition when you go job hunting, it's a rare employer who *asks* if you hold a degree. No client will care.

What part-time and summer jobs are good experience?

You'll learn something from any job in a photographic studio or the photography department of a publisher or manufacturer. You might be nothing more than an office clerk—still good experience—or you might land a spot as a junior darkroom technician, helping to process film and make prints.

If you're really skilled with a camera, even though you're still a student, you might be lucky enough to get a part-time or summer job actually taking pictures. Local portrait studios sometimes use part-time photographers, particularly for assignments like weddings and mass orders of portraits for school yearbooks. Summer camps and resorts sometimes hire photographers for a few months at the height of the vacation season. And you certainly might try to get freelance assignments from friends who want portraits, or even from local businesses.

Even if you can't get a job in photography, there are many worthwhile summer and part-time jobs in related fields. Any job in the communications business—advertising, publishing, publicity—will teach you something about a field where photography is used. If you're taking the kind of photography courses that include art training, you might try for a job in the *art* department of an agency, publishing house, publicity firm, store, manufacturing company, or printing plant. Just as art courses enrich the background of a future photographer, so will an art job.

What is a typical first job?

Photography students often dream of assisting a top-notch professional for the first couple of years after school. Such jobs aren't as rare as they sound, but nor are they as glamorous as you might expect. Assisting a photographer usually means helping your boss carry heavy equipment, handling lights, arranging backgrounds, mixing chemicals, keeping the darkroom and studio in order, filing negatives, processing film, retouching pictures, and perhaps helping to make prints.

You accept all these routine chores because they give you a chance to see how a professional operates. You absorb all you can, knowing that you'll never really take any pictures on such a job. You and your boss know that you'll part company as soon as you're good enough to get a job in which you *can* take pictures.

A glamour job assisting a big name photographer is *not* necessarily the ideal beginner's spot. An apprentice position in a studio, corporate photography department, or the photography staff of a publication will mean the same sort of routine chores; *but* you may also take pictures. These may be modest assignments at first—simple product shots, conventional portraits, nothing terribly exciting—but you might really learn more than you would learn by lugging equipment for a famous name.

Unlike most artists, photographers *can* sometimes start out doing fairly ambitious work right after they graduate. A really top graduate can sometimes skip the helper or darkroom technician stage and start taking pictures for a studio, company photo department, or magazine.

Many beginners start right out freelancing. This usually means trying to land assignments from clients *and* shooting lots of pictures on speculation. The freelance photo-journalist, for instance, shoots some stories on assignment from editors; but also does picture stories "on spec" and tries to sell them. Freelancing is inevitably a hectic business. It takes years to learn the ropes, to establish markets for your work, and to build up a reasonably dependable stream of assignments.

What are later jobs like?

As a staff photographer, if you have what it takes, you get more and more ambitious assignments as you advance. You may have an assistant—one of the younger staffers—and you may finally have a complete staff if you become head of a company photo department or photographic director of a publication. You may travel a lot, particularly if you're a photo-journalist. You may insist on processing and printing you own pictures, as many senior photographers still do. Or you may just shoot pictures and let your juniors do the darkroom work.

As a photographic director, you spend a large portion of your time planning assignments for other staffers and for freelances. You oversee their work, judge the results, select pictures, reject others. You may actually concentrate on photo-editing: choosing and organizing photos for publication. If you organize things properly, you can still spend a reasonable amount of time at the camera and save some juicy assignments for yourself. But you're as much an editor and administrator as a photographer.

For this reason, many photographers reject the idea of a staff job, even one with high pay and great prestige. These professionals prefer to take their chances on freelancing. The successful freelance normally has a variety of clients. If you're lucky, a few advertising agencies, magazines, manufacturers, or stores will use you regularly. But most of your clients will turn up with assignments sporadically, often when you least expect them. Most freelances must invest in a studio with darkroom facilities, which they may share with a colleague to cut down expenses. It may also be necessary to hire an assistant, at least part-time. This makes photography quite an expensive business.

As a freelance, you must expect to travel fairly often. You work irregular hours, particularly if an assignment requires night shooting and immediate delivery of prints for a publication deadline. You have a lot of precision equipment to keep in working order. You may carry your own portfolio around to prospective clients or you may have an agent who sells your pictures and collects a percentage of the price. Life alternates from calm to frenzy, depending upon the upon the amount of work on order and the deadlines that must be met.

Many freelances resolve that they'll work alone and take only as many assignments as they can handle. But other freelances are delighted to see their business mushroom into a studio, with a staff of photographers, darkroom technicians, and even sales reps. As a head of a portrait or commercial studio, like a photo department director, you have heavy administrative responsibilities. You must direct your staff, deal with clients, and take pictures too, if you have time. You have the profit and excitement of running your own business, but these are balanced by the burdens of running a small corporation.

Where can you get more information?

Many popular magazines cover photography for professionals and serious amateurs: *Modern Photography, U.S. Camera, Popular*

Photography, American Photographer, The Professional Photographer,
and *Photographer's Forum. Aperture* is a handsome scholarly magazine that deserves a much wider audience.

The Professional Photographers of America publishes a
school directory. The American Society of Magazines Photographers publishes a useful reference book called *Professional Business Practices in Photography.* Look in the back of *Art Career Guide*
for the addresses of both these groups.

Photography exhibits have become widespread in galleries.
Local camera clubs have shows in most major cities. There's often outstanding photography in the exhibitions of local Art Directors' Clubs. Many museums now have photography shows.

But the best way to learn more about the work of leading photographers is to follow the scores of magazines that carry good
pictures in ads as well as in articles.

13
Art teaching

In one sense, the most important art profession of all is art teaching. For it's teachers who discover and bring forth the hidden potential of the future artist, designer, or architect. Equally important, art teachers train the *art public*—building an audience for art by training people to understand and enjoy what the artist creates.

What does an art teacher do?

What subjects you teach depends upon *where* you teach. In a primary or secondary school, you'll probably be expected to teach a wide variety of subjects. Particularly if you're the only art teacher in your school, which often happens, you may teach any art subject under the sun. In the same class, you may teach drawing, painting, sculpture, ceramics, fabric design, stage design, fashion illustration, and perhaps even more. However, if the school is big enough to support more than one art teacher, then you may be able to specialize in a few favorite subjects, though you're still likely to carry a diversified teaching load.

Teachers in an art school or university art department are usually far more specialized. Painters teach painting, drawing, perhaps some printmaking if they *do* prints. Architects teach architecture, drafting, perhaps some experimental design. Art historians teach art history. You don't stray from your professional field unless you're unusually versatile.

Whom do you teach? Children and teenagers are the public school teacher's main audience, of course. But many public school systems now have adult education programs—usually in the evening—in which many students are the same age as the teacher, even older. Age limits have broadened in art schools, colleges, and universities. Though typical students in such schools are in their late teens or early twenties, many professional art schools now have children's classes, and adult education programs for older students.

Your students may be hobbyists *or* future professionals. Public school art programs are rarely planned for the future professional. Their purpose is to introduce students to the enjoyment and understanding of art, even when programs include professional-sounding subjects like fabric design. In many large cities, there are high schools that give real preprofessional courses, but the mass of public school art students will never become professional artists.

The four-year programs of most art schools are planned for the future professional. College and university art programs *may* be for professionals, but many are planned only for the advanced amateur or as part of the student's general education. On the undergraduate level, art history courses are also regarded as part of the student's general cultural background, although graduate art history courses (leading to a master's degree or to a Ph.D) are intended to train art historians, teachers of art history, and museum staff members. So if you teach art history to undergraduates, you're teaching non-professionals; but if you work with graduate students, you *are* teaching future professionals. Actually, this is true in all art fields: college and university courses for undergraduates may or *may not* be for future professionals, but graduate courses are always regarded as professional training.

As a teacher, you make your living by talking. You talk to individual students as you look over their shoulders and criticize their classwork or homework. You lecture to a class of twenty or thirty students. And you may address an auditorium crammed with several hundred students and teachers.

But for an art teacher, words are never enough. You must be able to pick up a pencil, a brush, or a modeling tool and *demonstrate*. This means that you must be a skilled artist, designer, craftworker, or architect in your own right. For this reason, some public schools and *most* art schools, colleges, and universities schedule teachers' working hours to allow free time for creative work in the teacher's own studio or office.

Few art history teachers are practicing artists—though a fair number started out that way in their student days—so they're not expected to produce studio work. But they *are* expected to work at scholarly writing, producing and publishing articles and books in the field of art history and criticism. And their advancement up the academic ladder (from assistant professor to associate professor and so on) depends, in part, on their record as published writers.

Classroom duties aren't the only way teachers earn their salaries. There are the inevitable committee meetings to plan programs, to solve administrative problems, and to find ways of helping students who may be having trouble. There are special events: conferences and exhibits to be organized; school plays that need sets and costumes designed; social events that need decorations. There's paper work at registration and examination time. You may have office hours for private meetings with students who need guidance. And there's always the job of grading student work.

Public school teachers usually get the summer off, but some schools have year-round sessions. More and more art schools, colleges, and universities have summer sessions too. This means that some faculty members work the year round, which means more money but less vacation time, though there are still vacations between terms, and a lot of holidays.

Where does an art teacher find work?

As I've already indicated, most art teachers work in primary schools, junior and senior high schools, art schools, colleges, and universities. But there are also many art teachers employed in adult education schools, educational divisions of art museums, community centers, YMCAs, YMHAs, settlement houses, vocational rehabilitation centers, and even mental hospitals where art is taught for its therapeutic value. Many artists also conduct classes in their own studios.

Art teaching is certainly the most decentralized of all art professions. Though not every primary or secondary school has an art teacher, there are jobs in every major public school system in *every* state. There are also college and university jobs in every state. Nearly every major city has an art school. Chapter 14 on "Art Museum Jobs" points out that museums are also a field for teachers.

But it's vital to keep in mind that *jobs aren't equally good everywhere*. Many public school systems are ill-equipped for art teaching and pay so badly that it's facetious to talk about "job opportunities" in such places. There may be jobs, but they can hardly be called opportunities. Some states invest more in their art programs than others do. Wealthy communities can obviously invest more money in art programs than communities that aren't so lucky.

In general, opportunities for art teachers are best in fairly sophisticated cities and their suburbs. Some notable exceptions are the colleges and universities that have made a special effort to build ambitious art programs in out-of-the-way places. And the quality of many rural schools has risen rapidly in recent years. But the fact remains that the greatest number of good jobs are in cosmopolitan centers and communities nearby.

What does an art teacher study?

Leading art schools, college and university art departments offer special programs for teachers, usually called art education or teacher training. These programs are planned for teachers in *public* primary and secondary schools, but *private* schools generally get their staff members from the same programs.

Public school teachers must be certified, which means that they take programs agreed upon by the state department of education and the university, college, or art school. Certification generally requires a thorough knowledge of several art subjects, plus a reasonable acquaintance with many others. Your own preferences, the school you choose, and the requirements of your state will determine which art subjects you choose for your specialties, and which ones you know casually.

Painting, drawing, and printmaking get a lot of attention in most teacher training programs. So do sculpture and ceramics. There's often a lot of time given to crafts like jewelry and metalwork. Courses in design fundamentals often lead into applied art subjects like fabric, interior, graphic, and industrial design, even architecture. Stage and fashion design are popular. Illustration may be part of drawing and painting, or it may be merged with graphic design under the heading, commercial art. Art history is always a must. Mechanical drawing is common and photography appears more and more frequently.

The bigger the art school or university art department, the more subjects you can study. Because primary and secondary school teachers are expected to teach a wide range of art subjects, their training *must* be diversified. However, art educators are aware that one person can't develop *real* skill in every art subject. The trend is toward greater specialization. Though training remains diversified, many schools require *real* professional competence in at least one field.

Courses in education are considered just as basic as art classes. These usually include the philosophy and history of education, educational psychology, educational theory, and individual research in educational problems. There are also specialized *art* education courses: art teaching methods for elementary and secondary schools, philosophy of art education, ways of using audio-visual aids, art education research.

Among your most important courses will be student teaching, which means going out to observe experienced teachers in action, then teaching full-time as a kind of apprentice.

Since a good teacher must have an exceptionally well-rounded education, teacher training programs are always heavy on required courses in the liberal arts and the sciences. Required courses include subjects like English composition, public speaking, literature, history, a foreign language, philosophy, mathematics, psychology, sociology, plus other sciences like biology, chemistry, geology, astronomy, and physics. You won't be forced to take *all* of these, but you'll take a fair number. You may also be obligated to take courses of local interest, such as the history of your state.

Educational requirements for teaching jobs in art schools are more flexible. Naturally, an employer will be interested in where you went to school and what you studied. Hopefully, you have a strong educational background in the subject you hope to teach. If your schooling was rich in the liberal arts and sciences, so much the better. But there's almost never a *list* of educational requirements that *must* be met, as there is in a public school system. Art schools are interested mainly in your *ability* as an artist, designer, craftworker, or architect. Your schooling counts less than your record of professional achievement.

Like art schools, college and university art departments *rarely* have a tight list of educational requirements for art teachers. Teachers' colleges sometimes insist on hiring graduates of teacher training programs, but other colleges are less interested in such training.

For teachers of *studio* classes, colleges and universities are strongly interested in a job applicant's record of achievement in art, design, crafts, or architecture. However, they're also strongly interested—more than art schools—in your formal education, both in your professional field and in the liberal arts and sciences. College and university graduates are preferred. So are graduates of four or five-year art school programs. For studio teaching jobs (painting, sculpture, printmaking, drawing) the Master of Fine Arts is the preferred degree.

An art school will often hire an artist whose education is fragmentary, who's knocked about from one school or private class to another. A college or university *might* hire this applicant if the artist has a *reputation*. But without an outstanding record of achievement in the art world, a teacher faces tough competition from job hunters who can point to a formal education.

For teachers of art history and art education, the doctoral degree is preferred and the right formal education means more than it would for studio teachers. Art history teachers are expected to have taken courses (undergraduate and graduate) in all the great periods of art, from ancient to modern. You also need a specialty, since the job opening may be for someone to teach something as specialized as medieval art and architecture or "primitive" art of Africa and the South Pacific; for your Ph.D., your doctoral dissertation is likely to be written about some aspect of this specialty. An art education Ph.D. means graduate courses in the specialized art education courses listed on the preceding page, plus a dissertation based on research in the field.

Does an art teacher need a degree?

From what I've just said, it's clear that degrees are important credentials in the teaching profession.

For a public school teaching job, a bachelor's degree is essential. No major school system anywhere in the country will consider hiring you without a degree. Furthermore, your status and income rise with each additional degree. A master's degree automatically gets you more money and possibly a higher position. A doctorate pushes you even higher. For top administrative jobs in major school systems, the Doctor of Philosophy or Doctor of Education degree swings a lot of weight.

In most states, four years of study lead to a bachelor's degree and certification. Some programs now take five years. A master's degree requires at least a year's additional study. A doctorate requires at least a couple of years more. If you're teaching full-time and just working on an advanced degree part-time, a master's may take several years and a doctorate can often stretch out to eight or ten years. Both these advanced degrees combine classwork and independent research, culminating in a sizable piece of writing called a master's thesis or a doctoral dissertation.

Art schools rarely *insist* on a degree, though they're pleased when a faculty member has one. But even here the trend toward degrees is gaining momentum. More and more art schools grant degrees and this obligates the schools to hire teachers with degrees. Years ago, our leading art school faculties included only a handful of teachers with even a bachelor's degree. Now bachelor's degrees are common, and more and more art school teachers have master's degrees.

College and university art departments prefer faculty members with a formal education, as I've said, which means that a bachelor's degree is a minimum requirement. A master's degree definitely improves your job prospects. Few artists, designers, craftworkers, or architects go on to a doctorate. But it's essential if you want to teach art history or art education. Department heads are often expected to hold the top degree. In fact, some colleges and universities have ruled that no one can become a department head or even a full professor without a doctorate. In such schools, an artist must remain an associate or even an assistant professor because he or she lacks the label of *doctor*.

This obsession with degrees has forced many of our finest artists—who often have no degrees at all—to teach in art schools, rather than college and university art departments. This is a major reason for the low level of art teaching in many colleges and universities that hire teachers for their advanced degrees, not their talent or achievement.

What part-time and summer jobs are good experience?

The nation's summer camps have become a training ground for future teachers. For a future art teacher, the best possible spot would be the job of arts and crafts counselor. Almost every camp has one. However, if you can't be an arts and crafts counselor, any camp counseling job is excellent teaching experience.

You might also look into summer job opportunities as arts and crafts director of a resort hotel. There are sometimes jobs of this sort in city-sponsored recreation programs conducted in local parks and playgrounds.

Throughout the year, there may be part-time counseling jobs open in community centers, settlement houses, recreation programs of churches and synagogues, YMCA's and YMHA's. In such a job, you may assist an experienced teacher or you may be given your own group of young people to work with.

A teaching or counseling job isn't the only part-time or summer experience that may be useful. If you're a skilled artist, you might land some other kind of art job. Skim back over the preceding seven chapters for ideas about jobs in other art fields. Any job that makes you a better artist makes you a more effective teacher.

What is a typical first job?

In teaching, unlike most art professions, there's no real apprenticeship period, aside from student teaching when you're in school. When you land your first job, you start right out teaching. You're in full charge of your classes, though you may be responsible to a department head or to the head of the school. In some schools, you plan your own curriculum, while other schools give you a program to follow. But the organization of each class hour is really up to you. From the very beginning, you're your own boss.

Teaching in an elementary, junior, or senior high school, you'll probably average five class hours each day. This means that you may have 350 to 400 students to teach and grade during a week. Getting to know this many students is no small task.

Your teaching schedule in an art school, college or university may not be as heavy. Classes are often longer, anywhere from an hour to an entire morning or afternoon, but you may not teach a full day, and you may not even teach every day. Good art schools, colleges, and universities try to arrange your schedule to allow time for outside work in your own studio or office. Your week may include half days, a free day, or even two free days if you're very lucky.

Beginning teachers are often asked to handle beginners' classes: freshman art classes in high school; or foundation year courses in an art school, college, or university. However, there's no reason to believe that introductory classes are less fun to teach than advanced classes. Many teachers feel that freshman and sophomore classes are *more* challenging just because students know so little at that stage.

What are later jobs like?

Advancement in primary and secondary school teaching is often invisible, though very real. You start out teaching and you simply go on teaching, doing a more mature job, gaining deeper satisfaction, and earning more money as the years go by. Unless you shift into administrative work, you probably won't move into a more luxurious office or get an impressive title. However, you may be given more advanced classes to teach as you gain experience. You may have more freedom to experiment in your classes. Aside from the bigger paycheck, your advancement consists mainly of intangibles: the respect of your students and colleagues, greater creative scope, and your own sense of achievement.

Many successful teachers in primary and secondary schools *do* move into administrative spots. They become department heads; supervisors of art programs in a group of schools or for an entire school system; even principals, the top job in an elementary, junior, or senior high school. In some administrative jobs—head of a high school art department, for example—you may do almost as much teaching as before, with the added responsibility of running the department. On the other hand, many supervisory jobs cut down your teaching hours and give you more time for committee meetings, desk work, hiring new teachers, and evaluating the work of present teachers. A principal's responsibilities are *entirely* administrative, of course.

In college and university art departments, the benefits of advancement are just as intangible as they are in public school teaching, and equally satisfying. However, the ladder of advancement *is* a bit more obvious. You start as an instructor, or possibly as an assistant professor if you have a particularly impressive background. As the years go by, your title changes to associate professor, then simply to professor, sometimes referred to as *full* professor. Colleges and universities often impose a limit on the number of full professors, which means some faculty members will never reach this top grade. The biggest difference between a beginning instructor and a full professor is usually that the senior faculty member teaches more advanced classes. Senior faculty members also head departments and committees. Like administrators in public school systems, they plan programs, hire new staff members, and evaluate current staff members for advancement.

On an art school faculty, advancement may be as invisible as it is in a public school, *or* there may be a distinct ladder to climb. In many art schools, faculty members have no titles and no precise distinction is made between junior and senior members. Seniority may just mean more money and perhaps more advanced classes to teach. However, some art schools have adopted the college hierarchy of instructor, assistant, associate, and full professor. Teachers may also be promoted to department heads and other administrative positions.

Administrative work may mean greater pay, power, and prestige, but it can be a mixed blessing. If you really love teaching, you may not want to switch to administration. Top notch teachers are often rewarded by offers of administrative posts, but frequently turn them down because they prefer the classroom to the office.

In most good public school systems, art schools, colleges, and universities, advancement means *tenure*. After a certain number of years, you become a permanent member of the faculty: your job is guaranteed.

Where can you get more information?

School Arts and *Arts & Activities* are widely read by elementary and secondary school teachers. *Art Education* and *Art Teacher* are the journals of the National Art Education Association, a department of the National Education Association. The NAEA also publishes a variety of career booklets. You'll find the NAEA's address at the back of this book.

What other magazines you read depends upon the subject you

plan to teach. In each of the previous chapters, I've named leading magazines in each art field. Art historians should read the magazines listed in Chapter 14 on "Art Museum Jobs." Use the listings in these chapters to make up your own reading list, based on your interests.

Certainly the best way to learn about teaching is to watch your own teachers in action. As you watch, put yourself in their shoes. Who are the teachers you admire and why? Why do some teachers inspire you to learn, while others put you to sleep? Each class hour is a new opportunity to learn about your future profession.

14
Art museum jobs

Like a teaching job, a job in an art museum rarely involves *producing* art. Museums, (like schools) are *educational* institutions that collect works of art, conduct research, and *teach* people about art. The main teaching medium of the museum is the exhibition, rather than classroom teaching, but organizing exhibitions is only one of many possible museum jobs.

What do museum staff members do?

The most publicized figures in the museum field, of course, are curators who buy works of art (or charm them away from wealthy collectors as gifts or legacies); assemble works of art for exhibitions; supervise the installation of these exhibitions; write exhibition catalogs, which are becoming more and more elaborate these days, like small-scale art books; and lecture on the exhibitions they organize.

Curators often use the phrase *collections management* to describe the expanding range and complexity of their job. Collections management encompasses cataloging (which often means knowing how to use computer services), planning and administering storage arrangements for the collection (which includes such problems as safety and climate control), and endless details that range from security to proper labeling of artworks on display.

Museum administrators must also know museum law and must know how to deal with governing boards and government officials. They must also have the public awareness, tact, and sheer political skill to deal with the community served by the museum.

Many museums employ art teachers in educational departments. Members of the education staff conduct classes of students sent to the museum by local elementary and secondary schools; conduct guided lecture-tours of the collections for groups of schoolchildren, teenagers, and adults; write educational publications distributed by the museum or by commercial publishers; supervise film programs for museum visitors; organize lecture series that feature visiting experts; even run radio and television programs on art. Some museum educational departments develop into full-scale art schools for young people, Sunday painters, and future professionals.

The design departments of museums offer job opportunities in exhibition design—for art school graduates trained in industrial or interior design—and jobs for others trained in graphic design, who design catalogs, pamphlets, posters, promotional literature, museum magazines, and the hundreds of signs and labels that guide visitors through the galleries.

Conservation departments are responsible for the preservation and repair of paintings, sculpture, drawings, prints, ceramics, fabrics, metalwork, and all the other fragile objects that fill the galleries and storerooms.

These are the jobs that most often attract graduates of art schools, college and university art departments. But there are still other administrative, research, and public contact jobs that you might not think of. The registrar's office is the nerve center of the museum, assembling the vital facts about every item in the collection—history, condition, even insurance value—and keeping track of its comings and goings to exhibitions, restorers, photographers, both inside and outside the house. The publications department (only bigger museums have them) edits, designs, and supervises the manufacture of catalogs, the museum magazine, art books, and other printed matter. The public relations department keeps the press and the broadcasting media informed about current events at the museum, usually by writing news releases and shooting photographs; distributing them to reporters, editors, and broadcasters; and maintaining personal contact with local and national news media.

In sorting out which of these jobs might be right for you, here are a few guidelines. Curatorial jobs—and research jobs like those in the registrar's office—are most often for people who have a special fascination with art history. If you want to teach in the *literal* sense (by talking to people, rather than via exhibitions), you're most likely to fit into the education department. As I said a moment ago, the design department is a logical place for the industrial, interior, or graphic designer. A conservator (as members of the conservation department are called) is usually a skilled artist or craftworker who's fascinated with the materials and techniques of *other* artists and craftworkers, past and present. Publications and public relations departments attract job candidates who know about art and want to *write* about it. And it should be obvious, from what I've said so far, that most museum jobs take administrative skill and a head for detail.

In the 1980s, museums have placed particular emphasis on more businesslike management, more aggressive public relations, and more ambitious development (which means fund raising) to solve their financial problems. So these are the fields in which there's been the greatest growth in museum jobs. There's also greater emphasis on conservation, with more work for conservators—although many of these professionals are self-employed specialists who have an ongoing relationship with a museum, *almost* like a steady job.

Where do museum staff members find work?

Every large city in America has an art museum and virtually every medium-sized one now has a museum too—or seems to be building one. An astonishing number of excellent museums, large and small, are now in small cities, towns, or rural settings. Building museums has become almost a craze, with municipal and state governments competing with one another for architectural honors, distinguished directors, prestigious collections, and publicity.

The museum boom has hit the colleges and universities, which have also made a substantial investment in new buildings, personnel, and collections. Campus museums are now scattered from coast to coast in urban and rural settings—including many of the liveliest museums in the country.

Nor should you overlook the many museums whose territory is *not* art. Historical and science museums often have art collections—paintings, sculpture, drawings, prints, furniture and other decorative art objects that have been collected as historical or scientific artifacts. Such museums also need curators, educational staff members, and conservators. And every well-run museum needs exhibition and graphic designers; in fact, the historical and scientific museums are particularly notable for the quality of their design work.

The museum building boom won't go on forever, of course. Whenever the economy slows down—as it does periodically—museums slow down too, as public and private funds become scarcer. Besides, how many art museums does a city or a university campus need? But the fact remains that there are more museums than ever *and* more people are working in museums than ever before in history.

What do museum staff members study?

Art museum curators *may* start out in art schools as painters, sculptors, or printmakers—and some *are* practicing artists—but the usual route is through a college or university art history program. Such programs normally include courses in the art of various historic civilizations and periods, like ancient Egypt, Greece, and Rome; medieval, renaissance, and baroque art in Europe; the art of China, Japan, India, Africa, and Latin America; and "modern" art, which means the art of 19th and 20th century Europe and America. Such courses are heavy on lectures, research, and scholarly writing.

An increasing number of colleges and universities offer professional programs in museum administration, which include the art history courses I've just desribed, but also dig into the nuts-and-bolts problems of exhibition planning and installation, collections management, community relations (which includes politics), publicity and fund-raising, finance and business management. To do the job properly, the university must have a museum on campus—or a link with a local museum where you can see your future profession in action. This blend of art history and practical museum management is the best training for a museum career—and the training most likely to get you a job.

A particularly important development is the appearance of degree programs in *arts management* on university campuses. Such programs are designed to train future administrators for positions in all kinds of cultural organizations, from museums to symphony orchestras, theatrical companies, and dance groups. A degree in arts management, with special emphasis on museum administration and a fair number of art history courses, can be another route to a museum career.

Graduates of teachers' colleges and the art education programs of art schools, colleges, and universities are the logical choice for jobs in educational departments of museums. This means the kind of training described in Chapter 13 on "Art Teaching." Such training is particularly important because many art museums coordinate their educational programs with the elementary and secondary schools, which often conduct classes at the museum. Even the TV programs of many museums are designed specifically for local school children.

Graphic, interior, and industrial design training—as described in Chapters 7, 9, and 11—are what museum design departments are looking for. If your art school, college, or university design program includes a course in exhibition design, then so much the better.

Although I've described a conservator as "a skilled artist or craftworker who's fascinated with the materials and techniques of *other* artists and craftworkers, past and present," that's not really enough. Conservation is a highly technical job—vastly more complex than cleaning a dirty canvas or modeling a new nose on a broken statue—and it's taught by just a handful of universities. The older generation of conservators may have learned their trade by a long apprenticeship, but now formal training is expected. Such training includes art history; research into the techniques of the past; the chemical and physical behavior of art and craft materials; scientific methods of evaluating the condition of a work of art; and methods of preserving, cleaning, repairing, and reconstruction.

Do museum staff members need degrees?

Although museums aren't *quite* as obsessed with higher degrees as colleges and universities, the bachelor's degree is regarded as the minimum educational requirement for an entry job. A high percentage of museum staff members have a master's, which is mandatory for higher level jobs. And the Ph.D. is still the best ammunition for a job at the top level.

For a designer, a bachelor's degree is all anyone expects, but an art school diploma is just as good, as long as you can demonstrate that you got through school and know your job.

The older generation of conservators often have no degrees, since there were practically no universities teaching conservation a generation ago. But now that a master's degree in conservation is available, it's the right degree to get.

What part-time and summer jobs are good experience?

Museums are usually tight on money, so it's common for the paid staff to recruit volunteers as supplementary manpower. (It's estimated that 40% of museum workers are volunteers.) Such volunteers may do *anything*: selling postcards and books, conducting lecture-tours, cataloging, or teaching. These jobs are often a training ground for future museum personnel. Although you won't be paid, you'll learn something about how a museum works, which puts you ahead of a job candidate who's never been behind the scenes.

For a future curator, the ideal volunteer work is helping with an exhibition, even if it means nothing more than typing labels. Independent research, like living on an Indian reservation to study their crafts or going on an archeological "dig" is good job ammunition, though it's still unpaid work. For a future education staff member, it pays to volunteer to conduct tour groups of school children; a summer as an arts-and-crafts counselor is also relevant experience. For a museum designer, any kind of display work, even sign painting, is worth doing.

What is a typical first job?

Curatorial jobs often follow a hierarchy similar to the hierarchy in universities: curatorial assistant, assistant curator, associate curator, and finally curator. Curatorial jobs frequently start in the registrar's department (particularly in the larger museums), which means research and scholarly record-keeping, the best way to learn about the collection. In a smaller museum, where everyone does a bit of everything, the beginning curatorial assistant may start out doing routine work for a curator, like combing old catalogs to track down material for a show, handling the paperwork necessary to borrow it, filling out the insurance forms, and doing research for the catalog, which the boss will write.

A common beginning job for curators and education staff members is serving as a lecture-tour leader who escorts groups of visitors and talks about the collection. But museums are so often understaffed that a junior staff member can be called upon to do almost everything—exhibition paperwork, leading lecture-tours, carting pictures, and manning the information desk.

Museum design and conservation departments are small—often no more than a department head and perhaps an assistant—so the beginner also gets a chance to do a little of everything. The junior designer may begin with signs, posters, and small displays before getting a chance to design a whole exhibition or catalog.

The junior conservator obviously starts with a comparatively simple project like relining (mounting a picture on a new canvas) before undertaking something as hazardous as repainting or reconstructing a fragile work of art.

What are later jobs like?

As you move up the curatorial ladder, you take full responsibility for selecting and installing exhibitions, which means living with budgets and schedules—learning to be an administrator as well as a scholar. You also purchase works of art for the museum collection, whether at auction, from galleries, from artists, or from private owners. Such purchases must be justified by research, proving the value of the object you want to buy, and must be negotiated with businesslike skill.

The road to the top—the directorship of the museum—is usually up the curatorial ladder. But as a future director, you must not only prove yourself as a scholar, you must be skilled in the complex financial management of an institution which the public is watching; you must be able to maneuver effectively in local politics; you must be able to "romance" collectors and turn them into donors; you must be able to organize a staff that ranges from dozens to hundreds; and above all, you must be able to raise money from governments, foundations, and private benefactors.

In the education department, the top of the ladder is the job of educational director, curator of education, or dean, as the job is sometimes called. This means planning the whole educational program of the museum, working with heads of school systems to meet the needs of the community, even running an art school—since many art schools are actually a branch of a museum, perhaps large enough to occupy a wing of the building. At times, the educational director may become the director of the museum.

The design director's job is to function as the "architect" of major exhibitions, working closely with the curator who organizes the show. As a designer, you plan the construction of display units and decide where they go; design the lighting and the color schemes; even work out the traffic flow of the people who attend the show. If you're versatile enough, you may also handle the major graphic design jobs, like catalogs and the museum magazine. Or you may oversee the work of another designer who handles the graphic design. At times, there are two top designers, one for exhibitions and one for graphics.

The chief conservator obviously gets to do the most demanding and most hazardous jobs, reserved for an experienced professional, like transferring a mural from a wall to canvas or cleaning and imperceptibly repainting a priceless picture.

In large or medium-sized museums, jobs are likely to become specialized. In a small museum, a curator may just be "in charge of the collection," which could contain anything from Chinese bronzes to American Indian pottery. But bigger museums have a curator of Far Eastern art or even a curator of Chinese art, a curator of American Indian art, a curator of European painting, and so on. In the same way, a conservator is likely to specialize in oil paintings or works on paper (like prints and drawings) or metalwork or pottery, simply because each field has its own intricate technology. Such specialties usually begin in school, where the student writes a master's thesis on a specialized subject, like some aspect of German medieval sculpture, or becomes fascinated with the restoration of watercolors.

Where can you get more information?

You can keep up with the major museum shows by reading magazines like *Art News, Arts,* and *Art in America,* which survey the current scene. The American Association of Museums publishes the journal of the profession, *Museum News,* plus a newsletter called *AVISO,* which carries job advertising. And your library may subscribe to the UNESCO magazine, *Museum,* a professional journal that reports on museum activities around the world.

More specialized magazines for scholars and collectors include *The Art Bulletin, The Art Journal, Apollo, Burlington Magazine,* and *Connoisseur,* which will give you some idea of the type of research and writing produced by professional art historians and curators.

Larger libraries should also have a big reference book called the *Official Museum Directory*, which will give you names and addresses of museums, and describe collections, programs, and staff functions. This book is the best source of facts about museums where you might find work.

The Office of Museum Programs of The Smithsonian Institution has published a survey of *Museum Studies Programs in the United States and Abroad*, available from the American Association of Museums, whose address you'll find at the back of *Art Career Guide*.

Finally, one of the best ways to learn about the great museum collections—short of buying more airplane tickets than most people can afford—is by reading art books. Practically every museum of any importance has published at least one massive art book that surveys its collection. And every good public library has a shelf-load of such books.

15 Crafts

To most people, "crafts" used to mean the same thing as "hobbies": spare-time amusements like knitting scarves and making bookends. The number of serious craftworkers—who wove tapestries or made pottery with the same dedication as painters or sculptors—was once very small. But the scene has changed radically. Just as there are more spare-time crafts enthusiasts (and Sunday painters) then ever before, there's been a dramatic increase in the number of men and women who want to devote their professional lives to crafts—who want to make a living at crafts if they can.

What do craftworkers do?

By far the largest number of professionals are producing ceramics: making objects out of clay, decorating them with glazes and textures, firing them in a kiln, and hoping to sell the finished product. The word "potter" usually means someone who makes utilitarian objects like dishes, bowls, jugs, mugs, pitchers, teapots, vases, planters, and other things that generally come under the heading of "containers." Other ceramists, to whom the word "potter" doesn't apply as well, make objects as diverse as architectural reliefs, figures, animals, and three-dimensional constructions, all of which might just as easily be considered sculpture that happens to be made out of fired clay.

There are plenty of reasons for the predominance of ceramists—the enormous number of schools with ceramic equipment and the speed of the process, for example—but it's also true that pottery is easier to sell than most crafts. A skilled, well-organized, hard-working potter can produce salable items quickly and sell them for a price that many people can afford. So potters have a better chance of making a living than weavers, for example, who spend weeks or months on a single project and then sell it (if they can) for a price that most people consider high for a blanket or a rug—although it turns out to be coolie wages for the number of work hours invested!

From what I've just said, it should be obvious that professional weavers are a much smaller group than professional potters—though *amateur* weavers are legion. Working on hand looms and other hand-operated equipment, weavers produce textiles for fashions and home furnishings. They may create finished garments like scarves, skirts, ponchos, jackets, coats, hats, belts, and bags. For residential and business interiors, they may produce things like blankets, rugs, tapestries, and wall hangings. Or they may simply weave yardage, as it's called, for other people to buy and use to make their own clothing, upholstery, and other household items. Weavers frequently spin their own yarns and dye them with man-made colors or natural dyes derived from plants.

The textile field has also grown to encompass a lot of crafts that were once spare-time fun for teenagers and their grandmothers. There are now first-rate professionals knitting and crocheting anything from scarves to wall hangings as elaborate as paintings. Batik and tie-dyeing—both methods of decorating fabics with dyes—are now the province of professionals who might once have been painters who regarded textiles as low-brow. Hand-painted fabrics are now an important art form for such people. There are distinguished craftworkers producing block printed and screen printed textiles, too. And the many crafts generally lumped into the category of needlework—embroidery, applique, patchwork, and quilting, among others—are now attracting attention from serious professionals.

Metalworkers create craft objects in precious metals like gold and silver—as well as not-so-precious materials like bronze, brass, steel, and copper. They make jewelry, hollow ware (which means utilitarian objects from dishes to coffee pots), and decorative objects which might really be called sculpture. Enameling is normally associated with metalworking, since enameling means decorating metal forms with molten, colored glass. Like the potter, the jeweler has a better chance in the marketplace than most craftworkers: a well-trained hard-working jeweler can produce small, salable items at a price that many buyers can afford. There's even been a surprising renaissance in the ancient craft of the blacksmith.

Professional woodworkers practice the slow, painstaking craft of making items as small as bowls or as big as furniture. Many professionals have rediscovered the ancient art of glass, working with molten glass to create bowls, bottles, and other objects that rival the fascination of ceramics. Because they depend upon architectural commissions for their work, there are fewer mosaicists and workers in stained glass, although both of these crafts are popular with nonprofessionals, working on a small scale.

Crafts professionals see themselves as essentially handworkers, creative artists in the same sense as the painter or sculptor, making art objects one at a time, leaving a personal imprint on each. Even if you make a *series* of dishes or bracelets or ponchos, all following the same design, each one bears the mark of your own hands.

Where do craftworkers find work?

What craftworkers "do" is one thing; what they do for a *living* is often something else. The fact is that most craftworkers are in the same boat as painters, sculptors, and printmakers: they rarely make a living at their art. They have got to do something else.

True, a handful of extremely well-trained, highly organized, businesslike professionals open their own pottery or jewelry or textile shops, and survive. But this takes more than artistic talent:

it takes businesslike skills in financial management, promotion, and selling, as well as the willingness to get into the nitty-gritty of record keeping, storage, packing, shipping, and the endless other details of being an entrepreneur as well as an artist.

Not all professionals feel capable of this sort of life and too few schools train craftworkers in business. So many professional craftworkers—like many of the country's best painters, sculptors, and printmakers—turn to teaching jobs. Most often, they teach in art schools, colleges, and universities, though an increasing number have found jobs in elementary and high schools, as well as in community centers, YMCAs, YMHA's, and adult education programs.

For craftworkers who *can* think in terms of mass production, there are jobs in the design departments of the ceramic, textile, glass, and furniture industries, or with manufacturers of metal products like silverware and jewelry. But such jobs are never plentiful and employers usually prefer job candidates with industrial design backgrounds—which means training and experience in mass production methods—rather than training in crafts. However, industry often values the craftworker's *ideas*, even if he or she may not be right for a staff job. So there are opportunities to serve as freelance designers for manufacturers who may not have a design staff or who may want to supplement an internal design department.

There are more and more opportunities to exhibit and sell to the growing public for crafts. There are now frequent craft fairs and festivals at which craftworkers display and market their work. Department stores and specialty shops are selling more crafts. Crafts shops and "galleries" are opening, not only in major cities that qualify as art centers, but in resort towns and tourist areas. For weavers and other textile workers who can create on a large scale, there are occasional commissions from architects and interior designers, who want rugs, tapestries, and hangings created specially for a particular setting. Similar commissions may be awarded for architectural decorations in stained glass, mosaic, and ceramic sculpture. Such projects have grown with the increase in federal, state, and local laws that require an art budget—usually a specific percentage of the total construction budget—for government buildings.

What do craftworkers study?

Each craft has its own specialized technology, which the well-trained worker must learn by long and painstaking study. At a time when thousands of spare-time craftworkers *call* themselves professionals after they've taken a few courses and sold their first scarf or pendant at a local bazaar, it's vital to recognize the fact that a true professional is the product of professional training. Whether you plan to make your living as a teacher, as a designer in industry, or as a full-time professional, your career will depend upon starting out with the right training in a good, four year art school, college, or university. The course at the local YMCA may be fun for amateurs, but cuts no ice when you're looking for a job.

The ceramist learns to "throw" pottery on a wheel and build clay forms by hand; how to construct abstract forms out of clay; how to decorate clay with glazes and textural effects; how to operate a kiln; how to deal with the complex chemistry and handling properties of various clays and glazes; and often how to build kilns and other equipment.

Weavers study the entire process of transforming raw fibers into finished textiles: carding and spinning the raw wool and other fibers into yarns; dyeing the yarns with natural and man-made colors; constructing various types of looms and operating them; designing and executing various kinds of weaves and textile constructions.

Textile workers may also learn how to executive the intricate waxing and dyeing technique called *batik*; how to construct and operate a screen for screen printing; how to cut and print linoleum blocks and woodblocks; how to handle the chemistry of dyes and all the additives that dyes are mixed with to adapt them for various textile processes; and how to evaluate textiles and fibers and select the right one for a particular project.

Metalworkers study the working characteristics of metals and alloys; learn how to operate hand and machine tools for cutting, shaping, welding, soldering, casting, texturing, polishing, and finishing metals in scores of ways, each depending upon the character of the specific material; and may go into such specialized skills as cutting and setting stones, enameling, blacksmithing, and combining metals with other materials like wood, ceramic, glass, or plastics.

Woodworkers must learn the behavior (often unpredictable) of various woods: how to use hand and machine tools to shape and assemble wooden forms, how to construct furniture, how to finish and preserve wooden objects. Glassworkers may study not only the ancient crafts of glassblowing and stained glass, but other means of fabricating, forming, casting, coloring, and texturing glass objects. Needleworkers learn an immense vocabulary of stitches; the behavior of scores of different yarns and fabrics; and the techniques of embroidery, knitting, crocheting, fabric collage, quilting, patchwork, appliqué, macramé, and still *other* methods, ancient and modern, that will be "rediscovered" by the time this book goes to press.

A good art school or college or university art department expects you to study more than your craft. In the foundation year, as well as in later years, your background is enriched with painting, drawing, sculpture, art history, and *especially* design courses that are meant to enhance creativity, even if you never again pick up a brush or a modeling tool. And crafts students are usually encouraged to explore other crafts outside their chosen field. It may be good for potters to try weaving, if only to broaden their color sense. Or metalworkers may be encouraged to try pottery to heighten their ability to deal with form and texture.

Do craftworkers need degrees?

Since many professionals teach for a living, degrees are inescapable. For art school, college, university, elementary, or high school teaching, a bachelor's degree is the minimum and a master's has a distinct edge. Few craftworkers go as far as the Ph.D.—it's rarely expected of practicing artists—but some *do* go on for the doctorate, because it's the ultimate "union card" in college teaching.

For a job in industry, a bachelor's degree tells the employer that you've stuck to school for four years and completed your training; but the employer usually won't expect you to have a master's degree.

If you're hoping to run your own workshop and sell directly to the public—or if you hope to freelance as a designer for industry—no one will ask about degrees. It's your *work* that counts. But the fact remains that four or five years in school is the best available way to get the professional training you need.

What part-time and summer jobs are good experience?

Although architectural and design students can often get part-time and summer drafting jobs, for example, it's particularly hard for crafts students to get short-term jobs in their chosen fields. A job in a commercial pottery or a textile plant is a possibility, but a remote one. For a future teacher, there's worthwhile experience in a summer camp job as an arts-and-crafts counselor. And there are good practical lessons to be learned about public taste if you can find a job selling in a crafts shop or in the right section of a good department store—textiles, furniture, glassware, pottery, housewares.

Actually, if you hope to "make it" as a full-time craftworker, *any* practical business experience may be useful. Dull as it may sound, you can learn something useful from any job that involves selling, record-keeping, or managing money.

What is a typical first job?

As I've already made clear, many professionals earn their bread by teaching; so, for many readers, the answer to this question is in Chapter 13 on "Art Teaching."

For professionals who find their way into industry, a beginning job is usually that of the junior designer, assisting a senior designer with chores and undertaking modest design projects. For a brief picture of the junior designer's role on a corporate design staff or in a consulting design office, turn back to Chapter 8 on "Fabric Design" and especially to Chapter 11 on "Industrial Design."

If you hope to open your own workshop and sell your own crafts, the best "first job," if you can get it, is doing chores in the shop of some more experienced professional. Here, in addition to practicing the skills you learned in school, you'll learn the business methods—ways of organizing production, inventory control, promotion, selling—without which your boss couldn't survive. These may be very primitive versions of the methods taught in the Harvard Business School, but if they work, they're worth learning.

What are later jobs like?

Once again, for many professionals, the answer to this question will be in Chapter 13 on "Art Teaching," while some will find their answers in Chapter 8 on "Fabric Design" and particularly in Chapter 11 on "Industrial Design."

For those rare professionals who have the talent and the business ability to run their own shops successfully, life is a combination of art and business. On the one hand, you must design and create works of art. But you must also exercise organizational skill; enforce budgets and work schedules; supervise and motivate assistants if you want to "manufacture" your designs, even on a small scale.

Whether you work alone, making everything one of a kind, or go into small scale production with a small staff, you have to decide how to sell what you make. You may have a retail shop, open to the public, which means advertising, window displays, and waiting on customers. You may decide to sell only to stores, which then resell your work; but this still means that someone (you or a representative) must call on stores to make the sale. Or you may produce just enough to sell at craft fairs and exhibitions—which are often very profitable—where you must be prepared to set up and manage a booth, and sell direct to the public.

Whatever route you take, you must keep track of inventory so that you *have* crafts to sell; keep accurate records of production costs (to make sure that you charge enough to make a profit); record operating expenses and income (for tax reasons and also to be sure that you're not going broke); pack, insure, and ship things if you're selling by mail order or filling orders from distant customers.

For many professionals, of course, a workable compromise is your own workshop *and* a teaching job. With a predictable salary coming in from school, you can afford to be casual about business—which is the way most craftworkers prefer to live.

Where can you get more information?

The nation's most widely read crafts magazine—which covers the current scene in all craft fields—is *American Craft,* published by the American Craft Council. The council also publishes good books on such practical subjects as *Craftsmen in Business: A Guide to Financial Management and Taxes* and *Pricing and Promotion: A Guide for Craftspeople.* (You'll find the address of the council at the back of *Art Career Guide.*) Another helpful book is *How to Start Your Own Craft Business* by Herb Genfan and Lyn Taetzsch, published by Watson-Guptill, New York.

Any well-stocked periodicals room in a good library will have a variety of specialized crafts magazines on ceramics, weaving, and other subjects too numerous to list here. But the best way to keep track isn't merely to read magazines, but to see crafts firsthand. There are craft shows at major museums, as well as collections of historic crafts from Europe, Africa, Asia, and the Americans. Crafts fairs, festivals, and gallery shows are on the increase, as I've said. Calendars, listing the dates and places of such fairs and exhibitions, appear in the various crafts magazines.

16
Earnings and job prospects

One September day, a woman stepped into my office with her teenaged son in tow and announced: "I want Harold to take a course in freelancing." "What do you mean, freelancing?" I asked. "I don't know," she said promptly, "but I hear the pay's good."

When you're a teen-aged artist living with—and *on*—your parents, finances may seem a rather distant problem as long as you have a bit of pocket money. But Harold's mother *had* put her finger on a fundamental requirement of any profession: the job must pay a living wage. Having explored the eleven most important art fields, we now must deal with the hard boiled question of money. How much do artists earn? And what are their long-term job prospects?

Reliable income figures for artists, designers, and architects are hard to find. When you do find such figures and put them into print, your information may be outdated before the ink dries.

Artists' incomes fluctuate more than you might think. In the industrial design field, for instance, I once watched beginners' salaries shoot sky-high, drop far back, then move upward again, all in less than four years. Why? Fluctuations in the economy had something to do with it. So did fluctuations in the number of young designers looking for work. Similar ups and downs seem to occur in most art professions.

Nevertheless, this book would be incomplete without some estimate of the earnings you can hope for as an artist, designer, craftworker, or architect. With the warning that no figures are reliable for very long, I'll try to suggest some income goals that *seem* realistic at the time I'm writing this.

The most widely quoted source of information on job opportunities and money is the United States government's massive *Occupational Outlook Handbook*, from which I've drawn many of the figures in this chapter.

Selling fine art

Since there's no such thing as a *steady job* producing fine art, it's impossible to quote salary figures as one might for a field like architecture or graphic design. As I explained in Chapter 5, most fine artists earn their living in teaching or in some applied art job. In the next few pages, we'll look over salary prospects in these fields. But at this moment, we must still deal with the question: what do fine artists earn from the sale of their work, even if this isn't their main source of income?

So far as I know, no one has compiled accurate figures on the average incomes of painters, sculptors, and printmakers. But as I said earlier, artists generally accept one bitter fact of life: not one artist in a hundred—including artists of national reputation—can live entirely by the sale of his or her work. Among the scores of artists I know, the best of them hope to make just a few thousand dollars a year from sales of paintings, sculpture, and prints—if they're lucky. Many refuse to *count* on making a cent and regard a sale as a happy accident. They paint or sculpt or draw for the pleasure of it and hope an occasional sale will cover the cost of frames, canvas, paper, or clay.

Yes, there *are* fine artists who hit the jackpot and live on a five-figure or even six-figure income for a while, as long as their work stays in vogue. But the lucky ones are terribly rare. Furthermore, they all know that public taste changes quickly and that the jackpot can suddenly disappear into thin air. For every artist who's *now* riding high, there's another who *once* rode high.

Prices of fine art are hopelessly unpredictable. I've seen big paintings, roughly equal in size and quality, tagged anywhere from $100 to $10,000. In theory, the zeros on a price tag grow with the artist's reputation. But some well-known artists keep their prices down to encourage sales, while little-known artists may try to impress the public with high prices.

In the world of fine art, pricing is a matter of guesswork. Purely by trial and error, you try to discover how much the public is willing to pay for your work and what price tag will drive purchasers away. For lack of a foolproof pricing yardstick, cautious artists suggest that you begin low and hope the demand for your work will force prices up.

For good advice on this subject, look into Betty Chamberlain's *The Artist's Guide to the Art Market* and Kenneth Harris' *How to Make a Living as a Painter*, which I've already recommended in Chapter 5 on "Fine Art."

Architects and landscape architects

According to the latest figures available at the publication date of this edition of *Art Career Guide*, architects and landscape architects have been starting somewhere between $12,000 and $15,000 per year, after graduating with a bachelor's or master's degree from a recognized school.

Beyond the beginners' level, salaries move into the $15,000 to $30,000 range for experienced employees, with the upper range of these figures reserved for job captains and other senior staff members. Architects who run their own offices successfully, and partners in large, well-known offices can earn upwards of $40,000 a year. Principals in major firms can earn salaries in six figures!

Architects are among the largest of the art and design professions. At this moment, there are something like 65,000 registered architects and 20,000 landscape architects in the field.

The *Occupational Outlook Handbook* simply rates job outlook in each profession as average, above average, or below average in comparison with trends in the total job market. Thus, job prospects for architects and landscape architects are rated above average, with two warnings; these professions are especially vulnerable to economic fluctuations; and the increase in architecture graduates could mean *very* stiff competition. The American Society of Landscape Architects projects roughly 900 new job openings each year.

Industrial design

Industrial designers with bachelors' degrees start at about the same level as architects and landscape architects, roughly averaging $15,000 a year. There are about 13,000 industrial designers at this moment and the *Occupational Outlook Handbook* expects stiff competition for jobs in a "relatively small occupation . . . expected to grow more slowly than the average." The Industrial Designers Society of America expects 450 graduates to compete for 250 to 300 entry level jobs each year.

Experienced industrial designers are apt to earn anywhere between $15,000 and $30,000 a year. A partner in a successful design office can earn upward of $50,000, with some going as high as $200,000. Design directors of manufacturing firms average around $40,000, but go as high as $75,000.

Photography

Photography turns out to be the largest of the practicing art professions, with over 90,000 members. Although the *Handbook* rates job prospects as average, the increase in graduates has made the job market highly competitive.

Since almost half the advanced professionals are freelances, often with great ups and downs in their incomes, it's hard to come by reliable figures on their earnings. But we do have some typical figures for salaried people. Rates for beginning newspaper photographers are in the $12,000-$15,000 range, while 4-5 years experience will bring $20,000-$25,000, and the top salary is about $30,000. Corporate salaries are higher still for industrial photographers, with the upper range probably $30,000-$40,000.

Heads of corporate photographic departments and chief photographers for magazines and news agencies often go above the $50,000 figure. So do successful freelance photographers, and a handful of highly publicized ones—top fashion photographers, for example—have astronomical incomes in six figures.

Of course, such six-figure incomes are far from typical of self-employed photographers. A survey of readers of *The Professional Photographer* reveals a wide range of gross billings—which means income *before* deducting expenses. Roughly 38% were above $50,000, with another 26% in the $25,000-$50,000 range, and 19% under $10,000.

Graphic design and illustration

The *Handbook* lumps these fields together as "commercial art" and estimates the number of professionals at 120,000. The *Handbook* says that the supply of new job hunters will exceed the demand. In this highly competitive job market there's room only for the best. "Average" graduates will have trouble finding jobs and moving up.

This seems to be a good field for women, who fill 40% of the jobs. But how many of them fill *top* jobs is another question. Most of the top art directors are still men; women tend to get stymied at the middle level. Many top freelances are women, which suggests that male employers may be more willing to trust women with freelance work than with top responsibilities in a staff job. But that's a subject for another book.

Beginners in "commercial art" jobs are scantily paid until they prove themselves. The *Handbook* points out beginners can literally start out at *barely* above the minimum wage, although top graduates of top schools can get $10,000 to $15,000 in major advertising and publishing centers. Several years of experience in a staff job can mean $20,000 to $30,000 for someone who's really good. And art directors in executive positions can earn $30,000 to $40,000 or more for well-known professionals.

As a graphic designer or illustrator, you probably can't afford to quit your job and start freelancing—nor does it make sense to freelance—unless you can make at least $12,000 a year on your own. For a *successful* freelance $25,000 to $40,000 a year is probably the most common range, although the numbers can go much higher for top people, sometimes into six figures.

Interior design

Traditionally, a great many women are also attracted to interior design, although the percentage actually turns out to be lower than in "commercial art." Roughly 25% of the nation's 35,000 interior designers are women. There are lots of graduates each year and competition is stiff. The *Handbook* labels job prospects as average, emphasizes that only the most talented will find jobs, and adds that the profession is sensitive to fluctuation in the economy.

Beginning graduates can earn as little as the minimum wage, which may be increased by commissions. Top graduates of top schools may earn a salary in the $8,000 to $14,000 range. Moderately experienced staff members in design offices and design departments of stores, manufacturers, and other firms can earn $15,000 to $25,000 a year. Heads of design offices and departments can earn $30,000 to $50,000 or more. As in other design fields, "stars" who run their own businesses can earn upwards of $100,000 a year. Remember that interior designers can make a profit on furnishings sold to a client. On a large job, involving large quantities of furnishings, this profit can be substantial.

Fabric design

Since there's no professional association of fabric designers and the *Occupational Outlook Handbook* has nothing on the subject, it's impossible to come up with dependable figures in this field. No one is really sure how many professionals there are, particularly if we assume that fabric designers work not only in the textile industry, but for manufacturers of floor coverings, paper products, plastics, and a variety of home furnishings, as well. Nor is it possible to offer any projection of job openings in the future.

Based purely on conversations with people in the field, I'd guess that beginning fabric design graduates are at the lower end of the salary scale, starting at $8,000 to $12,000. I'd guess that experienced designers on corporate staffs rarely go beyond $20,000 to $30,000 a year, with the exception of design directors, whose jobs are scarce and can be in the $30,000 to $40,000 range. The best-paid designers I know in the textile industry have "graduated" from design into executive positions like director of marketing, where it's possible to break the $40,000 barrier and go beyond it.

Crafts

Here's another field where figures are so scarce that they might just as well be nonexistent. No one really knows the incomes of those craftworkers who survive by selling what they make. Some barely subsist in backwoods retreats where life is inexpensive and a few thousand dollars go a long way. Others live in reasonable comfort, particularly if they earn their bread by teaching or working in industry.

Since many professionals teach, the income figures for teachers are the most reliable I can offer. For those who go into industry, consult the figures for industrial designers, although crafts graduates do seem to start out at slightly lower salaries than industrial design graduates.

Teaching

The 1960s and 1970s boom in teaching jobs is over. The era when the so-called "war babies"—born in the late 1940s and early 1950s—filled the schools, demanding unprecedented numbers of teachers, is past. The "war babies" have grown up and they're in the job market. Nor is there any prospect of so many young people flooding the schools in the foreseeable future. So the *Handbook* paints a very modest picture of the teaching job market for the 1980s and 1990s.

The projections are based on population trends, too complex

to go into here, but the picture is roughly this. In the 1980s there will actually be a decline in the number of secondary school students, which will mean a decline in secondary school teaching jobs. This doesn't mean a complete disappearance of jobs for new graduates, I hasten to add. But most job opportunities will be created by the need to replace teachers who retire, die, or leave the field for some other reason. There *will* be jobs, but competition will be stiffer than before.

In the elementary schools, student population will be fairly stable, or there may actually be moderate growth in enrollments. So the number of teaching jobs is apt to match the number of new job hunters or may even rise a bit. Still, most openings will be replacement spots, like the openings for secondary teachers.

On the college and university level, the *Handbook* expects declining enrollments, which means fewer jobs for teachers. Presumably, this means fewer jobs for art school teachers too. M.F.A. and Ph.D graduates will meet rugged competition for teaching jobs. There may be personnel cutbacks at big universities. And graduates of top schools may have had to "settle" for teaching jobs in out-of-the-way places. Job openings will be mainly replacement spots, as faculty members retire or move on—there will be few *new* jobs.

In the meantime, teachers' salaries continue to improve since the last edition of this book. Although the American Association of University Professors points out that much of the increase has been wiped out by rising living costs, teachers don't feel quite as underpaid as they used to feel, at least in the larger states where there's more money available for education.

The National Education Association places the average salary at roughly $17,000 a year for teachers in public elementary schools, with private school teachers earning a bit less. In the states that pay the highest salaries—such as Alaska, New York, California, Michigan, and Hawaii—the average is higher. The lowest salaries are in states like Mississippi, South Dakota, Arkansas, North Dakota, South Carolina, and Idaho. Bear in mind that these are *averages*, which means that beginning salaries are lower and salaries for seasoned teachers are higher.

Secondary school teachers are slightly better paid than elementary school teachers. The National Education Association places the national average at close to $18,000 a year. The highest paying states are in the northeast and the west. Again, remember that these are *average*. Starting salaries are lower and top salaries can be considerably higher.

In most public school systems, elementary and secondary school teachers get annual salary increases automatically. Eventually, you reach a maximum salary and the increments taper off or stop.

In college and university teaching, the National Center for Educational Statistics has published the following average figures for the various faculty ranks in four-year schools: just under $31,000 for full professors; just over $23,000 for associate professors; just under $19,000 for assistant professors; and just over $15,000 for instructors. The average for all ranks is about $23,000.

Art school salaries haven't been surveyed, as far as I can determine, but it's generally assumed that they're lower than college and university salaries. I doubt that many art school teachers get much beyond the salary level listed above for an associate professor. But again, salaries are better than they used to be.

Museum jobs

The salary figures for museum jobs are based on a salary survey made by the Association of Art Museum Directors. The AAMD points out that the survey represents figures given by its members—who don't include the smallest museums or nonart museums. Nonetheless, I think it's fair to say that these figures will give you a reasonable idea of your potential earnings in the museum jobs described in Chapter 14.

According to the AAMD, the average salary for an art museum director is about $49,000, with 75% of these top jobs paying over $38,000 and 25% paying over $56,000.

For chief curators, the average is roughly $29,000, with 75% of these jobs paying $20,000 or more, and 25% paying over $34,000.

A notch below this level is the chief curator's second-in-command or possibly the curator of some specific collection or department. The average salary then is a shade under $28,000, with 75% of them earning $33,000 or above.

The curator of exhibitions is a specialized job in larger museums, where this job pays an average of $23,000. Seventy-five percent of these curators command upward of $17,000, while 25% are paid $27,000 or more. The average for associate curators is around $22,000, with 75% of these positions paying $17,000 or more and 25% paying more than $25,000. Assistant curators average roughly $17,000, with 75% of these jobs paying over $14,000, and 25% paying $20,000 or above. And the entry job of curatorial assistant produces an average salary of $14,000, with 75% of these beginners earning $11,000 or more, and 25% earning above $16,000.

Chief conservators do about as well as chief curators, with an average salary of $29,000. Seventy-five percent of these top jobs in conservation pay roughly $22,000 or more, while 25% pay over $35,000. The next notch down is the senior conservator, with an average of $27,000. Seventy-five percent of them earn over $21,000, while 25% earn more than $31,000. Associate conservators average $25,000, with 75% of these jobs paying upward of $20,000, and 25% paying $26,000 or more. Assistant conservators get an average salary of $18,000, with 75% of this group getting over $14,000, and 75% earning roughly $21,000 or more. The beginning job in conservation is that of the conservation assistant, who averages $16,000.

It's worth mentioning that many conservators are self-employed; no figures are available, but successful freelance conservators certainly earn as much as salaried employees, and the top ones—who often have national or international reputations—may earn a great deal more.

Here are some more abbreviated figures for other museum jobs: Educational jobs in art museums—for professionals with teaching background—average $23,000 for the head of the education department; roughly $16,000 to $19,000 for experienced department members on the middle level; and about $13,000 for the entry job of the educational assistant. Development officers, who take command of museum fund-raising, are paid an average of $31,000, while public relations officers average about $20,000. Museum photographers earn an average salary of about $19,000, although freelance photographers, specializing in art, can earn a great deal more if they have an important reputation in the field. The chief editor or head of museum publications earns an average of $24,000, while the chief designer averages roughly $21,000.

Methods of payment

Artists, designers, craftworkers, and architects who work 9-to-5 for someone else normally get a paycheck each week or twice a month. You may get an annual bonus around Christmas or a percentage of the year's profits. Your check from the profit-sharing plan may come at Christmas or early the following year, when the past year's profits have been added up.

Teachers are always salaried unless they conduct private classes in their own studios, for which they usually charge by the hour, by the session, or for a *series* of sessions. School paychecks usually come once a month. Since the school year is normally nine or ten months, you may get your annual salary in nine or ten monthly payments. Some schools, however, feel that it's more considerate to make a dozen smaller payments, one each month throughout the year.

So-called fringe benefits are also part of your earnings, even though they may not show up in your paycheck. Your employer may provide medical insurance, life insurance, disability insurance, and a retirement plan, all of which can add up to a good deal of invisible income over the years. Although teachers aren't the best paid people in the art field, they generally get better fringe benefits than most: contracts and tenure—which means permanent employment after a trial period of several years— mean greater job security; insurance and retirement plans are practically universal.

Freelance pay arrangements may be simple or quite complicated. Most often, you're paid a flat fee for each assignment. Frequently, a freelance has a steady client who wants to make a more permanent arrangement. The client may ask you to work so many days a month for a fixed charge. This may turn into a *retainer* agreement, whereby the client pays a monthly or annual fee for your services, plus hourly charges for your working time, and additional charges to cover special expenses like travel.

The flat-fee-per-assignment arrangement is most frequent among illustrators, photographers, and graphic designers. Industrial designers also work on a flat fee basis, but retainers are also common. Interior designers may collect a flat fee, may agree on a retainer, *or* may charge nothing for their services, making their profit on the furnishings they sell to the client. Architects may collect a percentage of the total cost of each building they design, charge a fee, work on a retainer, or work out some combination of these methods.

Although the biggest incomes usually go to free lances and people who have their own businesses, like architectural or design offices, bear in mind that they have the heaviest business expenses. Thus, their incomes may not be as impressive as they look. I know one young architect who started his own office just five years after leaving school and soon had so many clients that he had six staff members working overtime and a "gross" in six figures; yet his weekly outlay for salaries, rent, and other overhead kept his *personal* income (after all the bills were paid) under $20,000 a year—a rather doubtful success story that underlines the importance of skilled financial management and efficient organization for the freelance professional.

PART THREE
Finding a Job

17
Writing your resume

Your school days are over. Now for the big test: you have to find a job in your chosen field. If you're lucky, a job may await you in the files of the school's placement office. Or one of your instructors may steer you to a job opening. If you're already in a job, you might get an offer from someone who's heard of your work. But there's no guarantee that a job will drop into your lap. I'm going to assume you have to *hunt*.

Job hunting procedures may vary a bit from one field to another. It's also true that each city has its own special problems for the job seeker. And, of course, the *seasoned* artist, designer, or architect isn't in the same boat as the recent graduate who's never held a job. Nevertheless, the recommendations in these next four chapters should be useful to almost everyone who pounds the pavements looking for an art job.

Since the fine artist can't hunt for a *job* as a painter, sculptor, or printmaker, these chapters will mean most to applied artists and art teachers. The fine artist's problems—dealer hunting in particular—have already been discussed in Chapter 5. But if you're a fine artist, you're usually forced to take a job in applied art or teaching, so you're likely to face a job hunt after all. These chapters should help fine artists too.

Why is a resume necessary?

Whether you're a seasoned professional or a complete beginner, the first step in your job campaign *must* be to write a resume. This is simply a fact sheet, usually one or two pages, that tells potential employers the main things they want to know about you. Few job hunters realize how vital this resume is. Yet your job campaign will be immeasurably harder without this simple fact sheet, which one employment consultant calls "the job seeker's basic weapon."

Why is the resume so important? First, because many employers won't talk to you without first seeing a resume. If you don't have one to mail off, you automatically eliminate lots of potential employers. Second, an employment agency needs your resume to get you interviews with its clients. Third, a resume is the only practical way to answer "help wanted" ads and reach out-of-town employers. You can't tell your story in person, so you must *send* it.

Finally, once you've landed an interview, the employer has only one way to remember you among the dozens of job hunters under consideration: your resume is in the file. There may not be an *immediate* opening. But weeks later there may be one *or* the employer may hear of an opportunity elsewhere. Naturally, the employer turns to the resume file. Yours had better be there.

Facts you should include

What items go on a typical resume? No two employment counselors agree completely on the scope and sequence of the ideal resume. But the following list combines the features of the best resumes I've seen. The items are listed in the order they should follow on the final printed fact sheet.

(1) *Name:* Your full name, including middle names or initials. Some resumes list the last name first—Jones, John—but this seems unnecessarily complicated. Avoid the affectation of putting your degree after your name—John Jones, B.A.—as

European job hunters sometimes do. No nicknames, please!

(2) *Address:* Street, city, state, and *country* if the resume is going abroad. Remember your zip code and be sure to include it: your mail will reach you faster. If you have *two* addresses, one temporary and one permanent, list both with *dates.* Your temporary address might carry the notation, "June 15 through August 15." Your permanent address might carry the words, "After August 15."

(3) *Phone number:* If you have more than one phone, perhaps one at your temporary home and one at your permanent location, list each number with the appropriate address. If the phone belongs to a neighbor, explain this and add the neighbor's name. If you can be reached by phone only during certain hours, list the hours. If you include a *business* phone, say so and indicate whether your present employer knows that you're job hunting. It's important for a potential employer to know whether you can talk freely on your business phone and whether it's safe to leave messages.

(4) *Portrait photo:* Some resumes include a small "head shot" of the job hunter. The main value of this photo is to help interviewers recall your face several weeks after they've seen you. The picture may help an employer pick you out of the crowd of job seekers. I don't think a photo is essential—it certainly makes your resume more costly—but it's an extra touch that may be useful.

(5) *Summary:* Most employers are busy. They may not have time to read every word of your resume. You'll help readers, and win their gratitude, if you lead off with a brief paragraph summarizing your background. This paragraph takes the most significant facts on the sheet and compresses them into a few lines that read like a "situation wanted" ad in the newspaper (which I'll discuss later in this chapter). You'll need a few lines about education and job experience, though you needn't *name* your schools and

employers unless they're well-known. You'll want to mention the sort of job you're looking for. And you should include your age and whether you're willing to relocate to another part of the country. Don't worry if you repeat these facts in more detail further down the page: the reader may not get that far. A typical summary paragraph appears in the sample resume further on in this chapter.

(6) *Education:* This section should list art schools, colleges, or universities you've attended. Give enrollment and graduation dates. Specify your degree or degrees, if any. List major and minor subjects, but don't list every class you took unless your program was rather unorthodox and needs explanation. Certainly include academic honors like Phi Beta Kappa, awards, scholarships, or fellowships.

Extracurricular activities are worth mentioning only if they prove professional or administrative skill. For example, few employers care that you were secretary of the Square Dance Club. But they *would* be interested to learn that you served on the committee that designed the annual student exhibition. You'll note that I've left elementary, junior, and senior high school out of the education section. High school is worth listing *only* if it's one of those rare ones specializing in art.

(7) *Experience:* List jobs you've held during school, during summers, or after graduation. Your latest job should come first, then the previous job, and so on back to your earliest. Name each employer and the city where the organization is located. It's helpful, but not mandatory, to give an address and phone number. If your employer's name doesn't explain the nature of the business, *you* explain it. Thus, if you worked for Smith Associates, you'll have to add "an interior design office specializing in stores." Specify the date you were hired and when you left.

List your title, if you had one, and briefly describe your duties, clients, projects, and any achievements you're especially proud of. For example, a future employer would be interested to read that you'd reorganized your department or brought in new business.

The recent graduate may have very little to put into the experience section. But even the briefest jobs—part-time jobs during school, summer jobs, small freelance assignments—are worth including if they were good experience for a future artist, designer, or architect.

(8) *Special skills:* Job hunters often have special qualifications they've never used on a job, but which might be valuable to a future employer. Can you read, write, or speak a foreign language? Someone might have clients abroad. Can you type? This could be valuable in a small office. What are your hobbies? You can never be sure what side interest might ring the bell. The weekend boat builder or sports car fan might be just right for an office specializing in transportation design. On the other hand, don't waste space listing hobbies like stamp collecting, with no visible link to your profession. Nor are vague hobbies like "reading" or "travel" much help to an employer.

(9) *Professional associations:* In many art fields, there are professional associations whose names mean something to a future employer. It's worthwhile to list your membership in groups like the American Institute of Architects, the Industrial Designers Society of America, the American Society of Magazine Photographers, the American Society of Interior Designers, or your local Art Directors Club. Your membership tells a future employer that you're making contacts and getting to know your way around the field.

(10) *Personal:* This final section is for odds and ends of personal data. Here's the place for date and place of birth; marital status; number of children; where you prefer to work and if you have a preference. It's not necessary to include details about health, unless you have some physical defect that would influence your work. Nor do I think it's important to give details about religion, color, or national origin.

No one ever reads "vital statistics" like height, weight, the color of your hair or eyes. Skip these.

You might add other sections if you have material to fill them. If you've done some writing, for instance, add a section for publications.

What to leave out

You'll note that I've avoided all mention of money. An interviewer will probably ask what you earned in your last job and what you *hope* to earn. But don't put these figures in the resume. If the figures in the fact sheet are high, you might scare off an employer you'd really like to work for. If the figures are low, you might not be considered for a high-salaried job that you're really qualified to handle.

Another thing to avoid is the supposedly picturesque detail that many job hunters sneak in to "individualize" their resumes. You'd be amazed how many resumes announce that the job hunter lives in "the oldest brick house in Circleville" or is "three-time winner of the horseshoe pitching trophy awarded biennially by the Perry Street Athletic Club."

Another sort of picturesque detail is the lofty statement of purpose that begins many resumes: "I am deeply dedicated to the cause of contemporary architecture and my professional goal is to associate myself with a growing firm to which I can contribute my enthusiasm, idealism, education, and professional experience in exchange for adequate remuneration and the opportunity to perform a creative, satisfying, and lasting service to the community and my colleagues in the field." This sort of thing may be good for a laugh, if it doesn't put the reader to sleep. But it never got anyone a job.

References are sometimes included in resumes, but I'd be inclined to leave them out. Instead, keep these names, addresses, and phone numbers handy in a pocket address book. Job hunters usually find that each employer wants different references. Some employers are particularly interested in your school record and ask for names of teachers who'll vouch for you. Other employers just want to talk to your former bosses and co-workers. Still others insist on character references: old friends and respected members of the community who'll say that you're a responsible person.

There are even employers who assume that *any* reference you give them is worthless because you're certain to name friends who'll stand up for you automatically. These employers won't ask for references, but they'll go out and dig up their own sources of information.

So then, since each employer will want a custom-made list of references, I think it's best to wait for the interview to give employers whatever names they want. I'd only list references in the resume if the names are so well known that an employer will immediately recognize them and be impressed.

You must remember that your resume is more than a cold collection of facts: it's a sales tool. It shouldn't read like advertising copy. Nor should it include false data merely to make an impression. But you must line up the most impressive facts that you can assemble, then present them in clear, dignified, literate prose that will win a future employer's respect. This prose, I might add, will be the first real test of what you learned in your English classes.

Sample resumes

On the following pages, you'll find two sample resumes: one for an industrial designer with eight years' experience, plus two years in the army; the other for a young graphic designer just out of school. Both are one-page fact sheets, the ideal length if you can cram all the facts onto a single sheet. Both have plenty of heads and subheads for employers who skim *before* they read.

A rather stenographic style of writing keeps sentence length to a minimum. You'll see that words like *and, the,* and *he* are dropped. Paragraphs are packed with information, but not crowded together. Plenty of lines are skipped so that paragraphs don't look dense and forbidding.

The industrial designer's fact sheet on page 211 doesn't stick to the sequence I suggested a moment ago. His jobs come ahead of his education, because a seasoned job hunter's main selling point is his experience. His military years come next because the army gave him job experience that will interest an employer. Then comes his education, which mentions a valuable year of engineering, plus academic honors and extracurricular activities. His hobbies and special skills take very little space, so these don't need a special section. They just go into the personal paragraph.

Luckily, he can fit everything onto one page. But there would be no harm in going onto a second page if he needed more space to describe additional background. If *you* need two pages, don't be worried by the old wives' tale that employers read only one-page resumes. However, it *is* true that few readers have the patience to wade through *more* than two pages.

The inexperienced graphic designer's resume on page 212 turns out to be as long as the fact sheet of the seasoned industrial designer. She gives two addresses to indicate that she's staying with a friend or relative while job-hunting in the New York area. She places schooling first, since this is the major part of her career so far. Normally, your school program doesn't need much description—your major subject tells employers what they need to know—but this graphic designer feels that an employer will want to know about her school's unusual emphasis on printing processes. She also has a lot to tell about extracurricular activities and honors.

She's had two good summer jobs, which she describes in some detail to prove that she's had a bit of practical experience. She doesn't mention her third summer job as a camp counselor: this has nothing to do with art. The personal section mentions her father for a logical reason: he was also an artist and presumably contributed to her training.

Both these resumes are typewritten. But this doesn't mean that you must sit up nights, like so many misguided job hunters, banging out dozens of typewritten originals, one for every interviewer. One typing job—use just one side of the page—will do. A few dollars should pay for 100 reproductions of your original, run on an office copying machine. A good machine will even reproduce your photo on the resume.

RALPH WILLIAM SNYDER   CONFIDENTIAL

221 North High Street
Centerville, Ohio 44646

(513) 226-2237

SUMMARY: Now assistant to product design director, nation-
ally known appliance manufacturer. Previously job
captain on business machine, appliance, transportation
accounts for independent industrial design office.
Northern State University, B.A. in industrial design.
Veteran, Corps of Engineers. Seek supervisory position,
client contact, in design office. Willing to relocate.
Age 32.

JOB EXPERIENCE 1975-Present

Allied Kitchens Corporation, Northburgh, Indiana, 1980
to present. Assistant to Director of Product Design for
manufacturer of kitchen appliances. Coordinate design
teams developing refrigerators, ovens, ranges, washer-
dryers., freezers. Consult with marketing, graphic
design departments on packaging. Handle liaison with
design office, suppliers, sub-contractors. Reorganized
model shop for low-cost production of prototypes.

Allison, Goldman & Webb Associates, Jasper, Ohio, 1975-
1980. Advanced from junior design draftsman to job
captain, responsible to partner. Major projects:
adding machine, microfilm reader, computer tape unit
for Wilson Business Machines: electric mixer, iron,
toaster, packaging for Hilldale Electric: bus interior,
exterior for Transport Division, Standard Products.

MILITARY SERVICE 1973-1975

Corps of Engineers, U.S. Army, Fort McNab, Kentucky,
1973-1975. Engineering, architectural draftsman.
Worked on new installations: barracks, storage facilities, hospital. Designed educational exhibit.
Illustrated technical publications.

EDUCATION 1968-1973

Northern State University, University Park, Ohio, 1968-
1973, B.A. Cum Laude. Major: transferred to industrial
design after one year mechanical engineering. Minor:
sculpture. Vice-president, industrial design
fraternity. Full tuition scholarship, senior year.

Harrington Art School, Harrington, Ohio 1971-1973.
Extension courses in photography, while attending
university.

PERSONAL

Born Columbus, Ohio, 1951. Married. Two children.
Speak German. Hobbies: photography, sculpture, building
and flying gliders. Willing to relocate U.S. or abroad.
Prefer New York area, Chicago area, West Germany, or
Holland.

ELEANOR A. RUSSO

Temporary address: 241 Holly Road
                   Westbrook, New York 14478
                   (914) 661-3903
                   (July 10 through October 5)

Permanent address: 6 Maple Drive
                   Green Ridge, New Hampshire 03580
                   (603) 478-4077
                   (After October 5)

SUMMARY: Recent graduate, graphic design, Central School
    of Fine and Applied Art. Summer jobs in retail adver-
    tising, printing. Seeks beginner's job in advertising,
    publishing, art studio, printing plant or related
    graphic arts field. Willing to relocate anywhere in
    East. Age 22.

EDUCATION 1979-1983

    Central School of Fine and Applied Arts, Concord
    Connecticut. Four Year Certificate in Graphic Design,
    June 1983. Course included not only diverse assignments
    in design of printed matter, but experience in type-
    setting, offset, letterpress printing. Minors:
    photography, printmaking.

    Extracurricular Activities: Poster designer, Publicity
    Committee, Central School Student Council, 1978-1983.
    Designed announcements, stationery, programs for Annual
    Jazz Concert Series.

    Academic honors: Lettering prize, Annual Student
    Exhibit, 1982. Student Honor Society, 1983. Graduated
    top quarter of class.

SUMMER JOBS 1980-1982

    Fox & Mendelsohn's Department Store, Green Ridge, New
    Hampshire, summer 1980. Art director's "girl Friday"
    in advertising department. Designed small newspaper
    ads, store posters, spot illustrations, lettering.

    United Printers and Engravers, Lynnfield, New Hampshire,
    Summer 1982. Graphic designer attached to sales depart-
    ment. Designed stationary, pamphlets, packaging,
    trademarks, logotypes for small clients of printing
    plant. Prepared paste-ups for offset. Developed
    knowledge of type, engraving, printing, binding.

PERSONAL

    Born Bangor, Maine, 1961. Daughter of Vincent Russo,
    book designer, illustrator. Single. Hobby: designing,
    illustrating, and printing children's books on
    hand press.

Problem resumes

The format I've recommended will fit most job hunters if it's not followed rigidly, but used with imagination. However, certain job hunters have special problems which this type of fact sheet may not solve.

What sort of resume should you write if you want to change fields? Let's say you're an engineer who wants to be an industrial designer, or you're an illustrator who wants to design printed fabrics. A straightforward list of jobs, schools, and special skills won't do. Your education and experience are in your *old* field, not your new one. Though I've warned against beginning a resume with a statement of purpose, such a statement might be in order here. You might help the reader by beginning your summary with an explanation of why you want to change fields and why you think you're qualified for a new profession.

"After six years as an illustrator, I'm convinced that my skills and interests would be better used in fabric design. My decorative drawings for children's books and greeting cards have been well received. It has been suggested that this style would lend itself to printed fabrics and wallpapers. I am keenly interested in fashion and home furnishings and have spent my spare time learning more about those fields in which fabric design plays an important part. During the past two years, I have done many experimental fabric designs and have sold four to local manufacturers. I have also taken extension courses in fabric design and technology at a nearby technical school."

At this point, you can list your jobs and freelance accounts. But don't describe each job in detail. Just pick out the aspects of the job that might relate in some way to your *new* field. The engineer might explain:

"The mechanical design of this product taught me a great deal about such human factors as comfort, ease of operation, and maintenance, all of which are essentially industrial design problems. Our engineering staff worked closely with our industrial design and marketing consultants."

The same thing could be done in the education section, where you might pick out courses that relate to your new field. There might also be special emphasis on the section devoted to skills and side interests. You have a complex story to tell, a difficult idea to sell. Don't be concerned if your resume grows to a couple of pages and your sentences become fuller, less stenographic, more personal.

A spotty job record represents another resume problem. What sort of resume is best if you've hopped from one short term job to another? You may have good reasons for "job hopping"—an uncongenial boss, a sudden cutback in business, an interruption for illness—but employers are uneasy about workers who don't hold jobs long enough to build up solid experience. Your problem is to prove that you *have* this experience despite your irregular professional history.

One effective way to present your case is not to list jobs, but *kinds of experience*. Let's say you're a photographer with a few short-term jobs as a darkroom technician, a brief stint with an industrial photographic service, and several years of diversified freelance work. After these last years on your own, you want a long-term job. When you examine your background, you find that you have good experience in black and white processing and printing, color processing, industrial magazine photography, product photography, portraiture, theatrical publicity, architectural photography, and even photo-editing. Your resume ought to have a brief paragraph about your work in each of these areas.

As usual, your resume should begin with a summary, but this should also emphasize types of experience, not jobs. Toward the end of the fact sheet, you can simply list employers and freelance clients in a single paragraph headed "Employers and Clients." No dates are needed for individual jobs or freelance assignments.

The problem resume can take many other forms. If you have a dazzling way with words, you may *not* feel that the cold, efficient fact sheet format does you justice. You may want to write an intriguing letter instead. Sometimes a job hunter has an idea for a kind of job nobody has ever done before, a job that has to be *created.* If this is your problem, you might want to spend the first page of your resume selling potential employers on the need for this job. Then the second page would present your professional history. I've even seen resumes that were three-quarters *pictures,* one-quarter text and captions.

The format of the problem resume depends on your personality and the nature of the problem. But these unorthodox resumes—letters, descriptions of new job ideas, picture stories, or whatever else you might try—must be terribly good. If they aren't really "stoppers," unorthodox resumes often end up in the wastebasket. *Most* job hunters will find it best to play it safe and stick to the fact sheet format I've outlined.

However, if you're eager to produce a resume that's *different,* try to choose a format that demonstrates your professional ability. One of the most memorable resumes I've seen was sent by a graphic designer who wanted a job in advertising. Her resume took the form of a handsome, full-page newspaper advertisement, not only well-designed, but attractively illustrated by the job hunter. The lettering was also her work. And to prove her skill as an all-round advertising woman, she'd written lively copy to tell her story. Not every resume can be this elaborate, of course. But if you take the trouble to design an unusual resume, the design should be *so* good that the resume could be carried in your portfolio as a sample of your work.

Too often, the unorthodox resume turns out to be *different,* but neither imaginative nor tasteful. One old chestnut—which looks like a fresh idea to a surprising number of job hunters—is the resume in the form of a press release. Job hunters sometimes carry this hackneyed idea a step further: they go to a local printer or novelty shop and order a fake newspaper page, complete with headlines that scream the job hunter's name. I've even heard of a job hunter who put his resume on a phonograph record and sent it to a potential employer. The employer was not impressed. There was no phonograph in the office and the employer had no intention of carrying the record home to play on the stereo set after dinner. Like most *gimmick* resumes, the record was ignored. Employers want to hire artists, designers, and architects, not press agents.

18
Organizing your job hunt

Most job hunts are haphazard affairs: a few phone calls one day, a visit to an employment agency, casual calls on a few potential employers, all on the spur of the moment with no particular plan. Sooner or later, you find a job. But it's often *later* and often the wrong job. This sort of unplanned job hunt can drag on for months. At last, discouraged and desperate, you grab the first thing that comes your way. Well, it's not exactly what you had in mind, but it's *something*.

To find the right job reasonably soon, you must organize your hunt as carefully as a general plans a military campaign. Like most military campaigns, yours won't always proceed as planned. Unpredictable things happen. But a well-organized job hunt gives you a sense of direction, a sense of achievement as you cover new ground each day. You'll find the actual *process* of job hunting satisfying. Above all you'll feel more confident of finding the spot you want.

Contact list

Having put the essential facts into your resume, your next step is to decide whom you want to reach with these facts. Like any good salesperson, you need a contact list: a list of people you'll want to see, phone, or write.

Who should be on this list? Most job hunters make the mistake of contacting just those people they want to work for. But many job offers come from unpredictable directions. If you contact only employers who interest you, you cut out many unforeseen job opportunities that *might* be just as good.

The first lesson in job hunting is that *everybody* in the field should know you're looking. If you're an interior designer, every department store decorating department, furniture store, decorating shop, interior design and architectural office in town should know you're hunting. True, most of these people won't have jobs for you. You may not *want* to work for many of them. But there's an old saying: "Everybody has an uncle." The employer who has no job for you *may* have a friend who needs you. The more people who know you're looking, the better your chance of stumbling on an unexpected opportunity.

Your most obvious source of names, addresses, and phone numbers is the classified phone directory. If you're hunting out-of-town—by mail or in person—your local phone company may have out-of-town directories. Professional organizations often make membership lists available to job hunters. If you're a graphic designer or illustrator, for example, try to get the lists of the local Art Directors Clubs in cities where you want to work.

One important source, often neglected, is your personal address book. You should certainly contact your friends, co-workers, and former teachers. They may know of jobs. They can also suggest names to add to your contact list. And they may have job hunting lessons to pass on. Don't be embarrassed to ask friends for help and advice. They'll be flattered.

Professional magazines in your field are a good source of names. Read these magazines regularly to learn who are the leaders and who are others to watch. The magazines will also give you some idea of the kind of work each person or organization does. This will help you decide which employers might want your type of education and experience. For example, if you're an architect with a special interest in schools and hospitals, it's helpful to read architectural magazines to see which offices specialize in these fields.

It's simplest to put your contact list on index cards, one name to a card. The standard small index card, three by five inches, fits the pocket perfectly, so that you can carry your contact list wherever you go. Each card includes the name of the person you want to reach, the person's title or function, the name of the firm, the address and phone number. You also have space for notations: Who steered you there? Did you write a letter? Did you get an answer? Did you talk to someone on the phone? Did the employer interview you? Did anyone else in the office talk to you? What were their comments on your background and portfolio? Did they steer you to any other contact in another firm? All these notations should be dated.

If you assemble your contact list in the way I've suggested, you may end up with a hundred or more index cards. These contacts may be scattered halfway across the country. Obviously, you can't just go and see them all. Yet you should try to reach every one of them somehow. Your goal is not only to spread the word, but to land as many interviews as you can get. Each interview *could* turn into a job offer, or at least give you a lead.

There are six ways of landing that all-important interview: through a personal introduction, phone call, or letter; by answering a "help wanted" ad or placing a "situation wanted" ad; or through an employment agency. You should be prepared to try each of these channels.

Personal introductions

When you write or phone an employer, it's enormously helpful if you can say, "Joe sent me." If only out of friendship for Joe, the employer has to interview you. Besides, the interviewer may respect Joe's judgment: Joe probably sent you because he thinks you're *worth* seeing. He may even have sent you to fill a current opening.

This is known as the grapevine method. A sends you to B. If B doesn't have a spot for you, B may still send you on to C. Somewhere down the line a job is waiting for you, though you're never sure where. This sounds like a pretty rambling way to look for work. You're sent to all sorts of people who may not interest you. Most of your interviews may turn out to be cordial chit-chat rather than job offers. These interviews are often pleasant, but you may wonder whether the grapevine is leading you anywhere. The amazing thing is that the grapevine method *does* work. A job materializes when you least expect it. Personnel experts often say, "The *best* jobs come through the grapevine."

The grapevine begins in the pages of your personal address book. All you need are two or three people to start the chain: a couple of friends in the field who'll introduce you to some of their associates; perhaps a former teacher who'll send you to a few employers who take a special interest in graduates of your school. The one important rule is that you *must* keep adding links to the chain. You must try to get each person you meet to send you to one or two others. You must be bold enough to ask: "Is there anyone else you think I ought to call on for a steer?"

Don't expect interviewers to make a phone call or dictate a letter of introduction, though some do. But they might come up with some names you can add to your index cards. It's considerate to ask: "May I say you suggested I call?" If you *can* use someone's name, that's all the introduction you need. Even if you *can't* use the name for some reason, the interviewer has still added a contact or two to your list. You *can* call without any introduction.

Phone or write ahead for an appointment. Never just drop in without advance warning. You'd be astonished at the number of job hunters who wander in during the busiest part of the day, with the sheepish explanation, "I just happened to be in the neighborhood with my portfolio." This marks you as rude and disorganized. Employers *might* see you if they're good-natured, but they have every right to throw you out.

If you phone ahead, you may be asked to send a resume and then call again for an appointment. Don't be insulted. Interviewers want to know more about you so they can talk to you more intelligently. If you write for an interview, instead of phoning, be sure to enclose a resume.

Phone calls

You certainly won't be able to get an introduction to everyone on your contact list. But you can still phone for an appointment. If you're trying to reach a busy person in a large organization, speak to the secretary and ask to arrange an interview.

So far, I've assumed that you know the *name* of the person you want to reach. But what if you know the name of the organization but not the person? In that case, it's simplest to phone the personnel department. In a large organization, you might be routed to one of several interviewers. In a smaller place, there may be no personnel department, just one person who's responsible for talking to job hunters. In a large, highly departmentalized organization, it may be best to ask for the head of the department where you want to work. If the department head doesn't do the hiring, then you'll be steered to the personnel department.

One warning about phone calls: don't just say, "I'm looking for a job." Be ready with two or three short sentences, explaining who you are, what kind of work you do, and when you'd like an appointment. A simple introduction would be: "I'm Edwin Wolf, a fabric designer with a degree from the Institute and two years' experience. Might I show you my portfolio sometime next week?" If you're in town for just a few days, say exactly how long. Don't expect *everyone* to grant you an interview. Some will, some won't. You may be asked to send a resume and phone again. When you land an interview, it's considerate to send a confirming note. The note might simply say:

> This is to confirm our appointment on Monday, April 3, at 11 A.M. I look forward to meeting you. Thank you for your interest in my work.

Closing with the stock phrase, "yours very truly" sounds archaic nowadays. So does "sincerely yours," though many letter-writers still use it. "Cordially" sounds a lot more friendly. I might add that "kind regards" is suitable *after* you've met someone and hit it off with him; it's an especially good closing for a thank-you note.

Letters

You can't reach everyone by phone. Out-of-town contacts are logical targets for letters. Local contacts should also be made by letter if they're hard to reach by phone or if there are so many that you can't possibly phone them all.

If you've made up the extensive contact list I've recommended, you probably have dozens of letters to write. Job hunters in big cities like New York and Chicago often find themselves turning out a hundred letters or more. How can you cover all this territory, get all these letters into the mail, without turning the project into a backbreaking chore?

This is a time when you're grateful for a good resume. Since the essential facts are in your resume, you needn't repeat them in a letter. All you do is clip your resume to a brief note. The note must be typed, of course, not hand-written. But you have only a few sentences to type, an envelope to address, and the job is done.

You needn't wrack your brain composing a fresh note to go with each resume you mail. You can simplify your mail campaign if you develop a few standard messages. You can then pick the right one for each employer. Let's say you're a graphic designer with a diversified background in advertising, packaging, and magazine layout. You'll need one standard note for advertising agencies and the advertising departments of corporations; another note for manufacturers of packaging and design offices specializing in packaging accounts; a third for employers in the publishing field. Each note might be written in two versions: one for local and one for out-of-town employers.

What should your note say? Since your resume carries the complete story, all you need are a few sentences similar to your phone introduction. Your note should start off with the simple statement that you're looking for a job. Then give a few high points of your background, details that will be relevant to this particular employer. Finally, you should indicate when an interviewer can meet you and see your work. A typical letter might read as follows:

After four years as an art director at Clark Advertising, I am interested in a new job with a similar organization.

The attached resume describes a fifteen-year career in advertising and editorial art direction, with substantial freelance experience in packaging. As you will see, many of my major accounts have been in the food field, which I believe to be one of the main interests of your agency.

I plan to be in your city on a business trip from Monday, November 3, through Friday, November 7. I would appreciate the opportunity to show you my work sometime during that week.

This five-sentence note will do very well when you write to an advertising agency specializing in the food field. If you're writing to an agency with a strong interest in packaging, you might emphasize packaging experience in the third sentence. You might also have to alter the dates in the final paragraph. But the rest of the note can be used more or less intact for all advertising agencies. Your other two standard notes can follow the same basic form.

The second paragraph demands some slight knowledge of the organization you're writing to. If you've gathered your contact list carefully, you *will* know something about many of your contacts. But if you don't know enough, you can still write paragraph two to fit the *type* of organization. For example, if you didn't know that the agency specialized in food accounts, the second paragraph could simply emphasize the breadth of your experience.

As you will see, my advertising agency background has brought me into close contact with clients manufacturing a wide range of consumer and industrial products, both here and abroad.

The beginner, just out of school, hardly has this impressive professional history to write about. However, you *can* call attention to your special interests, summer jobs, and school projects.

This June, I will receive a bachelor's degree in architecture from Northern State University. I am sending you my resume in hope that there might be a place for me in your office at that time.

As the resume indicates, my most ambitious school project was a multi-story office building, designed to meet the complex requirements of this city's west side business section. My summer jobs have also included work on multi-story buildings, as well as some contact with city planning.

I would be glad to show you my portfolio whenever you find it convenient to see me.

This note is for architectural offices with a major interest in big city office buildings and urban design. The same job hunter may have training and summer experience in residential architecture. This would be spotlighted in paragraph two of the note that goes to architects who specialize in houses.

Short notes like these can be banged out on a typewriter in ten or fifteen minutes; less if you're a good typist. You can easily turn out half a dozen each evening. Over a few weeks, you'll have a sizable mail campaign underway.

To whom should your letters be addressed? If you have a specific name on your contact list—a department head, personnel director, or even the head of the organization—there's no harm in addressing your letter to that person. But don't be surprised if your letter gets routed to someone down the line, who does the preliminary screening of job hunters.

If you *don't* have a specific person's name on your contact list, just the name of an organization, it's best to address your letter to the personnel department. If you can find out the personnel director's name, so much the better. But don't spend hours tracking down that name. The executive won't be slighted if your envelope simply says, "Personnel Director," and your letter begins, "Dear Personnel Director."

Don't expect everyone to answer you. They all *should,* but not everyone is polite. Some of your letters will go right into the trash basket. Others will be filed for future reference, but not answered until there's a job opening, perhaps months later, long after you've found your job. Some considerate employers will send you a polite, "Sorry, no openings." A reasonable number will want to meet you as a matter of interest. No job opening at the moment, but they'll want to remember you if they're impressed. A *small* percentage of employers will want to see you because they have a current job to fill.

Don't be discouraged by the low percentage of favorable replies to your mail campaign. You're like a general planning a bombardment. You assume most of your shells will miss, but if your barrage is heavy and well-planned, a few shells will hit dead center. Remember, all you have to find is *one* job.

"Help wanted" ads

Newspapers published in larger cities often carry "help wanted" ads that announce jobs open for artists, designers, and architects. Some job hunters mistakenly assume that these ads cover *all* the jobs available. Actually, only a small percentage of current openings are advertised. Not every employer believes in classified advertising. Many just rely on the grapevine and their resume files. It's worthwhile to read the classified section and answer the ads that seem to fit your qualifications. But don't spend *all* your time answering classified ads. "Help wanted" ads don't justify more than a small part of your job hunting time.

Classified ads often sound like miniature versions of the summary that heads your resume. They usually begin by naming the position, then go on to list the main qualifications:

> Interior designer, recent graduate. Good drafting, rendering, for beginner's spot, department store decorating staff. Some knowledge cabinetry helpful. Opportunity. Relocate.

Apparently this job will involve a lot of drafting and rendering. The employer adds that it's useful for the applicant to know something about cabinetry, but this isn't essential. The word "opportunity" is common sales talk in "help wanted" ads. The word implies that whoever gets the job will advance quickly.

This implied promise may or may not have any real meaning. But the sales talk reminds you that a "help wanted" ad is meant to *attract* you. Like all advertising, it can't be taken at face value. The word "opportunity" may sugar coat a low salary. It may also be a means of softening what might be a blow to some job hunters: you have to relocate. You answer such an ad the same way you conduct your mail campaign. Send just two things: your printed resume and a brief typewritten note. The note should begin by explaining where and when you saw the ad. The employer may have placed several ads in a number of papers and wants to know which ad attracted you. Then explain, in just a few lines, why you feel that you qualify for the job. The employer will read about your qualifications in more detail in the resume. Finally, you need a sentence telling the employer when you can come in for a talk and show samples of your work.

This resume is sent in response to your advertisement in the June 1 *Dispatch*, which describes a job I feel qualified to fill.

My interior design training at Western State College included a wide range of residential and commercial projects, with heavy emphasis on drafting and rendering. My grades in drafting were among the highest in my class. I also ranked high in my rendering classes and have done freelance rendering assignments for local design offices. Though our school does not emphasize cabinetry, I have designed and built my own furniture.

I will be glad to supply further details in a personal interview any time after June 9.

Replying to a "help wanted" ad is always a shot in the dark. The employer may get dozens of replies and arrange only half-a-dozen interviews. Most of the replies may go into the wastebasket. If the employer does write or phone you, it may take weeks. The executive may be snowed under with applicants from employment agencies and job hunters who've come via the grapevine. The firm may be too busy to start interviewing immediately. Someone may just be a procrastinator. Or the firm may not *want* to interview anyone: they may just be collecting resumes as insurance, in case a couple of people are planning to quit.

Many artists, designers, and architects get good jobs through "help wanted" ads, though *high level* jobs are more likely to be filled via the grapevine. Though a few papers like *The New York Times* often carry ads for top jobs, most classified columns are best for jobs on the lower and middle levels.

"Situation wanted" ads

We've examined classified ads written by the *employer* who's looking for talent. There are also classified ads—usually listed as "position wanted" or "situation wanted"—written by the job hunter. The "situation wanted" ad is a condensed version of the summary that heads your resume. It's a summary of a summary:

> Fabric designer, 16 years experience with manufacturers, converters. Knows fashions, home furnishings. Strong technical background. Heavy experience marketing, color research. Top contacts, U.S., abroad. Bring new business. Seeks executive position with manufacturer.

This job hunter is a heavyweight. In addition to substantial experience, the resume adds the bait of contacts and possible new business. The candidate wants a top job. This ad may appear in the classified columns in the usual small type. Or the job hunter might feel justified in paying the extra charge for a boxed ad in large type.

For the top-level job hunter, a "situation wanted" ad is often a good investment. The middle-level job hunter may also get good results. The ad might be placed in the classified or the business section. The Sunday paper is usually a better bet than weekday editions: more people read it and they cover it more thoroughly. The ad might also go into a professional or business magazine. The fabric designer, for example, would be wise to insert the ad in a textile industry publication. The job hunter might also try a fashion or home furnishings trade magazine.

For a beginner or a job hunter with limited experience, the value of a "situation wanted" ad is debatable. Boxed ads placed by heavyweights are surprisingly well read, often just for curiosity's sake. But I doubt that many employers read the "situations wanted"—straining their eyes over the long, gray columns of small type—as closely as job hunters read the "help wanted" ads.

Besides, classified advertising is costly. One insertion won't necessarily do. You may need several, repeated on successive Sundays or scattered among various professional publications. You have to land a job with a sizable salary to justify this expense.

Before you invest in a "situation wanted" ad, discuss the idea with some friends in the field. If a city has several daily and Sunday papers, one paper's classified section may be better read than the others. If there are several magazines in your field, which ones are best for your ad? Like an efficient advertising executive, you must do *media research* before you spend your money.

Employment agencies

Every large city has firms that earn their living by bringing employers and job hunters together. The employer calls an employment agency about a job opening. Job hunters also come in to be interviewed and listed with the agency. When the employment agency gets a job to fill, they dip into the file and pull out records of men and women who might fit. If there are no suitable people on file, the agency may advertise the job and interview candidates. The most promising candidates are sent to the employer. If a candidate is hired, the job hunter pays a fee to the agency. Occasionally, the employer pays the fee.

Few job hunters speak well of employment agencies. The typical agency seems to be a dingy, two-room office in a rundown building. No one greets you as you step through the door. You take your place on a bench or a battered chair and wait till your turn comes to be interviewed. While you wait, another job hunter motions toward a registration form you're to fill out. On the back of this form is a contract you don't understand, which commits you to pay the agent a couple of weeks' salary, maybe more, depending upon the job.

When your turn comes, you step into another small, drab room—or behind a partition—and hand your registration form to the interviewer, who scans the form and fires a few terse questions at you. If you fit a job in the agency's file, the agent gives you a few quick details, usually *too* few, then hands you a card to take to a certain address. Such agencies make no bones about it: they're flesh peddlers. They're not interested in you as a person. You're simply a salable object. Their purpose is to sell you, as quickly as possible, to the highest bidder.

This is a bitter stereotype, I know. But the appalling truth is that this stereotype fits most agencies I've seen. A few dedicated people have opened agencies based on more humane principles. Some call themselves *employment counselors* to dissociate them from their hard-boiled competitors. But now the hard-boiled agents are beginning to pick up the phrase. An increasing number of employment specialists are fighting the flesh peddlers by running a totally different kind of business: the employer pays the *personnel consultant* to find the right employee by an exhaustive talent hunt and elaborate psychological tests.

So it's not impossible to find an employment agent who will treat you as a human being. If you choose your agency carefully, you'll get an honest evaluation of your job prospects and good advice on your job campaign. More important, the agency will carry on its *own* campaign to get you a job if the agent believes in you. Agencies may call employers who *don't* have current openings, but who might be interested in seeing you anyway. They may send out copies of your resume. They may even advertise your talents if you're a heavyweight. Obviously, they're not doing this out of pure friendship: they'll collect a hefty fee if they place you, and they hope to win future business from you and from your new employer. But the services of the few *good* employment agencies are worth every cent you pay.

You can't tell good employment agencies from bad by skimming their ads in the papers. Go to friends for recommendations.

If you're just out of school, last year's graduates are a good source. If you're already out in the field, talk to co-workers who've been through job hunts recently. They'll remember which agencies treated them well. They'll also know which agencies specialize in art, design, or architectural jobs.

When you've selected an agency—more than one, if you can find a few good ones—treat your employment agent with the same consideration that you'd gove a potential employer. Don't just walk in; call for an appointment. Explain your background briefly and offer to send a resume in advance. Bring your portfolio (more about this in the next chapter) and several copies of your resume. When the agency sends you out to meet an employer, be sure to call the agent right after the interview and report how things went. Don't let two agencies send you to the same employer: tell your agent if someone else has already made the same contract for you.

When an agent tells you about a job opening, keep it to yourself. If you start sending your friends to the employer, you're cheating the agent out of the fee. If you trust an agency, you're morally bound to send your friends there. The agency will then arrange to have them interviewed for the job.

One tip: sometimes *you* are supposed to pay the agent's fee and sometimes the *employer* will offer to pay. Ask your agent whether there's a chance that the employer will handle this expense.

Personnel consultants operate in a different way from agencies, as I've said. The consultant is paid by the *employer* and may have a staff of talent scouts, psychologists, and other experts who find and evaluate people to fill jobs. Because consultants charge high fees, employers normally use professional talent hunters only for high-level jobs. Beginners' jobs don't justify the expense. Again, talk to your co-workers about consultants likely to be working for employers in the art field. But keep in mind that this is a long shot. Unlike an employment agency, personnel consulting firms won't campaign to find you a job. They fill only those jobs that clients hire them to fill. There's a slim chance that consulting firms will be looking for someone like you when they get your resume. More likely, they'll file your fact sheet in case one of their clients wants you *some day*.

Out-of-town trips

If you're hunting for a job far from home, you're up against a special problem. You'll have a tough time finding a job in a distant city without going there. The trip can be expensive. Your transportation costs something, and each day you spend hunting costs more. Therefore, it's vital to plan out-of-town trips well in advance, so you'll get the most out of every minute.

If possible, try to have plenty of appointments scheduled before you arrive in town. Don't wait till you arrive, then waste precious days trying to set up dates with busy people who may not be available on short notice. Write letters to the out-of-town employers on your contact list asking for an interview and specifying when you'll arrive and how long you'll stay.

A good employment agency can be especially helpful when you're hunting in an unfamiliar city. They'll have contacts you don't have, plus an intimate knowledge of the local job market. If you've found an agency you trust near home, ask them to recommend an agency in another city that you plan to visit. They may even have a working agreement with such an agency: the two agents might collaborate on finding you a job. If you can't get such a recommendation, write some of your out-of-town contacts and ask them to suggest an agency. When you've picked an out-of-town agency, tell them when you're coming and send half-a-dozen resumes so they can start making appointments with employers.

Out-of-town newspapers are sometimes a good source of information about distant job markets. The classified ads will give you a hint of the kinds of jobs available. Read the employment agency ads to see who handles jobs in art, design, or architecture. You may write ahead about a specific job that's advertised. If the employer is interested in your resume, the organization may absorb the expense of bringing you in for an interview.

When you arrive in an unfamiliar town, make sure it's easy to reach you. Your family and home town employment agency should know where you're staying, so they can relay messages by mail, wire, or phone. If there's no one to answer your home phone, it may be a good idea to invest in a telephone answering service while you're away, especially if you're expecting important calls. You might also have a friend collect your mail and send important items on to you. While you're away from home, be sure to stay in a hotel, rooming house, or YMCA, where someone's always on hand to take phone messages.

Carry your temporary phone number wherever you go—you'd be amazed how many employers get a blank stare when they ask for a phone number—and call this number several times a day for messages, while you're out pounding the pavements.

Secrecy

If you have a job and you're looking for a new one, it's usually necessary to keep your job hunt a secret from your present boss. You might be lucky and have a boss who won't resent it when you tell the truth: "I'd like to start looking for a new job." Some bosses will shake your hand, wish you luck, offer their help and tell you, "Stay on here as long as you like." But the natural tendency of *most* bosses is to start looking for your successor. So unless you know your boss awfully well, keep your job hunt under wraps.

This isn't easy to do, but you have to try. Be sure to tell every interviewer that your current employer doesn't know you're on the prowl. You might mention this in a postscript to your job hunting letters. Your resume can simply carry the word, CONFIDENTIAL. However, it's obvious that your secret can't be *very* secret once you've contacted several dozen employers. Some are probably friends of your boss. All you can do is keep your fingers crossed.

Freelance work

All these recommendations, so far, have been intended for the artist, designer, or architect who's looking for a 9-to-5 job. But what if you're a freelance, working in your own office or studio? You're not looking for a salaried job with a single employer, but for assignments and fees from several employers. How do you find freelance work? In many ways, your problems are quite different from those of the professional who's hunting for a 9-to-5 job. In other ways, your problems are the same.

The freelance rarely needs a resume unless a potential client asks for one. More useful than a resume is a list of your past and current clients, with brief descriptions of work you've done for them. This is your record of achievement, the most powerful sales talk you can assemble aside from your portfolio, which I'll discuss in the next chapter. It's worth a few dollars to produce a hundred lists on a copying machine. Try to stick to one page and be sure that the list carries your address and phone, so the client knows where to reach you at a moment's notice.

As a freelance, you can hardly exist without a contact list. You collect these contacts from colleagues and friends; from other clients who recommend you; from the classified phone directory and membership lists of professional groups; and from reading your professional and business press. Unlike the 9-to-5 job hunter, you have to keep these contacts alive year after year. You must re-contact each potential client regularly. Clients may not have an assignment for you today, but they might in a few months.

How do you make these contacts initially, then keep them fresh? You make your first approach in the same way as any job hunter: write or phone for an appointment. Your phone introduction or note is the same three-part message: (a) what sort of work you're looking for; (b) what background you have that will ring the bell with this particular contact; (c) when they can see samples of your work. Attach a client list to your note. If you phone, send a client list along with a note to confirm your appointment.

If you get a freelance assignment and do it well, you'll eventually hear from that client again. The contact renews itself. On the other hand, *you* must take the initiative and keep renewing contacts that didn't result in work. You can't insist on dropping in with the same portfolio every month. But you're justified in renewing a contact when you have some new samples. Several months after your first visit, you may phone for another appointment for a brief look at the new items in your portfolio *if* the prospective client is interested. Keep up any contacts who show interest, even if they have no work immediately. If your portfolio makes a good impression, you'll be remembered and called when the right assignment comes along.

A freelance has no need for an employment agency or personnel consultant, but graphic designers, illustrators, and photographers often employ an *artist's agent* to carry their portfolios and drum up business. A good agent can develop wider contacts than you can make for yourself. After all, the agent devotes *full time* to making contacts, while you have to spend most of your time in your office or studio.

Agents save you time and energy and they're well paid for it. When they win you an assignment, they get a sizable chunk of the price, usually a percentage agreed upon in advance. Good agents are worth what you pay them, but intelligent, trustworthy agents with good contacts are hard to find. The few good ones often have more portfolios than they can carry. To get a first-rate agent, you must have a solid record of professional achievement. Such agents rarely handle beginners. If you're looking for an agent, ask your colleagues if they can recommend one. But before you put your portfolio in the agent's hands, talk to other artists who've used this "rep" and find out what kind of service they've been given.

Successful freelancing isn't just sitting in your cozy office or studio, sending off your work by messenger and getting checks in the mail. You have to build a detailed knowledge of dozens of clients, how they work and what they need. You have to publicize yourself and cultivate contacts for future business. You have to develop rapid, efficient working methods, so you can meet deadlines and production schedules. You have to think about budgets and bookkeeping. You're not just a happy-go-lucky Bohemian. You're running a *business*, and this is something few beginners are equipped to do.

Before embarking on a freelance career, you have to know the ropes. The simplest way to learn these ropes is to work for someone else. Working 9-to-5 for a boss, you can afford to make some mistakes. Beginners are expected to fumble the ball occasionally, as part of the learning process. But once you're in your own business, you can't afford many mistakes or clients won't come back with more assignments. Most of your mistakes had better be behind you, in the half-forgotten days when you worked from 9-to-5.

19
Planning your portfolio

One of your job hunting letters has clicked. An employer has asked you to come for an interview. In a couple of days, you'll be headed for someone's office with your portfolio under your arm. For ten or fifteen minutes—initial interviews are usually short— you'll be alone in a room with your samples and an interviewer who may offer you a job. If you make an impression, you may be asked to show your portfolio to a *series* of critical interviewers before any offer is made.

Your future hinges on the contents of that traditional, big, black folder. In most professions, people are hired on their personality and professional history. But employers in the art field believe only what they *see*. An artist, designer, or architect must show samples. Employers realize that your portfolio can't possibly tell the whole story. Samples can't prove that you're easy to work with, for instance. But your portfolio is your *only* concrete evidence of professional ability. Though architects sometimes go job hunting without a portfolio (which I don't recommend), this is the only art field in which it's even *remotely* possible to find a job without showing samples.

What goes into this portfolio? What's the best way to display your samples? In this chapter, I'll make some suggestions for beginners, as well as for seasoned professionals. Anyone who's been through a job hunt knows that no two employers agree on what makes an ideal portfolio. But I think it's possible to set down some general recommendations that most employers would accept.

Beginners' portfolios: what to include

You're just out of school. You have no professional experience to point to, except summer jobs. You may have hundreds of school projects piled up in your room, but which ones belong in your portfolio?

Try to put yourself in the employer's place. What do employers want to know about you? Above all, they want to know something about the *scope* of your professional training. How many different things have you done? For example, if you majored in graphic design, chances are that you've done magazine and newspaper advertisements, posters, pamphlets and magazine layouts, packages, lettering, some illustration and photography, possibly some book design. If you're reasonably competent in all these spheres, better include two or three samples of each. Even if you hope to specialize in one of these areas, don't narrow your portfolio to just one field. A future employer usually wants to survey your total background.

Having argued against a specialized portfolio for a beginner, I think most employers *do* want to know your special interests. If you're an architect with a strong interest in historic preservation, you should certainly give this work a prominent place in your portfolio. Special interests help an employer remember you: "Oh yes, she's the one who's a bug on old buildings." You might even be lucky and get a job with an office that's working in this field. But don't count on it.

Employers pay particular attention to a beginner's *skills and techniques*. In selecting your samples, you must not only show a wide range of *projects*, as I suggested, but these projects must display all the skills and techniques that are standard in your field. Let's say you're an industrial designer whose portfolio includes appliances, automobiles, business machines, metalware, and toys. An appliance might be documented as a series of marker sketches, culminating in a finished, tight rendering. You might show photos of your clay model of a car design. A business machine might be shown in line drawings, then photos of a cardboard mock-up. The idea is to prove your skill in model-making, drafting, sketching, and rendering.

Of course, the toughest thing for an employer to judge is how well you *think*. How good are you at problem solving? What mental operations do you go through in developing your solution? Employers know that they'll get the full story only if they hire you and watch you work. But they like to see some evidence of your mental processes in your portfolio.

Employment experts sometimes recommend that every portfolio contain one case history, tracing a project from the earliest doodle to the final solution. This *could* turn your portfolio into a bulging suitcase, but with careful editing, you can tell your story in a nutshell. An interior designer might simply show a series of preliminary sketches for a piece of furniture, then spotlight the final design in a large photo of a scale model. Architects and industrial designers often document a project with quick-reading charts and diagrams that explain the practical reasons for the final design.

Does fine art belong in an applied artist's portfolio? Every student leaves school with stacks of life drawings, paintings, and abstract designs. But these rarely add much to a portfolio's selling power. In the middle of a batch of drafting samples, the interviewer may suddenly run into some abstract paintings that the job hunter "just couldn't resist tossing in." The interviewer has to pause over each one and say, "How nice!" even if they seem irrelevant. It's best to assume that an employer's time is precious. Stick to samples that relate *directly* to your profession.

However, you may feel that fine art samples do relate directly. A fabric designer may carry some abstract color experiments among the samples, to demonstrate a knowledge of color. Or an industrial designer might show sculpture to demonstrate a feeling for three-dimensional form. In short, you *may* show some fine art if it sheds light on your potential as an applied artist. But don't include more than two or three fine art samples. That's just icing on the cake.

Thinking over these portfolio recommendations, you'll discover that a beginner's samples must prove two things to a potential employer. First, your samples must demonstrate that you're a creative thinker, capable of solving big problems *someday*. Second, your portfolio must prove that *today* you're capable of handling the routine jobs that all beginners must do.

Too often, beginners are tempted to overload their portfolios with blue sky samples that prove the job hunter's *future* value, but not *immediate* usefulness. Young illustrators cram their portfolios with paintings for national advertising campaigns, but may forget to add small drawings in black and white. The photographer may have a vast, poetic picture story about Mexico, but no product pictures shot in the studio. Looking over such a portfolio, one New York art director told a job hunter: "Okay, some day you'll be a great chief, maybe. But this week I'm just looking for an Indian."

Portfolios for experienced job hunters and freelances

Reviewing the portfolio of a seasoned artist, designer, or architect, an employer is still interested in the points I've listed for beginners: scope, special interests, skills, techniques, and mental processes. But there *is* a difference in emphasis.

If you have some job experience, you'll find that an employer is less interested in the scope of your education and more interested in the range of things you've done on the job. When you organize your portfolio, it's important to include samples of work you've done for pay. School samples are no longer enough.

How do you get these job samples? Many former employers are considerate enough to open their files and let you take, or order at your own expense, photos of models or finished products; photostats of sketches and finished artwork; blueprints; samples; page proofs of published artwork; prints from file negatives; and occasionally an *original* piece of artwork. I might add that even if you're *not* planning to leave your present job, it's wise to collect samples for possible future use, if you can collect them tactfully.

However, you may not have access to these files because your job hunt is secret or because you're on bad terms with an ex-boss. If that's your problem, then you'll have to find some other way to collect samples. If you're an architect or interior designer, you can get a camera and shoot pictures of finished buildings or interiors. The owners will probably be flattered. If you're a graphic designer, illustrator, or photographer, you can buy the magazines and newspapers where your work has appeared. Many publishers have back issues departments and there are also back issues dealers. If you're a fabric designer, you've just got to go out and buy a yard of fabric or try to get cuttings. Industrial designers can use a camera or clip out ads featuring their products. These emergency methods may not give you perfect portfolio pieces, but they're better than nothing.

Experienced artists, designers, and architects *do* sometimes carry schoolwork in their portfolios, in addition to job samples. If you're out of school just two or three years, you may not have enough job samples to tell your whole story. Your school projects may *have* to be included to complete the picture.

After surveying your scope, the employer wants to know about special interests. Few beginners can claim to be specialists, but many artists, designers, and architects develop specialties as they move up. For this reason, employers are only moderately concerned with special interests when they see a beginner's portfolio. But they may be on the lookout for specialties in the portfolios of seasoned job hunters.

Whether you're looking for a 9-to-5 job or freelance work, an experienced professional's portfolio should give plenty of space to samples that show special interests. It may be simplest to divide your portfolio into sections: one for each specialty and a "miscellaneous" section to emphasize your versatility. The freelance, of course, may become so specialized that he or she skips the "miscellaneous" section and devotes the portfolio entirely to one or more specialties.

Employers are always interested in your skills and techniques, but as you advance in a 9-to-5 job, these may become less important. For example, it's vital for beginning architects, interior or industrial designers to include drafting samples in their portfolios. They'll do plenty of drafting in the early years. But fifteen years later, they may do less drafting on the job, possibly none. They may concentrate on design and let younger workers do the drafting. Portfolios may still include a few drafting samples, but these are less important than other samples that prove that the job hunter can solve problems and generate ideas.

For this reason, the portfolios of top-level architects, interior and industrial designers often consist mainly of photos of finished designs. It's always sensible to include a handful of drafting, model-making or rendering samples, just to prove you *can* do these things. But the interviewer is likely to assume, without being told, that a senior job hunter has these skills.

Of course, lots of 9-to-5 jobs require technical skill even when you're at the *top* of the ladder. A top illustrator in an art studio never outgrows the need to draw and handle a brush unerringly. These aren't routine chores that you can pass on to an assistant. The experienced illustrator knows that a portfolio *must* include original drawings and paintings.

If you're assembling a freelance portfolio, the nature of your work will decide how much space to give to skills and techniques. A freelance graphic designer, specializing in advertising layout, may carry nothing but proofs of printed pages. Clients aren't interested in seeing original layouts or pasteups. They want to see the final ad. But a freelance photographer had better show *actual prints,* made in the darkroom, to demonstrate professional craftsmanship.

When I discussed beginners' portfolios, I said that employers like to see case histories to get some idea of how your mind works. In a beginner's portfolio, case histories can be powerful selling tools. They're less important in an experienced job hunter's portfolio, which includes examples of real projects—not schoolwork—successfuly completed.

However, many seasoned professionals still include simple case histories. Often, these are nothing more than before-and-after pictures, showing a product before redesign, then after. An illustrator sometimes shows a few preliminary sketches, then the finished drawing or painting. A graphic designer might show alternative forms of a trademark design, leading up to the final trademark. Case histories like these aren't *essential* in the portfolio of an experienced job hunter or freelance, but they're worth including if they tell an interesting story and don't take too much space.

Portfolios for teaching jobs

The art teacher's portfolio presents a special problem. The employer doesn't buy drawings, paintings, photos, or other artwork. Art teachers are paid for a vague thing called knowledge and the ability to transmit this knowledge to students. The portfolio supplements your "credentials": your academic record, your license, and your references. The art teacher's portfolio does this in two ways: it demonstrates that you're a competent artist and suggests that you're a good teacher.

The way to prove your competence as an artist is simply to show samples of your work. If you're a *recent graduate*, your art school, college, or university samples are logical things to include. If you're a *seasoned teacher*, you've probably taught a variety of art subjects and you may not feel that you need a portfolio to prove it. Your record may speak for itself. But even then, a good portfolio has a lot of selling power.

The portfolio will naturally divide itself into two sections: specialties and other art subjects you're qualified to handle. Specialties will probably dominate, if only because they're your best samples. If your major interests are painting, drawing, and printmaking, let's say, you might include four or five examples of each. Then come your secondary interests, subjects you *can* teach, but that aren't your specialties. You'll need just one or two samples of each: perhaps a stenciled fabric; one or two photos of sculpture; a sketch for a stage set; or samples of a few crafts like metalworking, ceramics, or weaving. Keep in mind that if you're going to contact school systems in different parts of the country, you may have to meet different requirements each time you're interviewed. It's useful to have extra samples on hand, so that you can alter your portfolio when necessary.

Though scope is essential in an *elementary* or *secondary school* art teacher's portfolio, specialization means much more if you're hunting for a job in an art school, college or university art department. If you're a sculptor, you'll be expected to teach sculpture, three-dimensional design, and probably some drawing. Sculpture and drawings are the main things that interviewers expect to see in your portfolio, though they'll be interested in seeing *some* evidence of your other interests. Art schools, colleges, and universities are always interested in *some* versatility. An interviewer might be delighted to see samples indicating that you can teach a few classes outside your main field of interest. There are plenty of graphic designers whose portfolios include photographs and illustrations; sculptors who show ceramics; architects who show furniture. However, these portfolios are rarely as diversified as the samples of a public school teacher. Specialties still dominate.

The hardest thing to communicate in a portfolio is teaching ability. Most often, an employer looks at your portfolio for proof of your art background. To gauge your value as a teacher, employers depend on your record, references, and personality. Unfortunately, some interviewers assume that good samples make a good teacher and look no further. This explains the shocking number of distinguished artists, designers, and architects who get top school jobs and turn out to be mediocre teachers. Every art student has met them.

Since teaching skill is so difficult to document in a portfolio, few job hunters even try. Yet the few who *do* try are often remarkably successful. An obvious solution is to show a diversified selection of your students' work, whether originals or photos. I've seen memorable portfolios put together by public school teachers who took a camera into the classroom to record a lively class project. The photos were combined with samples of the children's work to document the case. I also recall an art school teacher who developed an experimental method of teaching life drawing: for his portfolio, he drew a series of charts to explain his theory. These are elaborate time-consuming ways to build a portfolio. No interviewer *insists* on seeing such unique portfolio pieces. But when interviewers do see something unique, they're not likely to forget.

Portfolios for job hunters who hope to switch fields

A few years ago, I was visited by an electrical engineer who wanted to be an industrial designer. He carried what *he* called a portfolio: a folder full of diagrams that meant very little to me, except that he seemed to be a skilled engineering draftsman. I asked if he had any art training. No, he'd never drawn or painted, outside of a few classes he'd been forced to take in high school. What were his hobbies? Did he build furniture, make ceramics, tinker with cars, try to redecorate his home or office? Did he do anything that was even remotely related to industrial design? Well, no, his only real hobby was collecting coins. All he knew was that he was unhappy in electrical engineering and "sort of thought" he might be happier as an industrial designer.

For all I know, he might have made a brilliant designer. But he had no evidence to support his case. We *might* have hired him for a year's tryout, but investing time and money in him seemed absurd when we could have a trained designer for the same salary. All I could suggest was that he stick to his present job and take night courses at a local art school to see if industrial design was really what he wanted. When he'd learned to draw and completed some classroom design problems, I'd be happy to see him again *with samples.* This seemed to discourage him. He never came back. I assume he's still griping about being an engineer.

The disgruntled engineer was typical of many job hunters who hope to switch fields. They want a new job, but they have no samples to prove their qualifications. Nor are they willing to make the effort needed to create this portfolio.

Of course, *some* job hunters have ready made samples. An architect can often use an architectural portfolio to get an interior design job. A mechanical engineer with lots of experience in product development, marketing, and human factors—plus the ability to draw freehand—might quality for an industrial design job. But these are the lucky few.

More common is the job hunter who has *some* relevant experience or training, but not enough. A common case is the illustrator who wants to be a graphic designer. If that's your problem, you *can* fill *part* of you portfolio with drawings or paintings, but you also have to show some layouts. If you're this type of job hunter, you can often fill the gaps in your portfolio by spending your spare time creating the necessary samples. This may mean months of evenings and weekends, but without these samples your job hunt will be long and your prospects dim.

Painfully common are job hunters with *no* relevant experience. Like the unhappy electrical engineer, they have *no* samples. The logical way for such job hunters to create a portfolio is to go back to school. This takes time and money, but the investment has to be made.

If you're hoping to switch into a new field, you must remember that you face stiff competition from job hunters *already* in that field. They have education and experience that you lack. They have portfolios filled with the right samples. You must convince an employer that you're as good as the competition. At home or back in school, you must build a portfolio that can stand comparison with other portfolios that cross an interviewer's desk. If this doesn't seem worth the effort, it's better to stick with your present job.

Some suggestions about format

The traditional portfolio looks like a huge, black file folder. Two sheets of black cardboard are hinged together along one edge, and frayed shoe laces appear at various points so you can tie the whole thing together. This coffin for artwork has only two advantages: it's cheap and it's light. But anybody who's carried one will remember its drawbacks for a lifetime. After a week of job hunting, the black folder looks as shabby as an old shoe. There's no handle and no way of carrying the folder comfortably *without* a handle. When you want to untie the shoe laces so an interviewer can see your samples, the knots won't give: someone seems to have dipped them in glue. When you want to *tie* them and make a graceful exit, the knots refuse to hold and your samples spill across the floor. Humidity in the air makes the boards curl like potato chips. And heaven help your samples if it rains!

There are much better ways of carrying and protecting samples. A large accordion envelope, usually the color of decayed salmon, is just as ugly as the traditional portfolio, but easier to open and shut, and cheap enough to replace when it gets ragged. This also gives you *some* protection against weather, particularly if you coat it with lacquer from a spray can. If you can afford to spend more, you can buy a large leather or plastic portfolio, something like a briefcase with zippers on three sides. The zippers are easy to open, though sometimes hard to close. But it's easy enough to throw in your samples, make a quick exit, and zip the folder afterward. If your samples aren't too big, an attaché case or a briefcase will do handsomely.

After a few years of seeing job hunters, interviewers are prepared for *anything* when a portfolio is opened. An *anything* is what they often get. An amazing number of portfolios contain dog-eared sheets of paper in all shapes and sizes. There are pages torn from sketchbooks; blueprints folded in devious ways and impossible to open without tearing; pencil, charcoal, and pastel sketches that the job hunter forgot to spray with fixative, so the color comes off on the other drawings *and* on the interviewer's fingers; small, out-of-focus snapshots that get left behind among the papers on the interviewer's desk; drawings on tracing paper that you can't figure out because the drawing underneath shows through. Half the samples are face down. Others are sideways. And out of the pile, when you least expect it, slips a tiny plaster model that smashes on the floor.

One designer swears that he's going to buy an electric fan and keep it going full blast on his desk: "When somebody opens a portfolio, all those loose scraps of paper will get blown back in his dumb face!"

Order is the interviewer's first requirement when you open your portfolio. Interviewers have neither time nor patience to riffle through a stack of odd-size sheets. The simplest way to create an orderly portfolio is to paste *everything* on standard-size cardboards, all the same weight if possible. With all your samples the same size, the interviewer will flip through your portfolio without effort or interruption. Paste samples on just one side of a board. This makes it easy to keep boards in the proper sequence, all facing in the same direction. Several small items can be pasted onto one board, if they're related, like a series of thumbnail sketches or small photos. Even color transparencies can be mounted on cardboards; just cut a hole in the board, so light can get through. The interviewer can hold the card up to a lamp or a window if the board isn't too big and heavy.

A more expensive way of doing the same thing is to buy a large looseleaf notebook in an art supply store or stationery store. These now come in enormous sizes especially designed for portfolios and they contain transparent acetate sleeves for artwork. You mount samples on sheets of thick paper and slip the sheets into the sleeves. Sturdy black paper is sometimes supplied with the book. If you prefer some other color or a *variety* of colors, art materials stores usually have a good stock of drawing papers in various tones. Keep in mind that acetate sleeves protect artwork, but tend to get scratched up. They also tear easily, particularly at the holes where the looseleaf rings come through. It's sensible to have extra sleeves on hand to replace damaged ones.

A big looseleaf notebook is luxurious, but nobody will call you a piker for using boards. In fact, boards have some advantages over a looseleaf book. As they thumb through the boards, interviewers can set aside some samples for a second look. Interviewers can stand them against the wall and back away to see them better. And you can quickly reorganize boards, deleting some, adding others, for your next interview. All these things are less convenient when samples are under acetate in a looseleaf book. Samples are also easier to see without acetate, just as paintings are easier to see without glass. On the other hand, bare boards give your samples less protection. Try spraying the boards with plastic lacquer, which art supply stores sell in a spray can.

By choosing boards or a looseleaf book, you'll make the interviewer's life easier. You'll also protect your precious samples from the crumpled, dog-eared look that dooms loose sheets of paper.

The only samples you can't protect this way are drafting samples that are too big to fit into a portfolio without folding or rolling. Don't roll them. The cylindrical shape won't fit into your envelope or briefcase, so you must carry the roll separately and risk having it crushed. Worse still, rolled drawings never lie flat on an interviewer's desk. All you can do is fold them neatly and *logically*, so interviewers can open sheets quickly and you can refold them without too much fuss. Be sure to fold them all the same way, according to some logical plan, so the interviewer doesn't tear them or open them in the wrong direction.

Another solution is to make small photostats of big drafting samples. Stats are a good way to show off your designs, but the quality of your drafting may be hard to judge. If you have lots of drafting samples, you might photostat the ones that show design ability and paste these on boards or looseleaf pages. Then carry folded, full size prints of drawings that show drafting skill. Big, unmounted drafting samples soon show signs of wear. Better have extra prints of each drawing.

How many samples should you include? There's no infallible answer. Some employers have more patience than others. But it's safe to assume that an interviewer has only a short time to spend with you. I don't think you should make an interviewer turn more than twenty boards or looseleaf pages. If you can tell your story in less, better still. An experienced artist, designer, or architect needs only a few samples to judge you. If employers want to see more than fifteen or twenty items, they'll ask for them. You might carry an envelope of extras just in case. But don't haul them out and flood your interviewer's desk unless your future boss *really* wants to see more.

Job hunters sometimes number pages or boards. But they regret the numbers when they decide to add or delete samples. Better leave the numbers off. However, it's often helpful to label samples. Some portfolio pieces explain themselves at a glance. But others may need clarification. For example, it may be obvious to an interviewer that you're showing him an upholstery fabric. But the most seasoned professional may not be able to guess the exact blend of fibers. You could *tell* the interviewer, of course, but it's considerate to label the sample.

An intelligent label does more than just identify something. It gives the interviewer some basis on which to judge your work. In an industrial designer's portfolio, the caption, "Power Lawn

Mower," tells the interviewer something that anyone could guess just by looking at a photo. But call the product a "Low-Cost Power Lawn Mower," and you help the employer judge its suitability for low-cost production and the mass market.

A label doesn't have to be hand-lettered unless you're skilled with a lettering pen. You can buy handsome paste-on letters in an art supply store. A sharp, clean typewritten caption is also good looking and unobstrusive.

Color slides

More and more job hunters carry color slides. These *can* be enormously effective portfolio pieces, but they can just as easily be a headache.

I once sat at my desk, grinding my teeth while a job hunter set up a suitcase full of equipment to show me two dozen slides. He spent ten minutes trying to figure out an expensive new projector he'd bought for his job hunt. Then he discovered he needed an extension cord. An office boy finally located one at the other end of the building. To set up a portable screen, we had to move my desk. At last, a tray of slides went click-click into the projector and I dimmed my lights. The first slide appeared on the screen sideways. The next four were upside down. Desperately, the job hunter tried to reverse the automatic mechanism to get his slides out and try again. The projector jammed. We smelled burning film. I pulled out the plug and suggested he come back later *without* slides.

If you're going to show slides, steer clear of projectors, screens, and other equipment that clutter up the interviewer's office. All this paraphernalia takes ages to set up and knock down, while your interviewer politely smothers the urge to throw you out. The more equipment you have, the greater your chances of a mechanical failure. You may not be invited back for another try, unless the interviewer takes pity on you.

A small, portable viewer—most of them look like tiny TV sets—is the most convenient device for showing slides. The best kind is a desk top unit that holds a tray or a cartridge of slides that pop through automatically. A battery operated viewer is infinitely better than a plug-in model. Don't make an interviewer wait while you crawl around the floor, looking for an electric outlet.

You may have to economize and buy a hand-fed viewer, one that requires you to insert and remove each slide by hand. Whether you get a desk top model or one that's held in your hand, be sure to test various models to make certain that the slides are easy to get in and out.

Another type of hand viewer actually has to be held against the eye. You look into it like a miniature telescope. Interviewers who wear glasses sometimes object. I think you're safer with the kind that looks like a TV set.

Many interviewers prefer to look at slides with the naked eye. This is hard to do with 35 millimeter slides, for which most viewers are designed. But it's perfectly practical with larger transparencies. Many job hunters shoot 2¼ by 2¼ slides, which can be seen with the naked eye *or* through a special viewer. You can carry a viewer just in case and let interviewers decide whether they want to use it.

Slides are best for three-dimensional subjects like buildings, interiors, products, packages, displays, and other samples that you can't carry. Most interviewers object to slides of two-dimensional objects like illustrations, fabrics, or drafting samples. It's hard to judge your technique without seeing the original. Thus, slides seem best for architects, interior designers, and industrial designers, not for artists who work in two dimensions.

It's difficult to put a complete portfolio on slides. A top-level architect or designer might show slides just of finished buildings, interiors, or products. But most job hunters divide their portfolios into two parts: slides of models or finished work; plus a folder of sketches, renderings, and drafting samples.

Models

A nervous young man once stepped gingerly into my office, balancing an immense cardboard box on his shoulder. He quickly announced his name, set the box on the floor, lifted out a delicate model of an exhibit and placed this carefully on the chair next to my desk. With a sigh of relief, he shook my hand, backed up to the same chair and sat down. That crunch still haunts my dreams.

Models belong in a portfolio only if they're small and tough. This automatically excludes most architectural and interior models. Industrial designers' product models sometimes fare better: wood, metal, and hard plaster are meant to take a certain amount of punishment. But if you carry product models, it pays to build a special padded box, as some industrial designers have done. Stick to small items that an interviewer can hold securely: things like an electric shaver or a hand mixer. Don't hand the interviewer some delicate gadget that slips out of the strongest fingers like a cake of wet soap.

The safest way to show a fragile model is in a photograph. This may not do *complete* justice to your craftsmanship, but a good, sharp close-up will give a reasonable idea of your model-making skill. If interviewers ask to see the actual model—they rarely do—then you have to take a chance and bring it in. Until then, keep it safe at home.

Unusual portfolios

Conventional portfolios—mounted samples, looseleaf books, and slides—are always a safe bet. But you may not be satisfied that a conventional presentation does your work justice. If you can devise a more unusual way to design a portfolio, don't let this chapter hold you back. But don't be carried away by gimmicks, like the graphic designer who brought me a looseleaf book full of packages that popped out like a Jack-in-the-box as I turned each page. Her trickiness defeated her. I can remember the gimmick, but I can't recall any of her samples.

An unusual portfolio format is worthwhile only if it's a *more logical* way of telling your story. One of the most memorable portfolios I've seen was a stack of blank index cards and a scissors. An interior designer had developed a line of furniture based on a unique principle: each item in the line could be made from a single sheet of metal, cut at several points and bent into shape. The designer felt that sketches and photos were too static to explain her manufacturing method. She was convinced that only a demonstration would do the job. She asked me to think of each index card as a sheet of metal. Taking a scissors out of her pocket, she quickly snipped a card at several points and bent it with her fingers. The operation took half a minute and was repeated till I had a complete line of furniture on my desk. She'd rehearsed the demonstration and knew it would take no more than five minutes to *construct her portfolio* before my eyes.

Another job hunter who felt the need for a less static portfolio was an architect whose major interest was trade fairs. He'd built extraordinary models of experimental displays, too fragile to bring and too complex to make sense in a *still* photograph. So he made a brief eight-millimeter motion picture. The camera roamed in and out among the colorful shapes, revealing dramatic details and structural innovations. The whole movie was on a four-minute film cartridge that he simply popped into a portable projector with a minimum of setting-up time. Everything went smoothly. No upside-down images and no burnt film. This portfolio was worth waiting for.

Not every job hunter has samples that lend themselves to demonstrations or motion pictures. Your samples must *justify* this unusual treatment. And your off-beat portfolio—like an off-beat resume—must be exceptionally good to win the interviewer's patience. Unless your samples really *demand* unorthodox presentation, think twice about departing from a conventional portfolio format.

Planning the portfolio to fit the interviewer

Before you step into someone's office with a portfolio under your arm, take another look at your samples. Chances are that you know a few facts about the person who's going to interview you. Though you may not know the interviewer *personally*, you can probably make some intelligent predictions about the kind of samples that particular employer would like to see. Would it be wise to delete some samples? Do you have some extras you might add?

Even if you know nothing about your interviewer except the nature of the business, you may be able to tailor your portfolio to fit the interests of that business. Let's suppose you're a graphic designer about to visit an advertising agency. You don't know the agency's accounts. You don't know how the art staff is organized or what sort of talent they're looking for. But glancing through your portfolio the evening before your interview, you're reminded that only half your samples are really advertising layouts. The other half is a blend of magazine layouts, book designs, packaging, and a few illustrations. You need more emphasis on the advertising samples, less on the other kinds of graphic design you've done.

First, it's probably safe to delete most of the book designs. This isn't your interviewer's field. Are you particularly proud of *one* book? Well, leave that one in as matter of interest. Now, what about the magazine layouts? Not really your interviewer's field, but closer to advertising than the book designs. Keep a few, but delete some others. Packaging samples? More agencies are getting into packaging. Better hang onto several; just delete a few. Illustrations? You like to draw and the agency might need a good illustrator for smaller ads that aren't farmed out to freelances. Better hold onto these samples. Having trimmed down the portfolio, what can you add? Not all your advertising layouts were in the original portfolio. There are some extra samples in your desk drawer. You can certainly add some of these to bring your samples back to the original number.

You can even alter the sequence of your samples. Perhaps the magazine layouts originally came first, then some advertising samples, packaging, then more ads. Now it seems advisable to concentrate advertising samples at the beginning, then follow with packaging and magazine layouts, saving your dramatic illustrations for an "upbeat" ending.

You've really made no drastic changes in your portfolio. Most of the samples are the same. A handful have been deleted, another handful added, and you've re-shuffled things to put the most important samples first. It's essentially the same portfolio, but with a *different emphasis*. With a few minutes work, you have a portfolio that will have *much more impact* on this particular employer. If you have a second interviewer that same day, it takes only a few more minutes to re-shuffle your samples again and come up with another custom made portfolio. You can carry extra samples and do your switching between appointments. You may even keep a list of each portfolio arrangement you've tried, so you can repeat a successful arrangement without struggling to remember the sequence.

Naturally, if you're just out of school, you may find it difficult to add or drop samples whenever you have an interview because you may not have enough samples. In that case, one set of samples will do. But after you've had a job or two, you'll have more material to choose from. Over the years, you should accumulate an arsenal of samples, so you can choose your weapons when you plan a job hunt.

20
Conducting job interviews

You'll be interviewed by many employers before you find the right job. When employers make an appointment to meet you, there *might* be a current job opening. If there's no current opening, they may be thinking about creating a new spot in the organization *if* they find the right job hunter. They may know of a spot somewhere else in town. Or they may be seeing you just out of curiosity. You can never tell. But each time you step into an interviewer's office, this *might* be the climax of your job hunt. As you open your portfolio, you always wonder if the conversation will end with a job offer.

You need more than a good portfolio and a good resume to win that job offer. The big moment also hinges on how well you conduct your job interview.

Are you surprised by the suggestion that *you* conduct the interview? Doesn't the *employer* do the interviewing? It may look that way. After all, the employer asks the questions and you answer them. But the interview is the *job hunter's* show. The employer is the audience. *Your own* words and actions determine whether the show is a hit. You must plan an interview as carefully as you plan your resume and portfolio.

This chapter makes some suggestions about how to plan and conduct a job interview. Though these suggestions will mean most to the job hunter who's looking for a 9-to-5 position, many of these recommendations will apply just as well if you're looking for freelance work. Whatever sort of work you may be seeking, you still must meet potential employers and be interviewed.

Twelve ways to irritate an interviewer

Interviews are often wrecked by small things. Even if you have an impressive portfolio and resume, you can still ruin your job prospects by a few thoughtless acts. Here are a dozen common ways to irritate a potential employer:

(1) *Don't arrive on schedule.* Job hunters are often late. They sometimes have good reasons. The previous interview may have taken longer than expected. But few job hunters have the courtesy to phone and say they're off schedule. They just walk in late and expect employers to see them anyway. Job hunters don't seem to realize that an interviewer's day may be tightly scheduled, allotting just so much time to each appointment. If you're half an hour late, the interviewer must re-shuffle other dates to see you. Getting there half an hour early can be almost as inconsiderate as arriving late. Interviewers must disrupt their schedules to see you immediately. Or they're forced to keep you waiting and they're embarrassed.

(2) *Mutter your name so the interviewer never really gets it.* Then continue to talk inaudibly throughout the interview. Your interviewers will wonder if they need a hearing aid. As you talk, the interviewer will search vainly for the slip of paper on which a secretary had scribbled your name when you phoned for an interview. When you leave, the employer will shake your hand awkwardly and bid you, "Goodbye, Mr. Ummm."

(3) *Get the interviewer's name wrong.* Keep calling him or her by this wrong name and use it in the thank-you note you send the following day. Few job hunters have the foresight to double check the interviewer's name with the receptionist.

(4) *Forget to bring an extra copy of your resume.* You mailed a copy, but this is filed, or on someone else's desk. So the inter-

viewer is forced to hear you repeat your resume aloud. If you'd brought the resume with you, the employer would spend a minute scanning the page, then move on to your portfolio. Instead, the poor devil has to spend an exasperating five minutes pulling facts out of you and trying to remember them.

(5) *Talk about everything but the subject.* A surprising number of job hunters act as if employment is the last thing they want to discuss. They'll use any excuse to avoid getting to the point. The weather is a favorite: "Boy, today's a scorcher. I was at the beach Saturday and . . ." Personalities are also a popular dodge: "Jack Doolittle sent me over. Say, have you heard about Jack's new . . ." At last the job hunter runs out of small talk and opens the portfolio with a resigned look that suggests, "Well, we had to get down to business sooner or later." By now, the intereviewer's time and temper are growing short. The employer is forced to race through your portfolio and skip a lot of questions that might have helped you land the job!

(6) *Dump your portfolio on the interviewer's desk without warning.* Don't ask where to put your portfolio. Just drop it with a thud, scattering papers and tipping over the ashtray.

(7) *Apologize for your samples.* Nothing discourages an interviewer more than the news that, "These aren't really my best samples. I'm still working on the best ones, so I left them home." Another common apology: "A lot of these samples aren't so hot. They're old stuff, but I haven't had a chance to weed them out." Still another apology: "I wasn't sure what you wanted to see, so I just threw everything into my briefcase." When you start an interview with an apology, interviewers wish they could say, "Go home and come back when you can show me your *best* samples and nothing else." But they may not give you a second chance.

(8) *Insist on turning the portfolio pages yourself,* with a detailed running commentary. Of all the ways to make an interviewer's blood boil, this is the best. Don't let the *employer* thumb

through your samples. You do it. Linger over each sample and tell its story in encyclopedic detail: "I remember starting this job on a Tuesday afternoon. It was the first thing I'd done for this client. The client had called my boss that morning and . . ." At this rate, it may take half an hour to get through your portfolio. But after ten minutes, the interviewer will probably interrupt you for another appointment.

(9) *Evade the interviewer's questions.* Never give a specific answer. Be vague and watch interviewers grind their teeth. When interviewers ask why you left your last job, don't explain that the staff was too small to allow room for advancement. Just say, "I wasn't happy there." If you're asked how you did in school, don't say that you graduated in the top third of your class, made consistent B's and some A's in your major subject. Just say, "Pretty well." At the end of the interview, employers won't know much more than they did when you walked in.

(10) *Know nothing about your prospective employer.* If you want to do more than irritate interviewers, you can really *antagonize* them by your total ignorance of their business. They don't expect you to know *much* about their work, of course, but they'll be shaken to find that you think that the company is a magazine publisher, when it's really a book publisher. You can also rattle them by admitting that you've never read any of the magazines. Employers may get a good laugh out of such interviews. But they may also take your ignorance as evidence that you don't *care* enough about the organization to work there.

(11) *Fiddle with the objects on the interviewer's desk.* Distract the interviewer's attention from your portfolio by picking up a paperweight and rolling it about in your hand. Scan the letters on the interviewer's desk. Pick at a frayed corner of the desk blotter. Employers will be so busy watching you fidget that they won't remember a word you say or a single item in your portfolio.

(12) *Forget to leave.* When the interviewer has finished looking at your portfolio and you've both asked all the essential questions, don't get up and go. Just sit there and keep talking about nothing in particular. Chat about baseball scores, politics, books you've read lately, anything to drag out the visit and waste the interviewer's time. Ignore the fact that the next guest is waiting outside. Make the interviewer get up and show you the door. Don't leave till your prospective boss seems on the verge of throwing you out.

This list of irritations is no joke. Job hunters commit these small sins every day. Interviewers develop thick skins and a good sense of humor, but no one really gets *used* to inconsiderate job hunters. A thoughtless act, no matter how small, is rarely overlooked.

Your personal appearance

The need for good grooming and good taste in your clothes seems so obvious that I was tempted to skip this section altogether. But since I began *Art Career Guide*, at least a dozen colleagues have complained about job hunters' paint-clogged fingernails, unshaven faces, fire-engine-red sportshirts, blue jeans that have never seen a laundry, baggy plaid sport jackets, jangling jewelry, and dresses cut so low that no male interviewer can concentrate on the portfolio. So here are a few suggestions that may seem unnecessary to *some* readers, but may be helpful to others.

Theoretically, at least, we all learn the elements of good grooming when we're children—hair combed, hands and face scrubbed, fingernails cleaned and trimmed—so there's no point in going into such picky details here. But many job hunters must race directly from their classrooms or other jobs to an interview, with no time for a shower or a change of clothes. Under these circumstances, how can you hope to appear well groomed?

A good solution might be to make yourself a portable cleanup kit. Buy a small tube of hand cleaner if you spend your day elbow deep in paint or clay. You can buy a tiny nail clipper with a built-in file. You can also get hair cream in a tube. For women, there are plenty of cosmetics in small packages. A soft cloth and perhaps a small bottle of liquid polish are useful for giving shoes a quick treatment. The list might go on to include things like a hairbrush, a mirror, spot remover, and anything else that occurs to you. The whole works should fit into a small box, a briefcase, or a shoulder bag. I think I can safely assume that running water, soap, and paper towels will be handy somewhere in your school or office.

One further tip: if you're wearing good clothes for an interview later in the day, protect them with a smock or an apron while you're working.

Now, what about clothes themselves. What should you wear? An artist, more than most job hunters, is expected to show good taste in clothes. This doesn't mean that you must go into debt to buy a suit from the finest London tailor or a dress from a Paris salon. But it does mean that your clothes should be well cut and harmonious in color and texture.

For a man, the traditional dark suit is always a safe bet. Some interviewers *insist* on a suit, but I see nothing wrong with a subdued sport jacket and dark slacks—or clean jeans. The thing to avoid is the jazzy plaid jacket that always turns up in foreign caricatures of American tourists. I'd also stick to dark shoes. In shirts, white, a subdued solid color, or a quiet stripe are all acceptable.

For a woman, a dark suit is also traditional and safe. So is a trimly tailored, dark dress. Though it's wise to dress conservatively when you're job hunting, a woman can always dress in more adventurous colors and styles than a man. If you're looking for a job in fashion—with a fashion magazine, let's say, or a store—your clothes become evidence of your imagination and your knowledge of the field. But even then, simplicity commands more respect than ostentation: classic styles, small patterns, dignified jewelry, subtle rather than dazzling colors. I might add that you needn't resort to decolletage or a dress that looks sprayed on. (Interviewers will notice your figure anyhow.) Frankly, your chances of a job offer are better if the interviewer isn't worried that you'll be a distracting influence on others around the office.

Yes, these recommendations are pretty square! There *are* lots of top professionals who wear jeans and sneakers to work, never wear a necktie, go for wild jewelry, and never cut their hair until it obstructs their hearing and eyesight. (In fact, your interviewer may be one of them.) All I'm suggesting is that you play it square until you get the job—if only to avoid scaring off a conservative interviewer. Later on, when you get the job, you can switch to jeans and sneakers, and leave the necktie home, if you find that your co-workers dress that way.

Planning the interview

Planning an interview really means deciding what you want a particular interviewer to know about you. What details of your education or experience will mean most to the employer you're going to visit tomorrow morning?

You plan an interview the same way you plan your job hunting letters. Your first step is to pin down one or two basic facts about the employer. Let's say tomorrow's appointment is with a commercial art studio. This single fact tells you a great deal. Like most consulting firms, your potential employer is likely to have a variety of clients. This means that the office is probably interested in job hunters with *diversified* training and experience, plus what employers sometimes call a "client contact personality."

Your second step is to examine your background for details that prove you can fill this bill. It's not enough to recite your resume. The interviewer has already read it. Besides, the resume doesn't necessarily play up the particular details you want to emphasize in tomorrow's conversation. What are these details? If you're a beginner, you'll want to think back over the diverse school assignments that prove your flexibility. If you have some job experience, you'll want to examine your employment history for projects that demonstrate your versatility and "contact skills."

This doesn't mean that you should stride into an interviewer's office with a prepared sales talk, like someone selling vacuum cleaners door to door. But you *should* have a mental outline of details that will appeal to your interviewer. A good interviewer will give you plenty of opportunity to talk about them. If not, you can steer the conversation in the right direction.

Once you're in the employer's office, watch the conversation for clues about facts that interest the interviewer. You can even pick up clues from the pictures on his walls. For example, architects often decorate their offices with photos of their new buildings. If one of these is a housing project and you've done some housing work, you have another sales point to bring up.

At times, you'll run across interviewers who give you no chance to steer the conversation in the right direction. Some interviewers will talk your ear off and barely allow you to begin the conversation. All you can do is take the bull by the horns and say, "Though you have my resume, I think I should tell you a bit more about my background." The tongue-tied interviewer will be relieved that you've broken the silence in such a forthright way. Even the chatterbox may be pleased. Some interviewers jabber merely because they feel awkward, and they may be delighted when you take the initiative.

Showing and interpreting your portfolio

One of your main purposes in visiting an employer is to show your portfolio. This will take a good part of the interview, perhaps most of it. In the previous chapter, "Planning Your Portfolio," I've talked about editing the portfolio to fit the interviewer. But you must also plan what you *say* about these samples. You must even plan your method of showing them.

If your portfolio is a looseleaf book or a stack of boards, showing your samples is simple. Just open your portfolio and let interviewers thumb through *at their own pace*. Don't be surprised if they flip through your samples more quickly than you'd expected. This doesn't mean that they're unimpressed. But they've probably seen hundreds of portfolios and learned to judge them in minutes. Before they're halfway through your samples, they've sized you up. They'll look through the remaining samples just to confirm the first impression.

If you're using slides, showing your portfolio becomes trickier. In the previous chapter, I recommended a slide viewer rather than a projector. If you're using a hand-fed model—not an automatic unit with a tray or cartridge of slides—you'd better rehearse the feeding operation. Is it best for *you* to insert the slides or should you let the interviewer put them in? It's considerate to give the interviewer the choice and have a few quick sentences ready to explain how the viewer works. How should the slides be stacked? Should you mark them in one corner so you'll know where to grip them when you pick them up?

The toughest thing to plan is the commentary. You can't predict how fast the interviewer will turn pages or run through slides. How much should you say? I don't think you'll find it necessary to interpret *every* item. Many will explain *themselves* and you can remain silent. On the other hand, if you *do* have a significant point to make, try to keep your explanation down to one or two sentences: just as long as it takes for the interviewer to glance at the sample and move on. Don't make employers pause politely while you launch into a lecture. If they want more details, they'll ask.

How do you decide which samples need interpretation? There are good reasons for adding explanatory comment. First, you should certainly explain if there's some essential point that the interviewer would never get if you didn't mention it. Let's say that a color transparencey was processed by a new, experimental method. Or perhaps a lush interior was done on an unusually low budget. The interviewer won't fully appreciate the sample unless you add this vital, but invisible detail.

The second reason brings us back to a question raised in the previous section: what do you want this particular interviewer to know about you? Does a sample embody some sales point that may ring the bell with this employer? Suppose you're applying for a job on the photographic staff of a magazine with a strong interest in science. You should certainly point out that a flower photo in your portfolio was part of a series on plant life. If you're showing graphic design samples to a book publisher, you may want to emphasize your schooling in book production. Wait till the interviewer turns to a page that you set in the school's typographic shop and printed on a hand press. Then mention that you had a year's course in production.

You may feel that it's difficult to pack such information into one or two sentences. There's so much you *could* tell. But you must condense your message and take your chances on the interviewer asking for more facts. Don't be insulted if the employer just nods and doesn't pursue the subject. Your point has gotten across.

This job of condensation takes planning. No need to memorize sentences or rehearse in front of a mirror. But go through your portfolio the day before the interview and decide what to say about each sample. Keep your running comments short and informal, like a one-line caption under a magazine picture. "Built that model myself. It's lifesize. Stands about so high."

Questions you should be prepared to answer

Until now, I've concentrated on what *you'll* say. But you must also anticipate what your *interviewer* will say. A good interviewer asks questions, often embarrassing ones. You must be prepared for these. Here are some questions frequently asked by interviewers. Before your first interview, you should do some serious thinking about the answers you'll give.

(1) What was your school record?

If you're just out of school, this is a terribly important question. You have no job experience, except for a few summer jobs, perhaps, so your school record and portfolio are the interviewer's only evidence of your ability. Be prepared to give the interviewer a detailed account of your grades in various subjects. You needn't pull out a stack of report cards or school transcripts and read them aloud. It's simplest to talk in averages: "I averaged C in most foundation year subjects, but by the senior year I'd worked up to a B average in my major."

If your grades were poor, you must say so. But you may feel that your grades don't tell the real story. You may have good reasons: health problems, financial headaches, philosophical conflict with your teachers. If you have a valid explanation, be ready to present it.

(2) What have you done on the job?

Though your resume lists past employers and your duties on each job, interviewers often want more details. They may fire specific questions at you: "How was your department organized?" "What ideas did you contribute to this project?" Some interviewers prefer to ask general questions: "What do you think you learned from that job?" "Tell me more about your work." These broad questions may be lazy interviewer's way of keeping up the conversation. But they may also be a sharp interviewer's way of saying. "The floor is yours. Tell me why I should hire you." This is the moment when your planning pays off. If you've examined your background for sales points that will appeal to this particular employer, you're well prepared.

Of course, not every question is an opportunity to raise a sales point. For some reason, the interviewer may want a particular fact, which you must be ready to supply. Before you step into someone's office, review your professional history carefully. Have you got all the names, dates, places, facts, and figures straight? You'd be amazed at the number of job hunters who can't recall bosses' names, projects, or dates of employment.

One effective way of marshalling your facts about a past job is to visualize a typical work day or work week. If an interviewer says, "Tell me more about that job," describing a typical day or week is a quick, logical way of covering a lot of territory.

(3) Why did you leave your last job?

There's nothing wrong with quitting because you're bored, underpaid, at odds with your boss, or stuck in a job with no future. Nor is there anything wrong with being laid off because business is bad or your department is being reorganized. You can speak frankly about these circumstances, though you should avoid *knocking* past employers, even if they deserve it. *Future* bosses often resent bitter words about *former* bosses.

But this becomes an awkward moment if you lost your job under unpleasant circumstances. What if you were fired because your boss was dissatisfied with your work? Many job hunters manage to conceal the reasons for losing a job. But a potential employer may respect you for telling the truth: "Yes, I was let go because the boss didn't like my work. But I'm confident that I *can* do good work. I was just in the wrong job." What seems like *bad* work in one office may be *good* work somewhere else. If you're working in an architectural office specializing in colonial houses and you want to do modern homes, you may feel like a total misfit. You become discouraged and your work may seem hopelessly inept. But if you're put to work in a different office, you may turn into a fireball.

What if you were fired for a really good reason? What do you tell an interviewer if you lost your job because of sloppy work, laziness, unwillingness to cooperate, or just plain bad manners? Like many job hunters, you can try to hide the unpleasant facts. But keep in mind that a future boss will probably contact your past boss to get the facts. You may be *forced* to come clean. On the other hand, your personal code of honor may prompt you to tell the truth, *without* being forced. Again, you may be surprised at the number of bosses who'll respect your courage if you tell them frankly, "I turned in a rotten performance on my last job. But I've learned a lot from being fired. I won't make the same mistakes twice. I *can* turn in a first-rate performance and I'd like another chance."

(4) What type of job are you looking for?

When employers have a job to fill, they often start out with a mental picture of the employees they want. Sometimes this is a written *job description*, prepared by the personnel department. More often, it's a sketchy list of qualifications, tucked away in the interviewer's head. Interviewers also expect *you* to have some sort of job description in *your* head: some concept of the ideal spot for you. When interviewers ask, "What type of job are you looking for?" They're really asking for some details of *your* job description. If your concept of the right job seems close to the employer's concept of the right job candidate, you may be offered the job, provided that your qualifications fill the bill. Of course, even if the two job descriptions don't match, the interviewer may be impressed and may want to hire you anyway.

You *must* have some specific ideas about the kind of job you hope to land. If you're a graphic designer, would you rather work in the fast-moving world of advertising and magazines or the more staid world of book publishing? As a teacher, would you be interested in doing some administrative work in addition to conducting your classes?

But how do you answer an employer when you're asked a question as vague as, "What sort of job do you want?" You've got to think for a moment and come up with an honest, but diplomatic answer. Thus, when you walk into a large organization, it obviously makes no sense to announce that you'd like to work in a small office. Nor is it honest to say that you'd like to work in a big place if you don't mean it. The diplomatic way to state your position is to say: "I'd prefer a fairly intimate set-up, either a small organization or a close knit department in a large organization." This is the truth, but tailored to the interviewer and stated flexibly, so that you don't discourage an offer. The offer *may* be too good to turn down.

(5) How much money do you want?

When interviewers ask about money, this doesn't necessarily mean that they're about to offer you a job. They *might* make you an offer. But more likely, they want a figure to compare with the income requirements of other candidates for the job, or possibly just a figure to keep in mind in case there's an opening in the future. Or they may just be curious.

Whatever their reasons for asking, you'd better have an answer ready, well in advance of the interview. In deciding your answer, you must consider several things.

First, how much money do you *need?* If you're single, living with your parents, you probably need less money than if you're married, with a couple of children. It's worthwhile to take a careful look at your living expenses and come up with a minimum figure, the lowest income you can accept without working nights or going into debt.

Second, find out the *going rate* for someone with your training and experience. Ask friends in the field what their offices would pay someone like you. The figure may vary from city to city, as well as from one organization to another. Your friends won't all come up with the same figure, but if you get enough figures they'll begin to form a pattern.

Third, you should certainly keep your previous earnings in mind, if you've already held a job. Unless your pay was far above or below the going rate, you can reasonably expect as much money in your *next* job, hopefully more.

Finally, you can use recent job offers—you may have *several* before you accept one—as an index of your current value in the talent market. Again, the figures will vary: one employer may be willing to pay more than another. But again you may find that the various offers form a pattern.

You can't feed all these figures into a computer and come up with the exact salary you can command. But by balancing these four factors, you can visualize a *potential salary range.* The bottom figure in this salary range is the minimum you think it's reasonable to accept. The top figure is the maximum you can ask without seeming *unreasonable.*

When the moment comes to name your salary requirements, I think there are two rules worth remembering. First, since most interviewers will ask about past earnings, be prepared to state these figures frankly. Second, give a good reason to justify the salary you're asking. Don't just say, "I'd like $20,000." It's far more persuasive to say, "I made $16,000 on my last job. My current offers average $20,000." To an interviewer, this indicates that you've come up with a realistic figure based on facts, not just on a hunch.

What if your last salary was unusually low? If you tell interviewers what you earned, won't they use this as an excuse to offer you less than you deserve? I still think the most effective method is to lay your cards on the table: "I accepted a low salary on my last job because the job was a good opportunity to learn the ropes. But the going rate for someone with my experience is much higher now and I feel justified in asking $4,000 more."

Not all employers will ask you to name your price. Some will simply make you an offer. But your advance calculations are still useful when it's the employer, not you, who begins the bargaining by naming a figure. If the offer seems low, you have good reasons for naming a higher figure—and you can state these reasons frankly.

As you can see, salary negotiations are often like old-fashioned horse trading. There may be lots of bargaining before you and the employer agree on the price. If your first asking price, or the employer's first offering price, seems fair to both of you, the negotiations may stop right there. You've made a deal. But if the two figures are far apart, one of you, or both, may have to yield a bit. If the organization wants you badly, they may raise the ante and meet your price. If the job is attractive enough, you may be willing to lower your price and accept the employer's offer. Or you may both give way and arrive at a compromise figure. Naturally, there are times when neither you nor the employer will budge. Your negotiations simply end at that point and your job hunt goes on.

(6) Who are your references?

In the chapter on writing your resume, I suggested that you leave out references. Instead, I recommended that you carry a variety of references in a pocket address book, so you can select names that will mean most to each employer. As I explained, there's no predicting what references an interviewer will want. Some prefer to contact your former bosses. Other interviewers may want the names of your teachers. Still others prefer so-called character references. Many ask for an assortment. It's wise to have a full list to choose from.

If you're *just* out of school, your teachers are important references. This also holds true if you've been out of school only a short time and you've had just one or two jobs. Which teachers will give you the best send-off? Naturally, you'll want to refer an employer to teachers who worked with you closely and gave you good grades. Selecting the right teachers is especially vital if your grades weren't uniformly good. Most students do good work in some subjects, but not in others. A teacher who saw you do good work in that particular class will be able to talk about your strong points. You can't expect teachers to *conceal* your weaker points. But having seen you at your best, they can explain your weaker points sympathetically.

Can your future employer contact *past* employers? If you left your past jobs on friendly terms, you won't hesitate to say: "Sure, my former bosses will tell you whatever you want to know." But what if you're not on friendly terms with an ex-boss? What if you're currently employed and you don't want your present boss to know that you're job hunting? In either case, you must explain the circumstances frankly to your potential employer. At the same time, you must suggest someone else who'll vouch for you. Can you count on a reference from a former co-worker who was fairly high on the ladder? Do you now have a high level co-worker who'll keep your secret and give you a good reference?

Whom can you turn to for a character reference? Are there respected members of the community who've known you and your family for many years? A good character reference needn't be an *obvious* pillar of the community, like your clergyman, a local political leader, or the president of the bank where you do business. An intelligent friend will do just as well.

In fact, local clergymen, political figures, or bank presidents may *not* be good character references unless they really know you well. Don't ask casual acquaintances for letters of recommendation just because they have impressive titles. Chances are that they'll write cordial, but lukewarm letters that prompt the reader to say: "Oh, anybody can get a polite letter out of a State Assemblyman."

There are many other people who might provide valuable references: former clients; officers of professional associations in your field; editors and critics who've written about you; museum curators and private collectors who've bought your work; distinguished professionals who know and respect you.

How many references should you have in your address book? Few employers want more than three or four. But you'd better be armed with more than you need. If you tap all the sources I've mentioned, your list may easily reach ten or twelve. On the other hand, a beginner won't be criticized if references include only a couple of teachers, a summer employer, and a respected friend of the family.

Be sure to let people know when you plan to give their names as references. You might even send them a copy of your resume to give them a clear idea of your professional goals. This is more than courtesy. With some advance notice, people can refresh their memories about your qualifications and be better prepared when your prospective boss inquires.

How useful is the traditional reference letter that an employer gives you when you leave a job? Most of these notes are practically form letters. They generally begin with the impersonal phrase, "To Whom It May Concern." Then they go on with cut and dried sentences like, "During the three years so-and-so was employed by us, this employee fulfilled the necessary duties in a satisfactory manner." There's no harm in showing these to a furture employer, but they don't really tell enough to be helpful. Unless these letters are unusually warm and detailed, your prospective boss must still contact previous employers for the vital facts that are needed.

Questions you will want to ask

Until now, we've assumed that the *interviewer* will ask the questions. But if you're offered a job, there are questions *you'll* want to ask before saying yes. Don't be shy about quizzing potential employers. They don't expect you to walk into a job with your eyes closed. They'll expect questions and they'll give you straight answers. If they don't, think twice before you accept the offer.

Here are some questions to clarify before you take any job:

(1) *Are there other financial benefits beside salary?* Your salary may not be your only income from a job. There may be a profit-sharing plan, annual bonuses, incentives for bringing in business, expense accounts, or overtime pay. Many employers have life, medical, and retirement insurance plans. They may divide the cost with you or foot the whole bill. This can add up to a lot of money over the years.

(2) *What are working hours, vacations, and holidays?* Some organizations work 9-to-5. Others stretch the day to 5:30 or 6. Still others work 8-to-4. These details can be important if you're commuting or going to school at night. It's also worthwhile to ask how much overtime is normal. Do you get paid for it or take equivalent time off? Some employers are more liberal than others about vacations and holidays. Though the normal summer vacation in a profit-making organization is two weeks for a new employee, some employers give you three or four weeks after a number of years.

(3) *What's the organizational set-up?* What are the various departments? Who works for whom and who does what? Who's your immediate superior and can you meet him or her if you haven't already? Are there other offices in other locations, or is this the only one? What do the other offices do? It's important to get some sense of the organization's scope and structure and see just where you will fit into the total picture.

(4) *What will be the nature of your work?* What sort of projects will you work on? If there are clients, who are they? How much initiative will you be given? What skills will you be expected to use? Will you have to travel? Where and how often? Can you see your future surroundings and the equipment you'll work with? Are you being hired for the duration of a specific project? For a limited probationary period? Or can you consider this a permanent job unless, of course, you don't pan out?

(5) *What are your prospects of advancement?* This is a tough question for employers to answer, but you must try to find out if this is a dead end job or a job with a future. Employers can't make you any promises the moment you're hired, but they *can* say: "We have salary reviews every six months. We try to give raises when they're deserved. And we usually fill our high-level jobs from our own ranks instead of bringing in an outsider." Or they might say: "This is a growing organization and good workers move up as soon as they prove they can take more responsibility." Neither statement guarantees you anything. It's too early. But both statements promise you the chance to rise when you prove your value. That's as much as you can expect. I might add that a job "with no future," but with an interesting *present*, can still be worth taking for a year or two if the experience will be valuable for your professional advancement in later jobs.

Circumstances may suggest other questions. If you must relocate from one city to another, you have a right to ask whether your new employer will pay the moving bill. If you've landed the job through an employment agency, you might ask tactfully whether there's any chance that the employer will pay your agency fee or split it with you. Many organizations absorb these expenses.

Follow-up letters

Most interviews *don't* end with a job offer. However, if you've made an impression, interviewers will do their best to remember you. When suitable jobs turn up, you may hear from them again.

You can help them remember you. Many personnel experts recommend that you drop a brief thank-you note to everyone who interviews you. This is a sound idea if you don't make a big, time-consuming campaign of it. A few minutes at the typewriter are all you need to bang out a brief, informal message:

Just a brief note of thanks for your time and interest when we met on Monday afternoon. I enjoyed talking with you and I appreciate your constructive suggestions about my portfolio.

That's all you need. This note won't win you a job, but this extra bit of courtesy will leave its small mark.

Someone else who deserves a note is the interviewer who told you: "Call Ellen Parker and mention my name. She might know of a job for you." When you've seen Ellen Parker, you owe a thank you note to the interviewer who steered you to her. This is more than just a courteous gesture. Your note serves as a reminder that you're still job hunting. You might get a second steer from the same source, a steer you might not get without such a note.

A third type of follow-up note might be written *after* you land a job. This is the time to review the names of all the interviewers who showed more than a casual interest: those who said, "I wish I had a job to offer you;" those who were generous with their time and advice; those who sent you to their friends. This may turn out to be quite a long list. But I think it's worth a few evenings of letter writing to tell these people:

> Remembering your generous interest in my job hunt, I thought you might be pleased to learn that I've landed an excellent position. I'm now assistant to the Design Director of the Kenney Furniture Company. Again, my warmest thanks for your encouragement.

Just three sentences. But enough to reinforce a favorable impression. You're not looking for a job any longer, but some day you may be job hunting again. When that day comes, you'll hope that people remember you from your *last* job hunt.

This suggests an important tip: hold on to the stack of index cards on which you've kept track of your contacts. Many of these names will be useful throughout your professional life.

The job offer

If you've conducted your job hunt intelligently, you'll soon face the decisive moment. You'll be offered a job and you must say "yes" or "no." If this is definitely the job you want, all you have to say is, "Fine! When do I start?"

But what if you have two conflicting job offers? You may not be prepared to decide between them on the spur of the moment. In this situation, you have every right to ask both employers: "May I have some time to think about your offer and discuss it with my family and friends?" If an organization is in a hurry, they may ask for an answer the following day. If they're less rushed, they may say, "Okay, how much time do you need?"

As always, I think you'll find it best to lay your cards on the table. What if Employer A offers you more money, but Employer B offers you a more exciting job? I think it's fair to go to Employer B and say: "I'd like to work for you, but frankly I'm in a spot. Another organization has offered me more money. With a family, I have no right to turn down a higher paycheck. Would you be willing to reconsider your salary figure?" No responsible employer will blame you for telling the truth. Your future boss will probably be just as straightforward and ask you frankly, "How much is your other offer?" The organization can then tell you whether they can match it or at least try to make a compromise offer.

Another complication may be the job offer that isn't *quite* an offer. The employer may say: "We're going to make our decision at a meeting on Friday morning. If you have any other offers pending, can you put off your decision until Friday?" This is a reasonable request. If you *can* wait until Friday for a decision, you should certainly agree, with the promise that you'll phone if you get a conflicting offer that demands a decision *before* Friday. If you can't wait till Friday—perhaps another employer wants you to say "yes" or "no" tomorrow—say so. It's possible that the Friday meeting can be scheduled earlier if you're wanted badly enough.

But at last the right offer comes and you accept. Your new boss says, "Congratulations! You start three weeks from Monday." Usually, these words and a handshake consummate the bargain. Except for teachers and some top executives, few artists, designers, or architects get an actual written contract. However, many employers make things official by sending you a confirming note stating salary, starting date, department, and your title, if you have one. If you receive no confirming note, I suggest that *you* send one, just for the record:

> Thanks again for your confidence in me. As we agree, I'll report for work in the package design department on Monday morning, November 7. I understand that my salary will be $1500 a month and that I'm on a six-month probationary period, at the end of which we'll review my work and salary. I look forward to joining you.

This brief letter summarizes the verbal agreement. The third sentence tactfully mentions a promise made by the employer. No one would call this letter a contract. But it puts the facts on record and it's morally, if not legally, binding.

Your job hunt is ended. On that Monday morning, a new phase in your life begins. Now no book can help you. Your fate is in your own hands.

PART FOUR
Schools and Professional Organizations

21
Directory of degree granting schools

What are the nation's major art schools and college art departments? What are the most important schools in your state and the states nearby? What subjects do they teach? The listings in this directory are meant to answer these basic questions, the first questions you'll ask when you begin the difficult job of choosing a school.

How was the list compiled?

All colleges and universities and *nearly* all leading art schools grant degrees. To most art educators and employers, the degree is a symbol (though certainly not a guarantee) of thorough professional training and a rich cultural background. Therefore, it seems reasonable to limit the list to degree-granting schools.

Since this is a directory of *major* schools, the list is restricted to schools that have a minimum of 100 students working toward a degree or an equivalent diploma. For this information, I've relied on the *American Artist Directory of Art Schools and Workshops* published in the magazine, *American Artist.*

Course lists and other data in the directory come from the schools themselves. The facts are based on a series of questionnaire surveys made by the editors of *American Artist* and published in the magazine's school directory issue.

Excluded from the directory are: (1) schools that grant no degrees, (b) schools that grant too few degrees, (c) junior colleges, (d) correspondence schools, (e) private classes conducted by an artist in his own studio, (f) community centers, YMCAs, YMHAs and adult education schools, (g) schools that operate only in the summer.

Also excluded are schools that failed to return questionnaires, despite repeated reminders, and schools that returned questionnaires so vague or incomplete that the material was useless. In some cases, I was able to find missing facts in the American Federation of Arts *American Art Directory*. But in other cases, I was forced to give up and simply publish an incomplete listing or exclude a school altogether, for lack of information.

How to use this list

The fact that a school appears on the list is no guarantee that the school is good. This is just a list of the schools that have enough students to *suggest* that the institution offers an art program of reasonable size. Before you pick a school, you must still write for catalogs, talk to your high school teachers and guidance counselors, interview alumni, and visit the schools themselves. No directory can answer the fourteen vital questions listed in Chapter 4 on "Choosing an Art School." You must find the answers yourself.

Nor can you assume that the schools in this directory are the *only* ones worth considering. There *may* be smaller, lesser known schools in your neighborhood that are as good. This may be particularly true in the fine art fields—painting, sculpture, and printmaking—which may be taught equally well on a large university campus or in an artist's attic studio.

In short, some *good* schools may be left out and some *bad* schools may be included. Furthermore, there's also a certain percentage of incomplete or inaccurate data, simply because someone wouldn't take the trouble to fill out a questionnaire carefully. And keep in mind that school programs often change: some of these listings may be out of date in a matter of months.

Like any school directory, this list must be read with an awareness of its limitations. This directory does nothing more than suggest *some* of the schools you should investigate. Your investigations may lead you to choose one of these schools or to reject the whole pack and pick one that's not on the list. The directory may actually help you choose an *unlisted* school. When you've investigated several well-known schools on the list, you'll be better equipped to judge little-known schools that may turn out to be just as good.

What the listings will tell you

Each art school, college, or university is represented by a little paragraph that gives the full name of the school, the town or city where it's located, the zip code and the art subjects taught there. The full name of the school, town or city, and zip code should be all you'll need to write the school for a catalog and further information.

The listings don't specify which degree (or degrees) may be offered by each school. There are so many different kinds of degrees that I think it would be hopelessly confusing to try to include them all here. Depending upon the school—or the division of the school—your bachelor's degree may be a bachelor of arts (B.A.), bachelor of science (B.S.), bachelor of fine arts (B.F.A.), bachelor of architecture (B.Arch.), or bachelor-of-something-else. Master's degrees are just as confusing. To make things worse, a school may grant a bachelor's degree in one subject, a master's in some other subject, and a Ph.D. in something else. The only way to puzzle out the situation is to read a school's catalog. In the meantime, you can assume that inclusion in the school directory of *Art Career Guide* means that a school grants *at least* a bachelor's degree.

After looking over thousands of completed questionnaires and catalogs, I finally decided to eliminate any mention of scholarships in these listings. It's impossible to find a school that doesn't *claim* to offer scholarships or financial aid of some sort. It's only when you read the catalogs that you find out *how much* financial aid you can get—some schools are richer than others—

and what strings are attached. Some scholarships are available to anybody, some to specific minority groups, some for students in a particular subject area, and some to students who pass a particular examination or hand in some kind of project. You've just got to read the catalog.

The schools in the United States are grouped by state so you can quickly locate those nearest home or in the region where you'd like to go. Canadian schools are listed at the end of the section and are grouped by province.

Accreditation

Four professional associations in the art and design field issue lists of accredited schools. The approval of the National Association of Schools of Art and Design is indicated at the end of the listing by the letters, NASAD. Schools approved by the National Architectural Accrediting Board carry the letters, NAAB. Accreditation by the American Society of Landscape Architects is indicated by the letters, ASLA. And schools recognized by the Industrial Designers Society of America carry the letters, IDSA.

Needless to say, not all accredited schools are equally good, but the approval of one or more of these accrediting groups does indicate that a school meets certain basic standards. Thus, the school directory includes *all* schools on the accredited lists of these four professional groups, even though a few have under 100 students, but excludes junior colleges and non-degree schools.

A note about degrees and certificates

Remember that degrees are often *optional* in so-called independent art schools. Although you must have a degree to graduate from a college or university, many degree-granting art schools will permit you to eliminate the liberal arts and sciences from your program. So you can just take art courses and graduate with a certificate.

Degrees are often granted jointly by two institutions. An art school may be affiliated with a nearby college or university, which provides the art school's courses in the liberal arts and sciences. Or the college or university may send its students to the art school for studio courses. Your degree may come from the art school, from the college or university, or from both.

Speaking of degrees, it's only fair to mention a few distinguished art schools that still don't grant them. America's most famous art school, The Art Students League of New York (215 West 57th Street, New York, New York 10019) and the National Academy School of Fine Arts (5 East 89th Street, New York, New York 10028) are two of the last holdouts against degrees. And three of the nation's finest schools are open only in the summer, so obviously can't offer degree programs: Haystack Mountain School of Crafts, Deer Isle, Maine 04627; Penland School of Crafts, Penland, North Carolina 28765; and the Skowhegan School of Painting and Sculpture, located in Skowhegan, Maine, but with administrative offices at 329 East 68th Street, New York, New York 10021.

Reading the listings

Subjects listed may be majors, areas of concentration *within* majors, minors, or just courses that form part of a general art major. In a large university, consisting of many different schools, these subjects may be taught in several divisions or departments. Ridiculous as it may sound, architecture is sometimes part of a university's school of agriculture or engineering. Or painting and sculpture may come under the school of architecture. Interior design, oddly enough, is often taught in the school of home economics. Read catalogs carefully to find out *how many* classes are given in a subject and *where* they're taught.

Now let's look more closely at the subjects listed in the directory on the pages that follow.

Architecture may actually include separate curricula in landscape architecture or urban design. If a school offers architecture, but isn't marked NAAB, signifying accreditation by the National Architectural Accrediting Board, the program may really be pre-architecture; such courses prepare the student for later enrollment in the professional program of an accredited architectural school.

Art history may mean professional training, leading to a master's degree or a Ph.D. that qualifies you for a museum job or a job teaching art history. Or it may just mean background courses for students in other art fields.

Art teaching usually means a so-called art education program, leading to a career in elementary or secondary school art teaching. An art education program frequently includes one or two courses in each art or design subject described in this book. This doesn't mean that the teacher receives professional training in each of these fields; in most cases, these are merely introductory courses.

Arts management may mean a program for future executives in the visual arts or the performing arts or arts institutions in general. So it's especially important to read the catalog—and do all the homework described in Chapter 4—to find out what sort of arts management program you might be getting into.

Crafts courses are growing and changing so rapidly that each school is likely to define its crafts program quite differently. Most crafts programs do include ceramics and weaving, but crafts *may* also include subjects as diverse as jewelry and metalworking, plastics, woodworking, glass, fabric printing and dyeing, needlework, or still others that may suddenly appear in the catalog.

Fabric design sometimes means just weaving—which might as easily come under the heading of crafts—or it could mean fabric printing, dyeing, or even textile engineering, depending upon the scope of the program.

Film may mean a motion picture photography course in the photography program or it may mean a full-scale major in film-making. This is one of the fastest growing subjects on art school, college, and university campuses. It sometimes includes animation.

Graphic design may mean a complete program in the design of all types of printed matter or it may mean specialized subjects like book design, advertising design, or packaging. In the better schools, it includes TV graphics. Graphic design is often taught in conjunction with illustration as a major in "commercial art."

Illustration may mean a general course, a course combined with graphic design, or a specialty like fashion drawing, cartooning, or technical illustration.

Industrial design may cover the entire field or may emphasize a specialty like automotive design or packaging.

Interior design may be a general program or may focus on a specialty like furniture design.

Landscape architecture may also include urban design.

Painting, printmaking, and sculpture are listed separately, rather than grouped under "fine arts," because these are often separate majors or areas of concentration. It's also worth remembering that "fine arts" means art history, not studio courses, in some college and university catalogs.

Photography usually means still photography, but may include motion-picture photography in some programs.

In short, the highly condensed listings are nothing more than a quick look at what various schools offer. For the full story, you must read the catalog carefully and ultimately visit the school.

UNITED STATES

Alabama

Alabama State University, Montgomery, AL 36111. Art history, art teaching, crafts, fabric design, graphic design, painting, photography, printmaking, sculpture.

Auburn University, Auburn, AL 36830. Architecture, art history, art teaching, crafts, graphic design, illustration, industrial design, interior design, landscape architecture, painting, printmaking, sculpture. NASAD. NAAB. IDSA.

Troy State University, Troy, AL 36081. Art history, art teaching, crafts, fabric design, film, graphic design, painting, photography, printmaking, sculpture.

Tuskegee Institute, Tuskegee, AL 36088. Architecture, art history, art teaching, crafts, fabric design, illustration, landscape architecture. NAAB.

University of Alabama, Tuscaloosa, AL 35496. Art history, art teaching, crafts, graphic design, painting, photography, printmaking, sculpture.

University of Alabama in Huntsville, Huntsville, AL 35899. Art history, art teaching, film, graphic design, illustration, industrial design, interior design, painting, photography, printmaking, sculpture.

University of South Alabama, Mobile, AL 36688. Art history, crafts, graphic design, painting, photography, printmaking, sculpture.

Alaska

University of Alaska at Anchorage, Anchorage, AS 99504. Art history, art teaching, crafts, painting, photography, printmaking, sculpture.

Arizona

Arizona State University, Tempe, AR 85281. Architecture, art history, art teaching, crafts, fabric design, film, graphic design, industrial design, interior design, landscape architecture, painting, printmaking, sculpture. NAAB. IDSA.

Northern Arizona University, Flagstaff, AR 86001. Art history, art teaching, crafts, fabric design, graphic design, illustration, painting, photography, printmaking, sculpture.

University of Arizona, Tucson, AR 85721. Architecture, art history, art teaching, crafts, fabric design, graphic design, landscape architecture, painting, photography, printmaking, sculpture. NAAB. ASLA.

Arkansas

Arkansas State University, Jonesboro, AK 72467. Art history, art teaching, crafts, graphic design, illustration, landscape architecture, painting, photography, printmaking, sculpture. IDSA.

Harding University, Searcy, AK 72143. Art history, art teaching, crafts, fabric design, graphic design, illustration, painting, printmaking, sculpture.

University of Arkansas, Fayetteville, AK 72701. Architecture, art history, art teaching, crafts, graphic design, landscape architecture, painting, photography, printmaking, sculpture. NAAB.

University of Arkansas at Little Rock, Little Rock, AK 72204. Art history, art teaching, arts management, crafts, graphic design, illustration, painting, photography, printmaking, sculpture.

University of Central Arkansas, Conway, AK 72032. Art teaching, crafts, painting, photography, printmaking, sculpture.

California

Academy of Art College, San Francisco, CA 94102. Art history, arts management, crafts, film, graphic design, illustration, interior design, painting, photography, printmaking, sculpture.

Art Center College of Design, Pasadena, CA 91103. Art history, film, graphic design, illustration, industrial design, interior design, painting, photography. NASAD. IDSA.

California College of Arts & Crafts, Oakland, CA 94618. Architecture, art history, art teaching, arts management, crafts, fabric design, film, graphic design, illustration, interior design, painting, photography, printmaking, sculpture. NASAD.

California Institute of the Arts, Valencia, CA 91355. Art history, graphic design, painting, photography, printmaking. NASAD.

California Polytechnic State University, San Luis Obispo, CA 93407. Architecture, art history, arts management, crafts, graphic design, illustration, landscape architecture, painting, photography, printmaking, sculpture. NAAB. ASLA.

California State College at San Bernardino, San Bernardino, CA 92407. Art history, art teaching, crafts, fabric design, film, graphic design, painting, photography, printmaking, sculpture.

California State College at Stanislaus, Turlock, CA 95380. Art history, arts management, crafts, painting, photography, printmaking, sculpture.

California State Polytechnic University, Pomona, CA 91765. Architecture, art history, art teaching, crafts, fabric design, graphic design, illustration, landscape architecture, painting, photography, sculpture. NAAB. ASLA.

California State University at Chico, Chico, CA 95929. Art history, art teaching, arts management, crafts, fabric design, painting, printmaking, sculpture. NASAD.

California State University at Dominguez Hills, Carson, CA 90747. Art history, art teaching, crafts, graphic design, illustration, painting, photography, printmaking, sculpture. NASAD.

California State University at Fresno, Fresno, CA 93740. Art history, art teaching, crafts, fabric design, painting, photography, printmaking, sculpture.

California State University at Fullerton, Fullerton, CA 92634. Art history, art teaching, crafts, fabric design, graphic design, illustration, industrial design, interior design, painting, photography, printmaking, sculpture. NASAD.

California State University at Hayward, Hayward, CA 94542. Architecture, art history, arts management, crafts, painting, photography, printmaking, sculpture. NASAD.

California State University at Long Beach, Long Beach, CA 90840. Art history, art teaching, arts management, crafts, fabric design, graphic design, illustration, industrial design, interior design, painting, printmaking, sculpture. NASAD. IDSA.

California State University at Los Angeles, Los Angeles, CA 90032. Architecture, art history, art teaching, crafts, fabric design, graphic design, illustration, interior design, painting, printmaking, sculpture. NASAD.

California State University at Northridge, Northridge, CA 91324. Art history, art teaching, crafts, fabric design, film, graphic design, industrial design, interior design, painting, photography, printmaking, sculpture. IDSA.

California State University at Sacramento, Sacramento, CA 95819. Art history, art teaching, arts management, crafts, fabric design, film, painting, photography, printmaking, sculpture. NASAD.

Humboldt State University, Arcata, CA 95521. Art history, art teaching, crafts, graphic design, painting, photography, printmaking, sculpture. NASAD.

Immaculate Heart College, Hollywood, CA 90027. Art history, art teaching, crafts, fabric design, film, graphic design, painting, photography, printmaking, sculpture.

Mills College, Oakland, CA 94613. Art history, art teaching, crafts, film, painting, photography, printmaking, sculpture.

Otis Art Institute of Parsons School of Design, Los Angeles, CA 90057. Art history, crafts, film, illustration, interior design, painting, printmaking, sculpture. NASAD.

San Diego State University, San Diego, CA 92182. Architecture, art history, art teaching, arts management, crafts, fabric design, graphic design, illustration, interior design, painting, printmaking, sculpture. NASAD.

San Francisco Art Institute, San Francisco, CA 94133. Art history, crafts, film, painting, photography, printmaking, sculpture. NASAD.

San Francisco State University, San Francisco, CA 94132. Art history, art teaching, crafts, fabric design, film, illustration, painting, photography, printmaking, sculpture.

San Jose State University, San Jose, CA 95192. Architecture, art history, art teaching, arts management, crafts, fabric design, graphic design, illustration, industrial design, interior design, painting, photography, printmaking, sculpture. NASAD. IDSA.

Sonoma State University, Rohnert Park, CA 94928. Art history, art teaching, arts

management, crafts, film, graphic design, painting, photography, printmaking, sculpture.

Southern California Institute of Architecture, Santa Monica, CA 90404. Architecture. NAAB.

Stanford University, Stanford, CA 94305. Art history, art teaching, crafts, fabric design, graphic design, industrial design, painting, printmaking, sculpture. IDSA.

Stanislaus State College, Turlock, CA 95380. Art history, art teaching, crafts, film, painting, photography, printmaking, sculpture.

University of California at Berkeley, Berkeley, CA 94720. Architecture, art history, art teaching, graphic design, landscape design, painting, printmaking, sculpture. NAAB. ASLA.

University of California at Davis, Davis, CA 95616. Architecture, art history, crafts, film, interior design, landscape architecture, painting, photography, printmaking, sculpture. ASLA.

University of California at Irvine, Irvine, CA 92717. Architecture, art history, crafts, interior design, painting, photography, printmaking.

University of California at Los Angeles, Los Angeles, CA 90024. Architecture, art history, crafts, fabric design, graphic design, industrial design, landscape architecture, painting, photography, printmaking, sculpture. NAAB.

University of California at Riverside, Riverside, CA 92521. Art history, film, painting, photography, printmaking, sculpture.

University of California at San Diego, San Diego, CA 92093. Art history, film, painting, photography, sculpture.

University of California at Santa Barbara, Santa Barbara, CA 93106. Art history, crafts, painting, photography, printmaking, sculpture.

University of California at Santa Cruz, Santa Cruz, CA 95064. Architecture, art history, arts management, crafts, film, illustration, landscape architecture, painting, photography, printmaking, sculpture.

University of the Pacific, Stockton, CA 95211. Art history, art teaching, crafts, graphic design, illustration, painting, photography, printmaking, sculpture. NASAD.

University of San Diego, San Diego, CA 92110. Art history, art teaching, arts management, crafts, fabric design, graphic design, painting, photography, printmaking, sculpture.

University of Southern California, Los Angeles, CA 90007. Architecture, art history, art teaching, arts management, crafts, landscape architecture, painting, photography, printmaking, sculpture. NAAB.

Colorado

Colorado State University, Fort Collins, CO 80523. Art history, art teaching, crafts, fabric design, illustration, interior design, landscape architecture, painting, photography, printmaking, sculpture.

Fort Lewis College, Durango, CO 81301. Art history, art teaching, crafts, fabric design, painting, photography, printmaking, sculpture.

Metropolitan State College, Denver, CO 80204. Art history, art teaching, crafts, graphic design, illustration, industrial design, painting, photography, printmaking, sculpture.

University of Colorado at Boulder, Boulder, CO 80309. Art history, art teaching, crafts, film, landscape architecture, painting, photography, printmaking, sculpture.

University of Colorado, Denver Center, Denver, CO 80202. Architecture, art history, film, landscape architecture, paint-

ing, photography, printmaking, sculpture. NAAB. ASLA.

University of Denver, Denver, CO 80208. Art history, art teaching, arts management, crafts, fabric design, film, graphic design, painting, photography, printmaking, sculpture. NASAD.

University of Northern Colorado, Greeley, CO 80639. Art history, art teaching, arts management, crafts, fabric design, painting, printmaking, sculpture.

University of Southern Colorado, Pueblo, CO 81001. Art history, art teaching, arts management, crafts, fabric design, film, industrial design, painting, photography, printmaking, sculpture.

Western State College, Gunnison, CO 81230. Art history, art teaching, crafts, fabric design, painting, printmaking, sculpture.

Connecticut

Central Connecticut State College, New Britain, CT 06050. Art history, art teaching, crafts, fabric design, graphic design, industrial design, painting, photography, printmaking, sculpture.

Hartford Art School of the University of Hartford, West Hartford, CT 06117. Art teaching, crafts, film, graphic design, painting, photography, printmaking, sculpture. NASAD.

Southern Connecticut State College, New Haven, CT 06515. Art history, art teaching, crafts, fabric design, graphic design, painting, photography, printmaking, sculpture.

University of Bridgeport, Bridgeport, CT 06602. Art history, art teaching, crafts, fabric design, film, graphic design, illustration, industrial design, interior design, painting, photography, printmaking, sculpture. NASAD. IDSA.

University of Connecticut, Storrs, CT 06268. Architecture, art history, crafts, graphic design, illustration, painting, photography, printmaking, sculpture.

University of New Haven, New Haven, CT 06505. Art history, crafts, fabric design, film, graphic design, interior design, painting, photography, printmaking, sculpture.

Wesleyan University, Middletown, CT 06457. Architecture, art history, art teaching, crafts, film, industrial design, painting, photography, printmaking, sculpture.

Yale University, New Haven, CT 06520. Architecture, art history, graphic design, painting, photography, printmaking, sculpture. NAAB.

Delaware

University of Delaware, Newark, DE 19711. Art teaching, crafts, fabric design, graphic design, interior design, landscape architecture, painting, photography, printmaking, sculpture.

District of Columbia

American University, Washington, DC 20016. Art history, crafts, graphic design, painting, printmaking, sculpture.

Catholic University of America, Washington, DC 20064. Architecture, art history, art teaching, crafts, landscape architecture, painting, photography, printmaking, sculpture. NAAB.

Corcoran School of Art, Washington, DC 20006. Art history, crafts, film, graphic design, illustration, painting, photography, printmaking, sculpture. NASAD.

George Washington University, Washington, DC 20052. Art history, art teaching, crafts, fabric design, film, interior design, landscape architecture, painting, photography, printmaking, sculpture.

Howard University, Washington, DC 20059. Architecture, art history, art teaching, crafts, graphic design, illustration, landscape architecture, painting, photography, printmaking, sculpture. NASAD. NAAB.

University of District of Columbia, Washington, DC 20001. Art history, art teaching, crafts, fabric design, illustration, interior design, painting, printmaking, sculpture.

Florida

Florida A & M University, Tallahassee, FL 32307. Architecture, art history, art teaching, crafts, fabric design, graphic design, painting, printmaking, sculpture. NAAB.

Florida Atlantic University, Boca Raton, FL 33432. Architecture, art history, art teaching, crafts, film, painting, photography, printmaking, sculpture. NAAB.

Florida International University, Miami, FL 33199. Art history, art teaching, crafts, fabric design, painting, printmaking, sculpture.

Florida State University, Tallahassee, FL 32306. Art history, art teaching, arts management, crafts, fabric design, film, graphic design, illustration, interior design, painting, photography, printmaking, sculpture.

Ringling School of Art & Design, Sarasota, FL 33580. Art history, graphic design, illustration, interior design, painting, photography, printmaking, sculpture.

University of Central Florida, Orlando, FL 32816. Art history, crafts, fabric design, film, graphic design, illustration, painting, photography, printmaking.

University of Florida, Gainesville, FL 32611. Architecture, illustration, landscape architecture, painting, photography, printmaking, sculpture. NAAB. ASLA.

University of Miami, Coral Gables, FL 33124. Architecture, art history, crafts, fabric design, graphic design, illustration, landscape architecture, painting, photography, printmaking, sculpture. NAAB.

University of South Florida, Tampa, FL 33620. Art history, art teaching, crafts, film, painting, photography, printmaking, sculpture.

Georgia

Atlanta College of Art, Atlanta, GA 30309. Art history, art teaching, crafts, fabric design, graphic design, painting, photography, printmaking, sculpture. NASAD.

Columbus College of Art, Columbus, GA 31907. Art history, art teaching, crafts, fabric design, graphic design, interior design, painting, photography, printmaking, sculpture.

Georgia Institute of Technology, Atlanta, GA 30332. Architecture, industrial design, landscape architecture. NAAB. IDSA.

Georgia Southern College, Statesboro, GA 30458. Art history, art teaching, crafts, fabric design, painting, photography, printmaking, sculpture.

Georgia State University, Atlanta, GA 30303. Art history, art teaching, crafts, fabric design, graphic design, illustration, interior design, painting, photography, printmaking, sculpture. NASAD.

University of Georgia, Athens, GA 30602. Art history, art teaching, crafts, fabric design, graphic design, interior design, landscape architecture, painting, photography, printmaking, sculpture. NASAD. ASLA.

Valdosta State College, Valdosta, GA 31698. Art history, art teaching, crafts, fabric design, graphic design, painting, photography, printmaking.

West Georgia College, Carrollton, GA 30117. Art history, art teaching, crafts, fabric design, graphic design, painting, photography, printmaking, sculpture.

Hawaii

University of Hawaii at Manoa, Honolulu, HI 96822. Architecture, art history, crafts, fabric design, graphic design, illustration, painting, photography, printmaking, sculpture. NAAB.

Idaho

Boise State University, Boise, ID 83725. Architecture, art history, art teaching, crafts, fabric design, film, graphic design, illustration, interior design, painting, photography, printmaking, sculpture.

University of Idaho, Moscow, ID 83843. Architecture, art history, art teaching, crafts, graphic design, interior design, landscape architecture, painting, photography, printmaking, sculpture. NAAB. ASLA.

Illinois

Barat College, Lake Forest, IL 60045. Art history, art teaching, crafts, fabric design, illustration, painting, photography, printmaking.

Bradley University, Peoria, IL 61625. Art history, art teaching, crafts, film, graphic design, illustration, painting, photography, printmaking, sculpture.

Columbia College, Chicago, IL 60605. Art history, art teaching, arts management, crafts, fabric design, film, graphic design, illustration, interior design, painting, photography, printmaking, sculpture.

Eastern Illinois University, Charleston, IL 61920. Art history, art teaching, crafts, fabric design, graphic design, painting, photography, printmaking, sculpture.

Illinois Institute of Technology, Chicago, IL 60616. Architecture, art history, film, graphic design, industrial design, landscape architecture, photography. NASAD. NAAB. IDSA.

Illinois State University, Normal, IL 61761. Architecture, art history, art teaching, arts management, crafts, fabric design, film, graphic design, illustration, interior design, painting, photography, printmaking, sculpture. NASAD.

Northeastern Illinois University, Chicago, IL 60625. Art history, art teaching, crafts, fabric design, graphic design, industrial design, painting, photography, printmaking, sculpture.

Northern Illinois University, De Kalb, IL 60115. Art history, art teaching, arts management, crafts, fabric design, film, graphic design, illustration, interior design, painting, photography, printmaking, sculpture. NASAD.

School of the Art Institute of Chicago, Chicago, IL 60603. Art history, art teaching, crafts, fabric design, film, graphic design, illustration, interior design, painting, photography, printmaking, sculpture. NASAD.

Southern Illinois University at Carbondale, Carbondale, IL 62901. Architecture, art history, art teaching, arts management, crafts, fabric design, film, graphic design, illustration, industrial design, painting, photography, printmaking, sculpture. NASAD.

Southern Illinois University at Edwardsville, Edwardsville, IL 62025. Art history, art teaching, crafts, fabric design, painting, photography, printmaking, sculpture.

University of Chicago, Chicago, IL 60637. Art history, arts management, crafts, film, painting, photography, printmaking, sculpture.

University of Illinois at Chicago Circle, Chicago, IL 60680. Architecture, art teaching, crafts, film, graphic design, illustration, industrial design, landscape architecture, painting, photography, printmaking, sculpture. NAAB.

University of Illinois at Urbana-Champaign, Champaign, IL 61820. Architecture, art history, art teaching, arts management, crafts, film, graphic design, illustration, industrial design, landscape architecture, painting, photography, printmaking, sculpture. NASAD. NAAB. ASLA. IDSA.

Western Illinois University, Macomb, IL 61455. Architecture, art history, art teaching, arts management, crafts, fabric design, graphic design, illustration, interior design, painting, printmaking, sculpture.

Indiana

Ball State University, Muncie, IN 47306. Architecture, art history, art teaching, crafts, fabric design, graphic design, interior design, landscape architecture, painting, photography, printmaking, sculpture. NAAB. ASLA.

Hanover College, Hanover, IN 47243. Art history, art teaching, crafts, film, painting, photography, printmaking, sculpture.

Herron School of Art of Indiana University—Purdue University at Indianapolis, Indianapolis, IN 47243. Art history, art teaching, crafts, graphic design, illustration, painting, photography, printmaking, sculpture. NASAD.

Indiana State University, Terre Haute, IN 47809. Art history, art teaching, graphic design, painting, photography, printmaking, sculpture.

Indiana University, Bloomington, IN 47401. Art history, crafts, graphic design, painting, photography, printmaking, sculpture.

Indiana University-Purdue University at Fort Wayne, Fort Wayne, IN 46804.

Art history, art teaching, arts management, crafts, graphic design, painting, printmaking

Purdue University, West Lafayette, IN 47907. Art history, art teaching, crafts, fabric design, film, graphic design, industrial design, interior design, landscape architecture, painting, photography, printmaking, sculpture. ASLA. IDSA.

St. Francis College, Fort Wayne, IN 46808. Art history, art teaching, crafts, fabric design, graphic design, illustration, painting, photography, printmaking, sculpture.

St. Mary's College, Notre Dame, IN 46556. Art history, art teaching, arts management, crafts, fabric design, painting, photography, printmaking, sculpture. NASAD.

University of Notre Dame, Notre Dame, IN 46556. Architecture, art history, crafts, fabric design, graphic design, industrial design, interior design, landscape architecture, painting, photography, printmaking, sculpture. NAAB. IDSA.

Iowa

Drake University, Des Moines, IA 50311. Art history, art teaching, crafts, fabric design, film, graphic design, illustration, interior design, painting, photography, printmaking, sculpture. NASAD.

Iowa State University, Ames, IA 50010. Architecture, art history, art teaching, crafts, fabric design, graphic design, illustration, interior design, landscape architecture, painting, printmaking, sculpture. NAAB. ASLA.

Luther College, Decorah, IA 52101. Architecture, art history, art teaching, crafts, fabric design, graphic design, illustration, painting, photography, printmaking.

University of Iowa, Iowa City, IA 52242. Art history, art teaching, crafts, fabric design, industrial design, interior design, painting, photography, printmaking, sculpture.

University of Northern Iowa, Cedar Falls, IA 50614. Art history, art teaching, crafts, graphic design, illustration, painting, photography, printmaking, sculpture. NASAD.

Kansas

Emporia State University, Emporia, KS 66801. Art history, art teaching, crafts, fabric design, illustration, interior design, painting, photography, printmaking, sculpture.

Fort Hays State University, Hays, KS 67601. Art history, art teaching, crafts, fabric design, graphic design, illustration, interior design, painting, photography, printmaking, sculpture.

Kansas State University, Manhattan, KS, 66506. Architecture, art history, art teaching, crafts, fabric design, graphic design, landscape architecture, painting, printmaking, sculpture. NAAB. ASLA.

University of Kansas, Lawrence, KS 66045. Architecture, art history, art teaching, crafts, fabric design, graphic design, illustration, industrial design, interior design, landscape architecture, painting, photography, printmaking, sculpture. NASAD. NAAB. IDSA.

Kentucky

Louisville School of Art, Louisville, KY, 40223. Art history, crafts, fabric design, painting, photography, printmaking, sculpture. NASAD.

Morehead State University, Morehead, KY 40351. Art history, art teaching, crafts, fabric design, graphic design, illustration, painting, photography, printmaking, sculpture.

Murray State University, Murray, KY 42071. Art history, art teaching, crafts, fabric design, film, graphic design, illustration, painting, photography, printmaking, sculpture.

Northern Kentucky University, Highland Heights, KY 41076. Art history, art teaching, crafts, graphic design, painting, photography, printmaking, sculpture.

University of Kentucky, Lexington, KY, 40506. Architecture, art history, art teaching, crafts, graphic design, landscape architecture, painting, photography, printmaking, sculpture. NAAB. ASLA.

University of Louisville, Allen R. Hite Art Institute, Louisville, KY 40292. Art history, art teaching, crafts, fabric design, painting, photography, printmaking, sculpture.

Western Kentucky University, Bowling Green, KY 42101. Art history, art teaching, crafts, fabric design, graphic design, painting, printmaking, sculpture.

Louisiana

Louisiana State University, Baton Rouge, LA 70803. Architecture, art history, art teaching, crafts, fabric design, film, graphic design, interior design, landscape architecture, painting, printmaking, sculpture. NAAB. ASLA.

Louisiana Technical University, Ruston, LA 71270. Architecture, art history, art teaching, crafts, fabric design, film, graphic design, interior design, painting, photography, printmaking, sculpture. NASAD. NAAB.

Northeast Louisiana University, Monroe, LA 71203. Art history, art teaching, crafts, fabric design, graphic design, painting, photography, printmaking, sculpture.

Southeastern Louisiana University, Hammond, LA, 70402. Art history, art teaching, crafts, painting, sculpture.

Southern University & A&M College, Baton Rouge, LA 70813. Architecture, art teaching. NAAB.

Tulane University/Newcomb College, New Orleans, LA 70118. Art history, art teaching, crafts, fabric design, illustration, landscape architecture, painting, photography, printmaking, sculpture. NASAD.

University of New Orleans, New Orleans, LA 70122. Art history, painting, photography, printmaking, sculpture.

University of Southwestern Louisiana, Lafayette, LA 70501. Architecture, art history, art teaching, crafts, film, graphic design, interior design, painting, photography, printmaking, sculpture. NAAB.

Maine

Portland School of Art, Portland, ME 04101. Art history, crafts, graphic design, illustration, painting, photography, printmaking, sculpture. NASAD.

University of Maine at Orono, Orono, ME 04469. Art history, art teaching, painting, printmaking, sculpture. NASAD.

University of Southern Maine, Gorham, ME 04038. Art history, art teaching, arts management, crafts, fabric design, film, painting, photography, printmaking, sculpture. NASAD.

Maryland

Frostburg State College, Frostburg, MD 21532. Art history, art teaching, crafts, painting, photography, printmaking, sculpture.

Maryland College of Art & Design, Silver Spring, MD 20902. Art history, graphic design, illustration, painting, photography, printmaking, sculpture. NASAD.

Maryland Institute, College of Art, Baltimore, MD 21217. Art history, art teaching, crafts, fabric design, film, graphic design, illustration, interior design, painting, photography, printmaking, sculpture. NASAD.

Morgan State University, Baltimore, MD 21239. Architecture, art history, art teaching, arts management, crafts, fabric design, film, graphic design, illustration, interior design, painting, photography, printmaking, sculpture. NASAD.

St. Mary's College of Maryland, St. Mary's City, MD 20686. Art history, art teaching, arts management, crafts, fabric design, painting, photography, printmaking, sculpture.

Towson State University, Towson, MD 21204. Architecture, art history, art teaching, crafts, fabric design, graphic design, painting, photography, printmaking, sculpture.

University of Maryland, College Park, MD 20742. Architecture, art history, art teaching, arts management, landscape architecture, painting, printmaking, sculpture. NAAB.

Massachusetts

Art Institute of Boston, Boston, MA 02215. Art history, crafts, film, graphic design, illustration, painting, photography, printmaking, sculpture.

Boston Architectural Center, Boston, MA 02215. Architecture, art history, interior design, photography. NAAB.

Boston University School of Visual Arts, Boston, MA 02215. Art history, art teaching, graphic design, illustration, painting, photography, printmaking.

Clark University, School of the Worcester Art Museum, Worcester, MA 01608. Art history, crafts, graphic design, illustration, painting, photography, printmaking, sculpture.

Framingham State College, Framingham, MA 01701. Art history, art teach-

ing, arts management, crafts, fabric design, film, interior design, painting, photography, printmaking, sculpture.

Harvard University, Cambridge, MA 02138. Architecture, art history, film, graphic design, interior design, landscape architecture, painting, photography, printmaking, sculpture. NAAB. ASLA.

Massachusetts College of Art, Boston, MA 02215. Architecture, art history, art teaching, arts management, crafts, fabric design, film, graphic design, illustration, industrial design, interior design, painting, photography, printmaking, sculpture. NASAD.

Massachusetts Institute of Technology, Cambridge, MA 02139. Architecture, art history, film, graphic design, interior design, photography, printmaking. NAAB.

Salem State College, Salem, MA 01945. Art history, art teaching, crafts, film, painting, photography, printmaking, sculpture.

School of the Museum of Fine Arts, Boston, MA 02215. Art history, art teaching, crafts, film, graphic design, painting, photography, printmaking, sculpture. NASAD.

Smith College, Northampton, MA 01063. Architecture, art history, arts management, graphic design, landscape architecture, painting, photography, printmaking, sculpture.

Southeastern Massachusetts University, North Dartmouth, MA 02747. Art history, art teaching, arts management, crafts, fabric design, film, graphic design, illustration, painting, photography, printmaking, sculpture. NASAD.

Swain School of Art, New Bedford, MA 02740. Art history, graphic design, painting, printmaking, sculpture. NASAD.

Tufts University, Medford, MA 02155. Art history, crafts, painting, photography, printmaking, sculpture.

University of Lowell, Lowell, MA 01854. Art history, art teaching, crafts, graphic design, illustration, painting, photography, printmaking, sculpture.

University of Massachusetts, Amherst, MA 01003. Architecture, art history, art teaching, arts management, crafts, interior design, landscape architecture, painting, photography, printmaking, sculpture. ASLA.

Wellesley College, Wellesley, MA 02181. Art history, film, painting, photography, printmaking, sculpture.

Williams College, Williamstown, MA 01267. Architecture, art history, painting, photography, printmaking, sculpture.

Michigan

Calvin College, Grand Rapids, MI 49506. Architecture, art history, art teaching, crafts, film, graphic design, painting, photography, printmaking, sculpture.

Center for Creative Studies, Detroit, MI 48202. Art history, crafts, fabric design, film, graphic design, illustration, industrial design, interior design, painting, photography, printmaking, sculpture. NASAD. IDSA.

Central Michigan University, Mount Pleasant, MI 48859. Art history, art teaching, crafts, fabric design, film, graphic design, painting, photography, printmaking, sculpture.

Cranbrook Academy of Art, Bloomfield Hills, MI 48013. Architecture, crafts, fabric design, industrial design, painting, photography, printmaking, sculpture. NASAD. IDSA.

Eastern Michigan University, Ypsilanti, MI 48197. Art history, art teaching, arts management, crafts, fabric design, graphic design, painting, printmaking, sculpture.

Ferris State College, Big Rapids, MI 48307. Art history, art teaching, crafts, graphic design, illustration, painting.

Grand Valley State College, Allendale, MI 49401. Architecture, art history, art teaching, crafts, fabric design, painting, photography, printmaking, sculpture. NASAD.

Hope College, Holland, MI 49423. Architecture, art history, art teaching, crafts, painting, photography, printmaking, sculpture. NASAD.

Kendall School of Design, Grand Rapids, MI 49502. Art history, graphic design, illustration, industrial design, interior design, painting, photography, printmaking. NASAD.

Lawrence Institute of Technology, Southfield, MI 48075. Architecture. NAAB.

Michigan State University, East Lansing, MI 48824. Art history, art teaching, crafts, film, graphic design, industrial design, landscape architecture, painting, photography, printmaking, sculpture. ASLA. IDSA.

Northern Michigan University, Marquette, MI 49855. Art history, art teaching, crafts, fabric design, film, illustration, industrial design, painting, photography, printmaking, sculpture.

Siena Heights College, Adrian, MI 49221. Art history, art teaching, crafts, fabric design, graphic design, interior design, painting, photography, printmaking, sculpture.

University of Detroit, Detroit, MI 48221. Architecture, art history, landscape architecture. NAAB.

University of Michigan, Ann Arbor, MI 48109. Architecture, art history, art teaching, crafts, fabric design, film, graphic design, illustration, industrial design, interior design, landscape architecture, painting, photography, printmaking, sculpture. NASAD. NAAB. ASLA. IDSA.

Wayne State University, Detroit, MI 48202. Art history, crafts, fabric design, film, graphic design, illustration, industrial design, interior design, painting, photography, printmaking, sculpture.

Western Michigan University, Kalamazoo, MI 49012. Art history, art teaching, crafts, fabric design, graphic design, painting, photography, printmaking, sculpture. NASAD.

Minnesota

Bemidji State University, Bemidji, MN 56601. Art history, art teaching, crafts, fabric design, film, graphic design, industrial design, painting, photography, printmaking, sculpture.

Carleton College, Northfield, MN 55057. Architecture, art history, art teaching, arts management, crafts, film, painting, photography, printmaking, sculpture. NASAD.

Hamline University, St. Paul, MN 55104. Architecture, art history, art teaching, crafts, painting, photography, printmaking, sculpture.

Mankato State University, Mankato, MN 56001. Art history, art teaching, crafts, fabric design, graphic design, illustration, painting, photography, printmaking, sculpture. NASAD.

Minneapolis College of Art & Design, Minneapolis, MN 55404. Art history, film, graphic design, illustration, industrial design, painting, photography, printmaking, sculpture. NASAD.

Moorhead State University, Moorhead, MN 56560. Art history, art teaching, arts management, crafts, film, graphic design, illustration, painting, photography, printmaking, sculpture. NASAD.

St. Cloud State University, St. Cloud, MN 56301. Art history, art teaching, arts management, crafts, fabric design, film, graphic design, interior design, painting, photography, printmaking, sculpture. NASAD.

St. Olaf College, Northfield, MN 55057. Architecture, art history, art teaching, crafts, film, graphic design, interior design, painting, photography, printmaking, sculpture. NASAD.

University of Minnesota at Duluth, Duluth, MN 55812. Art history, art teaching, arts management, crafts, film, graphic design, painting, photography, printmaking, sculpture.

University of Minnesota, Minneapolis, MN 55455. Architecture, art history, arts management, crafts, graphic design, illustration, landscape architecture, painting, photography, printmaking, sculpture. NAAB. ASLA.

Mississippi

Delta State University, Cleveland, MS 38733. Art history, art teaching, crafts, fabric design, graphic design, illustration, interior design, painting, photography, printmaking, sculpture.

Jackson State University, Jackson, MS 39217. Art history, art teaching, crafts, graphic design, painting, printmaking, sculpture. NASAD.

Mississippi State University, Mississippi State, MS 39762. Architecture, art history, art teaching, crafts, graphic design, landscape architecture, painting, photography, printmaking, sculpture. NAAB. ASLA.

Mississippi University for Women, Columbia, MS 39701. Art history, art teaching, crafts, fabric design, graphic design, illustration, interior design, painting, photography, printmaking, sculpture.

Mississippi Valley State University, Itta Bena, MS 38941. Art teaching, graphic design, painting. NASAD.

University of Mississippi, University, MS 38677. Art history, art teaching, arts management, crafts, graphic design, interior design, painting, photography, printmaking, sculpture.

University of Southern Mississippi, Hattiesburg, MS 39401. Art history, art teaching, crafts, fabric design, film, graphic design, illustration, industrial design, interior design, painting, photography, printmaking, sculpture.

Missouri

Central Missouri State University, Warrensburg, MO 64093. Art history, art teaching, crafts, graphic design, illustration, industrial design, interior design, painting, printmaking, sculpture.

Kansas City Art Institute, Kansas City, MO 64111. Art history, crafts, fabric design, film, graphic design, illustration, industrial design, interior design, painting, photography, printmaking, sculpture. NASAD. IDSA.

Maryville College, St. Louis, MO 63141. Architecture, art history, art teaching, crafts, graphic design, interior design, painting, photography, printmaking, sculpture.

Northeast Missouri State University, Kirksville, MO 63501. Art history, art teaching, crafts, fabric design, graphic design, painting, photography, printmaking, sculpture.

Northwest Missouri State University, Maryville, MO 64468. Art history, art teaching, crafts, fabric design, painting, photography, printmaking, sculpture.

Southeast Missouri State University, Cape Giradeau, MO 63701. Art history, art teaching, crafts, fabric design, graphic design, painting, photography, printmaking, sculpture.

Southwest Missouri State University, Springfield, MO 65802. Art history, art teaching, crafts, fabric design, graphic

design, illustration, painting, photography, printmaking, sculpture.

Stephens College, Columbia, MO 65201. Architecture, art history, art teaching, crafts, film, graphic design, illustration, interior design, painting, photography, printmaking, sculpture.

University of Missouri at Columbia, Columbia, MO 65211. Art history, art teaching, arts management, crafts, fabric design, film, graphic design, illustration, landscape architecture, painting, photography, printmaking, sculpture.

University of Missouri at Kansas City, Kansas City, MO 64110. Art history, art teaching, graphic design, painting, photography, printmaking, sculpture.

University of Missouri at St. Louis, St. Louis, MO 63121. Art history, art teaching, illustration, painting, photography, printmaking.

Washington University, School of Fine Arts, St. Louis, MO 63130. Architecture, art history, art teaching, crafts, graphic design, illustration, landscape architecture, painting, photography, printmaking, sculpture. NASAD. NAAB.

Webster College, St. Louis, MO 63119. Art history, art teaching, arts management, crafts, film, painting, photography, printmaking, sculpture.

Montana

Eastern Montana College, Billings, MT 59101. Art history, art teaching, crafts, fabric design, graphic design, painting, photography, printmaking, sculpture. NASAD.

Montana State University, Bozeman, MT 59717. Architecture, art history, art teaching, crafts, fabric design, film, graphic design, illustration, industrial design, landscape architecture, painting, photography, printmaking, sculpture. NASAD. NAAB.

University of Montana, Missoula, MT 59812. Art history, art teaching, crafts, painting, photography, printmaking, sculpture.

Nebraska

Kearney State College, Kearney, NE 68847. Art history, art teaching, crafts, fabric design, graphic design, illustration, painting, photography, printmaking, sculpture.

University of Nebraska at Lincoln, Lincoln, NE 68588. Architecture, art history, art teaching, crafts, fabric design, film, graphic design, landscape architecture, painting, photography, printmaking, sculpture. NAAB.

University of Nebraska at Omaha, Omaha, NE 68182. Art history, art teaching, crafts, painting, printmaking, sculpture.

Nevada

University of Nevada at Las Vegas, Las Vegas, NV 89154. Art history, crafts, fabric design, film, painting, photography, printmaking, sculpture.

University of Nevada, Reno, Reno, NV 89557. Art history, art teaching, crafts, painting, photography, printmaking, sculpture.

New Hampshire

Notre Dame College, Manchester, NH 03104. Art history, art teaching, crafts, graphic design, illustration, painting, printmaking, sculpture.

Plymouth State College, Plymouth, NH 03264. Art history, art teaching, crafts, painting, printmaking.

University of New Hampshire, Durham, NH 03824. Architecture, art history, art teaching, arts management, crafts, fabric design, painting, photography, printmaking, sculpture.

New Jersey

Glassboro State College, Glassboro, NJ 08028. Art history, crafts, fabric design, illustration, painting, photography, printmaking, sculpture.

Jersey City State College, Jersey City, NJ 07305. Art history, art teaching, crafts, fabric design, graphic design, illustration, interior design, painting, photography, printmaking, sculpture. NASAD.

Kean College of New Jersey, Union, NJ 07083. Art history, art teaching, arts management, crafts, fabric design, film, graphic design, illustration, interior design, painting, photography, printmaking, sculpture.

Monmouth College, West Long Branch, NJ 07764. Art history, art teaching, crafts, fabric design, graphic design, painting, photography, printmaking, sculpture.

Montclair State College, Upper Montclair, NJ 07043. Art history, art teaching, arts management, crafts, fabric design, film, graphic design, illustration, painting, photography, printmaking, sculpture.

New Jersey Institute of Technology, Newark, NJ 07102. Architecture. NAAB.

Rutgers, The State University of New Jersey at New Brunswick, New Brunswick, NJ 08903. Architecture, art history, art teaching, arts management, crafts, fabric design, film, graphic design, landscape architecture, painting, photography, printmaking, sculpture. ASLA.

William Patterson College, Wayne, NJ 07470. Art history, art teaching, arts management, crafts, fabric design, film, graphic design, illustration, industrial design, painting, photography, printmaking, sculpture.

Princeton University, Princeton, NJ 08540. Architecture, art history, crafts, landscape architecture, painting, photography, printmaking, sculpture. NAAB.

Trenton State College, Trenton, NJ 08625. Art history, art teaching, crafts, fabric design, graphic design, illustration, interior design, painting, photography, printmaking, sculpture.

New Mexico

Eastern New Mexico University, Portales, NM 88130. Art history, art teaching, crafts, fabric design, illustration, painting, photography, printmaking, sculpture.

New Mexico State University, Las Cruces, NM 88003. Art history, art teaching, arts management, crafts, fabric design, graphic design, painting, photography, printmaking, sculpture.

University of New Mexico, Albuquerque, NM 87131. Architecture, art history, crafts, film, landscape architecture, painting, photography, printmaking, sculpture. NAAB.

New York

Adelphi University, Garden City, NY 11530. Art history, crafts, fabric design, interior design, painting, photography, printmaking, sculpture.

Alfred University (New York State College of Ceramics), Alfred, NY 14802. Art history, art teaching, crafts, film, painting, photography, printmaking, sculpture. NASAD.

Brooklyn College, City University of New York, Brooklyn, NY 11210. Architecture, art history, crafts, graphic design, interior design, painting, photography, printmaking, sculpture.

City College, City University of New York, New York, NY 10031. Architecture, art history, landscape architecture. NAAB. ASLA.

College of New Rochelle, New Rochelle, NY 10801. Art history, art teaching, crafts, fabric design, film, graphic design, illustration, painting, photography, printmaking, sculpture.

College of St. Rose, Albany, NY 12203. Art history, art teaching, crafts, fabric design, graphic design, painting, photography, printmaking, sculpture.

Columbia University, New York, NY 10027. Architecture, art history, art teaching, crafts, landscape architecture, painting, printmaking, sculpture. NAAB.

Cooper Union School of Art & Architecture, New York, NY 10003. Architecture, art history, crafts, film, graphic design, illustration, landscape architecture, painting, photography, printmaking, sculpture. NASAD. NAAB.

Cornell University, Ithaca, NY 14853. Architecture, art history, arts management, fabric design, interior design, landscape architecture, painting, photography, printmaking, sculpture. NAAB. ASLA.

Daemen College, Amherst, NY 14226. Art history, art teaching, crafts, fabric design, painting, photography, printmaking, sculpture.

Fashion Institute of Technology, New York, NY 10001. Art history, crafts, fabric design, graphic design, illustration, interior design, painting, photography, printmaking, sculpture.

Hofstra University, Hempstead, NY 11550. Art history, art teaching, crafts, fabric design, painting, photography, printmaking, sculpture.

Hunter College, City University of New York, New York, NY 10021. Art history, art teaching, crafts, fabric design, film, graphic design, painting, photography, printmaking, sculpture.

Herbert H. Lehman College, Bronx, NY 10468. Art history, crafts, painting, photography, printmaking, sculpture.

Manhattanville College, Purchase, NY 10577. Art history, art teaching, crafts, fabric design, film, graphic design, painting, photography, printmaking, sculpture.

Marymount College, Tarrytown, NY 10591. Art history, art teaching, crafts, fabric design, illustration, painting, photography, printmaking, sculpture.

Munson-Williams-Proctor Institute School of Art, Utica, NY 13502. Art history, art teaching, crafts, painting, photography, printmaking, sculpture. NASAD.

Nazareth College of Rochester, Rochester, NY 14610. Art history, art teaching, arts management, fabric design, graphic design, painting, photography, printmaking, sculpture.

New York Institute of Technology, Old Westbury, NY 11568. Architecture, art history, art teaching, arts management, fabric design, film, graphic design, industrial design, painting, photography, printmaking, sculpture. NAAB.

New York School of Interior Design, New York NY 10022. Art history, interior design, photography.

New York University, New York, NY 10003. Architecture, art history, art teaching, arts management, crafts, fabric design, film, industrial design, painting, photography, printmaking, sculpture.

Parsons School of Design, New York, NY 10011. Architecture, art history, art teaching, arts management, crafts, fabric design, film, graphic design, illustration, industrial design, interior design, painting, photography, printmaking, sculpture. NASAD.

C. W. Post Center of Long Island University, Greenvale, NY 11548. Art history, art teaching, arts management, crafts, fabric design, graphic design, illustration, painting, photography, printmaking, sculpture.

Pratt Institute, Brooklyn, NY 11205. Architecture, art history, art teaching, arts management, crafts, fabric design, film, graphic design, illustration, industrial design, interior design, landscape architecture, painting, photography, printmaking, sculpture. NASAD. NAAB. IDSA.

Pratt-Phoenix School of Design, New York, NY 10016. Fabric design, graphic design, illustration, photography.

Queens College, Flushing, NY 11367. Architecture, art history, art teaching, crafts, graphic design, illustration, painting, photography, printmaking, sculpture.

Rensselaer Polytechnic Institute, Troy, NY 12181. Architecture, art history, art teaching, crafts, painting, photography, sculpture. NAAB.

Rochester Institute of Technology, Rochester, NY 14623. Art history, art teaching, crafts, fabric design, graphic design, illustration, industrial design, interior design, painting, photography, printmaking, sculpture. NASAD.

School of Visual Arts, New York, NY 10010. Architecture, art history, art teaching, arts management, crafts, fabric design, graphic design, illustration, painting, photography, printmaking, sculpture. NASAD.

Skidmore College, Saratoga Springs, NY 12866. Art history, art teaching, crafts, fabric design, graphic design, painting, photography, printmaking, sculpture. NASAD.

Southampton College of Long Island, Southampton, NY 11968. Art history, art teaching, arts management, crafts, fabric design, graphic design, illustration, painting, photography, printmaking, sculpture.

State University College of New York at Brockport, Brockport, NY 14420. Art history, art teaching, arts management, crafts, painting, photography, printmaking, sculpture.

State University College at Buffalo, Buffalo, NY 14222. Art history, painting, photography, printmaking, sculpture.

State University College at Fredonia, Fredonia, NY 14063. Art history, arts management, crafts, film, graphic design, illustration, painting, photography, printmaking, sculpture.

State University College at Geneseo, Geneseo, NY 14454. Art history, crafts, fabric design, film, painting, photography, printmaking, sculpture.

State University College at New Paltz, New Paltz, NY 12561. Art history, art teaching, arts management, crafts, film, painting, photography, printmaking, sculpture.

State University College at Oswego, Oswego, NY 13126. Art history, arts management, crafts, graphic design, interior design, painting, photography, printmaking, sculpture.

State University College at Plattsburgh, Plattsburgh, NY 12901. Art history, crafts, fabric design, film, painting, photography, printmaking, sculpture.

State University College at Potsdam, Potsdam, NY 13676. Art history, art teaching, arts management, crafts, painting, photography, printmaking, sculpture.

State University College at Purchase, Purchase, NY 10577. Art history, painting, photography, printmaking, sculpture.

State University of New York at Albany, Albany, NY 12222. Art history, film, painting, photography, printmaking, sculpture.

State University of New York at Binghamton, Binghamton, NY 13901. Art history, arts management, film, industrial design, painting, photography, printmaking, sculpture.

State University of New York at Buffalo, Buffalo, NY 14214. Art history, graphic design, painting, photography, printmaking, sculpture. NASAD.

State University of New York at Stony Brook, Stony Brook, NY 91794. Architecture, art history, crafts, painting, photography, printmaking, sculpture.

State University of New York-College of Environmental Science & Forestry, Syracuse, NY 13210. Architecture, art history, landscape architecture, photography. ASLA.

Syracuse University, Syracuse, NY 13210. Architecture, art history, art teaching, arts management, crafts, fabric design, film, graphic design, illustration, industrial design, interior design, painting, photography, printmaking, sculpture. NASAD. NAAB. IDSA.

University of Rochester, Rochester, NY 14627. Art history, painting, photography, sculpture.

North Carolina

East Carolina University, Greenville, NC 27834. Art history, art teaching, arts management, crafts, fabric design, film, graphic design, illustration, interior design, painting, photography, printmaking, sculpture. NASAD.

North Carolina Central University, Durham, NC 27707. Art history, art teaching, arts management, crafts, fabric design, graphic design, painting, photography, printmaking, sculpture.

North Carolina State University, Raleigh, NC 27650. Architecture, fabric design, illustration, industrial design, landscape architecture, photography, printmaking. NAAB. ASLA. IDSA.

University of North Carolina at Charlotte, Charlotte, NC 28223. Architecture, art history, art teaching, crafts, fabric design, illustration, painting, photography, printmaking, sculpture. NAAB.

University of North Carolina at Greensboro, Greensboro, NC 27412. Art history, art teaching, crafts, fabric design, film, illustration, painting, photography, printmaking, sculpture.

Western Carolina University, Cullowhee, NC 28723. Art history, art teaching, arts management, crafts, fabric design, graphic design, illustration, painting, photography, printmaking, sculpture.

North Dakota

North Dakota State University, Fargo, ND 58102. Architecture, art history, art teaching, arts management, crafts, fabric design, illustration, industrial design, interior design, landscape architecture, painting, photography, printmaking, sculpture. NAAB.

University of North Dakota, Grand Forks, ND 58202. Art history, art teaching, crafts, fabric design, painting, photography, printmaking, sculpture. NASAD.

Ohio

Antioch College, Yellow Spring, OH 45387. Art history, art teaching, crafts, film, painting, photography, printmaking, sculpture.

Art Academy of Cincinnati, Cincinnati, OH 45202. Art history, graphic design, illustration, painting, photography, printmaking, sculpture. NASAD.

Bowling Green State University, Bowling OH 43403. Art history, art teaching, crafts, fabric design, film, graphic design, illustration, industrial design, interior design, painting, photography, printmaking, sculpture.

Cleveland Institute of Art, Cleveland, OH 44106. Art history, art teaching, crafts, fabric design, film, graphic design, illustration, industrial design, painting, photography, printmaking, sculpture. NASAD. IDSA.

Cleveland State University, Cleveland, OH 44115. Art history, art teaching, crafts, fabric design, painting, photography, printmaking, sculpture.

College of Mount St. Joseph, Cincinnati, OH 45051. Art history, art teaching, arts management, crafts, fabric design, film, graphic design, illustration, interior design, painting, photography, printmaking, sculpture.

College of Wooster, Wooster, OH 44691. Architecture, art history, art teaching, crafts, painting, photography, printmaking, sculpture. NASAD.

Columbus College of Art & Design, Columbus, OH 43215. Art history, arts management, crafts, fabric design, film, graphic design, illustration, industrial design, interior design, painting, photography, printmaking, sculpture. NASAD. IDSA.

Denison University, Granville, OH 43023. Art history, crafts, film, painting, photography, printmaking, sculpture.

Edgecliff College, Cincinnati, OH 45206. Art history, art teaching, crafts, fabric design, interior design, painting, printmaking, sculpture.

Kent State University, Kent, OH 44242. Architecture, art history, art teaching, crafts, fabric design, film, illustration, industrial design, painting, photography, printmaking, sculpture. NASAD. NAAB.

Kent State University at Stark, Canton, OH 44720. Art history, crafts, fabric design, painting, photography.

Kent State University at Trumbull, Warren, OH 44483. Art history, art teaching, crafts, fabric design, painting, printmaking, sculpture.

Marietta College, Marietta, OH 45750. Art history, art teaching, crafts, graphic design, painting, photography, printmaking, sculpture.

Miami University, Oxford, OH 45056. Architecture, art history, art teaching, crafts, fabric design, graphic design, landscape architecture, painting, photography, printmaking, sculpture. NAAB.

Oberlin College, Oberlin, OH 44074. Architecture, art history, film, painting, photography, printmaking, sculpture. NASAD.

Ohio State University, Columbus, OH 43210. Architecture, art history, art teaching, crafts, fabric design, graphic design, industrial design, interior design, landscape architecture, painting, printmaking, sculpture. NAAB. ASLA. IDSA.

Ohio University, Athens, OH 45701. Art history, art teaching, crafts, fabric design, graphic design, illustration, painting, photography, printmaking, sculpture.

Ohio Wesleyan University, Delaware, OH 43015. Art history, art teaching, crafts, fabric design, film, graphic design, painting, photography, printmaking, sculpture.

University of Akron, Akron, OH 44325. Art history, art teaching, crafts, fabric design, graphic design, illustration, interior design, painting, photography, printmaking, sculpture. NASAD.

University of Cincinnati, Cincinnati, OH 45221. Architecture, art history, art teaching, crafts, fabric design, film, graphic design, illustration, industrial design, interior design, landscape architecture, painting, photography, printmaking, sculpture. NASAD. NAAB. IDSA.

University of Dayton, Dayton, OH 45469. Art history, art teaching, crafts, fabric design, graphic design, painting, photography, printmaking, sculpture.

University of Toledo, Toledo, OH 43697. Art history, art teaching, crafts, painting, printmaking, sculpture.

Wittenberg University, Springfield, OH 45501. Art history, art teaching, crafts, graphic design, illustration, interior design, painting, photography, printmaking, sculpture.

Wright State University, Dayton, OH 45435. Art history, arts management, crafts, fabric design, film, graphic design, painting, photography, printmaking, sculpture.

Youngstown State University, Youngstown, OH 44555. Architecture, art history, art teaching, arts management, crafts, fabric design, graphic design, interior design, painting, photography, printmaking, sculpture.

Oklahoma

Central State University, Edmond, OK 73034. Art history, art history, crafts, fabric design, graphic design, illustration, painting, printmaking, sculpture.

Northeastern Oklahoma State University, Tahlequah, OK 74464. Art history, art teaching, crafts, fabric design, painting, printmaking, sculpture.

Oklahoma State University, Stillwater, OK 47078. Architecture, art history, art teaching, crafts, graphic design, illustration, landscape architecture, painting, printmaking, sculpture. NAAB.

Southwestern Oklahoma State University, Weatherford, OK 73096. Art history, art teaching, crafts, graphic design, illustration, industrial design, painting, photography, printmaking, sculpture.

University of Oklahoma, Norman, OK 73019. Architecture, art history, arts management, crafts, film, graphic design, industrial design, landscape architecture, painting, photography, printmaking, sculpture. NAAB.

University of Tulsa, Tulsa, OK 74104. Art history, art teaching, crafts, fabric design, graphic design, illustration, painting, photography, printmaking, sculpture.

Oregon

Oregon State University, Corvallis, OR 97331. Art history, art teaching, crafts, fabric design, graphic design, illustration, landscape architecture, painting, photography, printmaking, sculpture.

Pacific Northwest College of Art, Portland, OR 97205. Art history, crafts, graphic design, interior design, painting, photography, printmaking, sculpture. NASAD.

Portland State University, Portland, OR 97207. Architecture, art history, art teaching, crafts, fabric design, graphic design, illustration, painting, photography, printmaking, sculpture.

Southern Oregon State College, Ashland, OR 97520. Art history, art teaching, crafts, fabric design, painting, photography, printmaking, sculpture.

University of Oregon, Eugene, OR 97403. Architecture, art history, art teaching, crafts, fabric design, film, interior design, landscape architecture, painting, photography, printmaking, sculpture. NAAB. ASLA.

Pennsylvania

Beaver College, Glenside, PA 19038. Art history, art teaching, crafts, fabric design, graphic design, illustration, interior design, painting, photography, printmaking. NASAD.

Carnegie-Mellon University, Pittsburgh, PA 15235. Architecture, art his-

tory, crafts, fabric design, graphic design, illustration, industrial design, landscape architecture, painting, photography, printmaking, sculpture. NASAD. NAAB. IDSA.

Drexel University/Nesbitt College, Philadelphia, PA 19104. Architecture, art history, fabric design, interior design, painting, photography, printmaking, sculpture. NAAB.

Edinboro State College, Edinboro, PA 16444. Art history, art teaching, arts management, crafts, fabric design, film, graphic design, illustration, painting, photography, printmaking, sculpture.

Indiana University of Pennsylvania, Indiana, PA 15705. Art history, art teaching, crafts, fabric design, painting, photography, printmaking, sculpture.

Kutztown State College, Kutztown, PA 19530. Art history, art teaching, crafts, fabric design, film, graphic design, illustration, painting, printmaking, sculpture.

Marywood College, Scranton, PA 18509. Art history, art teaching, crafts, fabric design, graphic design, illustration, interior design, painting, photography, printmaking, sculpture.

Millersville State College, Millersville, PA 17064. Art history, art teaching, crafts, fabric design, graphic design, illustration, painting, photography, printmaking, sculpture.

Moore College of Art, Philadelphia, PA 19103. Architecture, art history, art teaching, crafts, fabric design, graphic design, illustration, interior design, painting, photography, printmaking, sculpture. NASAD.

Pennsylvania Academy of the Fine Arts, Philadelphia, PA 19102. Painting, printmaking, sculpture.

Pennsylvania State University, University Park, PA 16802. Architecture, art history, art teaching, arts management, crafts, fabric design, film, graphic design, landscape architecture, painting, photography, printmaking, sculpture. NAAB. ASLA.

Philadelphia College of Art, Philadelphia, PA 19102. Architecture, art history, art teaching, crafts, fabric design, film, graphic design, illustration, industrial design, interior design, painting, photography, printmaking, sculpture. NASAD. IDSA.

Philadelphia College of Textiles & Science, Philadelphia, PA 19144. Art history, fabric design, interior design, photography, printmaking.

Point Park College, Pittsburgh, PA 15222. Architecture, art history, film, graphic design, illustration, interior design, painting, photography.

Temple University/Tyler School of Art, Philadelphia, PA 19126. Architecture, art history, art teaching, crafts, fabric design, film, graphic design, landscape architecture, painting, photography, printmaking, sculpture. NASAD. NAAB.

University of Pennsylvania, Philadelphia, PA 19104. Architecture, art history, film, landscape architecture, painting, photography, printmaking, sculpture. NAAB. ASLA.

West Chester State College, West Chester, PA 19380. Architecture, art history, crafts, fabric design, film, landscape architecture, painting, photography, printmaking, sculpture.

Puerto Rico

University of Puerto Rico at Rio Piedras, Rio Piedras, PR 00931. Architecture, art history, crafts, graphic design, painting, photography, printmaking, sculpture.

Rhode Island

Rhode Island College, Providence, RI 02908. Art history, art teaching, arts

management, crafts, fabric design, film, illustration, painting, photography, printmaking, sculpture. NASAD.

Rhode Island School of Design, Providence, RI 02903. Architecture, art teaching, crafts, fabric design, film, graphic design, illustration, industrial design, interior design, landscape architecture, painting, photography, printmaking, sculpture. NAAB. ASLA. IDSA.

University of Rhode Island, Kingston, RI 02881. Art history, film, painting, photography, printmaking, sculpture.

South Carolina

Clemson University, Clemson, SC 29631. Architecture, art history, crafts, graphic design, illustration, industrial design, landscape architecture, painting, photography, printmaking, sculpture. NAAB.

Bob Jones University, Greenville, SC 29614. Art history, art teaching, crafts, film, graphic design, painting, photography, printmaking, sculpture.

University of South Carolina, Columbia, SC 29208. Art history, art teaching, arts management, crafts, fabric design, film, graphic design, illustration, interior design, painting, photography, printmaking, sculpture.

Winthrop College, Rock Hill, SC 29733. Art history, art teaching, crafts, fabric design, illustration, painting, photography, printmaking, sculpture.

South Dakota

Northern State College, Aberdeen, SD 57401. Art history, art teaching, crafts, fabric design, graphic design, illustration, interior design, painting, photography, printmaking, sculpture.

University of South Dakota, Vermillion, SD 57069. Art history, art teaching, arts management, crafts, fabric design, painting, photography, printmaking, sculpture. NASAD.

Tennessee

Austin Peay State University, Clarksville, TN 37040. Art history, art teaching, crafts, fabric design, graphic design, illustration, industrial design, painting, photography, printmaking, sculpture.

East Tennessee State University, Johnson, TN 37601. Art history, art teaching, crafts, fabric design, film, graphic design, illustration, painting, photography, printmaking, sculpture.

Memphis Academy of Arts, Memphis, TN 38112. Art history, crafts, fabric design, graphic design, illustration, painting, photography, printmaking, sculpture. NASAD.

Memphis State University, Memphis, TN 38152. Art history, art teaching, arts management, crafts, fabric design, graphic design, illustration, interior design, painting, photography, printmaking, sculpture.

Middle Tennessee State University, Murfreesboro, TN 37132. Art history, art teaching, crafts, fabric design, film, graphic design, illustration, painting, photography, printmaking, sculpture.

Tennessee State University, Nashville, TN 37203. Art history, art teaching, arts management, crafts, fabric design, film, graphic design, illustration, industrial design, interior design, landscape architecture, painting, photography, printmaking, sculpture.

University of Tennessee at Knoxville, Knoxville, TN 37916. Architecture, art history, crafts, fabric design, illustration, painting, photography, printmaking, sculpture. NAAB.

Vanderbilt University, Nashville, TN 37235. Art history, film, painting, photography, printmaking, sculpture.

Texas

Stephen F. Austin State University, Nacogdoches, TX 75962. Art history, art teaching, crafts, fabric design, film, graphic design, illustration, interior design, painting, photography, printmaking, sculpture.

Baylor University, Waco, TX 76703. Art history, art teaching, arts management, crafts, fabric design, graphic design, illustration, industrial design, painting, photography, printmaking, sculpture.

East Texas State University, Commerce, TX 75428. Art history, art teaching, crafts, fabric design, film, graphic design, illustration, industrial design, interior design, painting, photography, printmaking, sculpture.

Lamar University, Beaumont, TX 77710. Art history, art teaching, crafts, fabric design, illustration, painting, photography, printmaking, sculpture.

Midwestern State University, Wichita Falls, TX 76308. Art history, art teaching, arts management, crafts, graphic design, painting, photography, printmaking, sculpture.

North Texas State University, Denton, TX 76203. Art history, art teaching, crafts, fabric design, graphic design, illustration, interior design, painting, photography, printmaking, sculpture.

Pan American University, Edinburg, TX 78539. Art history, art teaching, crafts, graphic design, illustration, painting, printmaking, sculpture.

Rice University, Houston, TX 77001. Architecture, art history, film, landscape architecture, painting, photography, printmaking, sculpture. NAAB.

Sam Houston State University, Huntsville, TX 77340. Art history, art teaching, crafts, fabric design, graphic design, illustration, painting, printmaking, sculpture.

Southern Methodist University, Dallas, TX 75275. Art history, art teaching, crafts, fabric design, film, painting, photography, printmaking, sculpture.

Southwest Texas State University, San Marcos, TX 78666. Art history, art teaching, crafts, fabric design, graphic design, illustration, painting, printmaking, sculpture.

Sul Ross State University, Alpine, TX 79830. Art history, art teaching, crafts, fabric design, interior design, painting, printmaking, sculpture.

Texas A & M University, College Station, TX 77843. Architecture, landscape architecture. NAAB. ASLA.

Texas Christian University, Fort Worth, TX 76129. Art history, art teaching, crafts, fabric design, film, graphic design, illustration, interior design, painting, photography, printmaking, sculpture.

Texas Southern University, Houston, TX 77004. Art history, art teaching, crafts, fabric design, graphic design, painting, printmaking, sculpture.

Texas Tech University, Lubbock, TX 79409. Architecture, art history, art teaching, crafts, fabric design, film, graphic design, illustration, interior design, landscape architecture, painting, photography, printmaking, sculpture. NASAD. NAAB. ASLA.

Texas Woman's University, Denton, TX 76204. Art history, art teaching, crafts, fabric design, graphic design, illustration, interior design, painting, photography, sculpture.

University of Houston, Houston, TX 77004. Architecture, art history, arts management, crafts, graphic design, interior design, landscape architecture, painting, photography, printmaking, sculpture. NAAB.

University of Texas at Arlington, Arlington, TX 76019. Architecture, art his-

tory, art teaching, crafts, fabric design, film, graphic design, illustration, interior design, landscape architecture, painting, photography, printmaking, sculpture. NAAB.

University of Texas at Austin, Austin, TX 78712. Architecture, art history, art teaching, crafts, fabric design, film, graphic design, illustration, interior design, landscape architecture, painting, photography, printmaking, sculpture. NAAB.

University of Texas at El Paso, El Paso, TX 79968. Art history, art teaching, crafts, fabric design, painting, printmaking, sculpture.

University of Texas at San Antonio, San Antonio, TX 78285. Architecture, art history, crafts, painting, photography, printmaking, sculpture. NASAD.

University of Texas at Tyler, Tyler, TX 75701. Art history, art teaching, arts managment, crafts, film, graphic design, industrial design, interior design, painting, photography, printmaking, sculpture.

West Texas State University, Canyon, TX 79016. Art history, art teaching, crafts, fabric design, illustration, painting, printmaking, sculpture.

Utah

Brigham Young University, Provo, UT 84602. Art history, art teaching, crafts, industrial design, landscape architecture, painting, printmaking, sculpture. IDSA.

University of Utah, Salt Lake City, UT 84112. Architecture, art history, art teaching, crafts, fabric design, film, graphic design, painting, photography, printmaking, sculpture. NAAB.

Utah State University, Logan, UT 84322. Art history, art teaching, crafts, fabric design, graphic design, illustration, landscape architecture, painting, photography, printmaking, sculpture. ASLA.

Weber State College, Ogden, UT 84408. Art history, art teaching, crafts, fabric design, graphic design, illustration, painting, photography, printmaking, sculpture.

Vermont

University of Vermont, Burlington, VT 05405. Architecture, art history, art teaching, crafts, fabric design, landscape architecture, painting, photography, printmaking, sculpture.

Virginia

Hampton Institute, Hampton, VA 23666. Architecture, art history, art teaching, crafts, film, graphic design, illustration, landscape architecture, painting, photography, printmaking, sculpture. NAAB.

James Madison University, Harrisonburg, VA 22801. Art history, art teaching, crafts, fabric design, film, graphic design, industrial design, interior design, painting, photography, printmaking, sculpture. NASAD.

George Mason University, Fairfax, VA 22030. Art history, art teaching, film, painting, printmaking, sculpture.

Norfolk State University, Norfolk, VA 23504. Art history, art teaching, crafts, graphic design, illustration, painting, photography, printmaking, sculpture.

Old Dominion University, Norfolk, VA 23508. Art history, art teaching, crafts, fabric design, painting, photography, printmaking, sculpture.

Radford University, Radford, VA 24142. Architecture, art history, art teaching, crafts, fabric design, graphic design, illustration, painting, photography, printmaking, sculpture.

University of Virginia, Charlottesville, VA 22903. Architecture, art history, art teaching, arts management, graphic design, landscape architecture, painting, photography, printmaking, sculpture. NAAB. ASLA.

Virginia Commonwealth University, Richmond, VA 23284. Art history, art teaching, arts management, crafts, fabric design, film, graphic design, illustration, interior design, painting, photography, printmaking, sculpture. NASAD.

Virginia Polytechnic Institute & State University, Blacksburg, VA 24061. Architecture, art history, art teaching, crafts, fabric design, film, graphic design, industrial design, interior design, landscape architecture, painting, photography, printmaking, sculpture. NAAB. ASLA.

Washington

Cornish Institute, Seattle, WA 98102. Architecture, art history, arts management, crafts, graphic design, illustration, interior design, painting, photography, printmaking, sculpture.

Eastern Washington University, Cheney, WA 99004. Art history, art teaching, arts management, crafts, film, illustration, painting, photography, printmaking, sculpture.

Pacific Lutheran University, Tacoma, WA 98447. Art history, art teaching, crafts, fabric design, film, graphic design, illustration, painting, photography, printmaking, sculpture.

University of Washington, Seattle, WA 98195. Architecture, art history, art teaching, crafts, fabric design, film, graphic design, industrial design, interior design, landscape architecture, painting, photography, printmaking, sculpture. NASAD. NAAB. ASLA.

Washington State University, Pullman, WA 99164. Architecture, art history, art teaching, crafts, graphic design, landscape architecture, painting, photography, printmaking, sculpture. NAAB. ASLA.

Western Washington University, Bellingham, WA 98225. Art history, art teaching, arts management, crafts, fabric design, graphic design, illustration, industrial design, painting, photography, printmaking, sculpture. IDSA.

West Virginia

Marshall University, Huntington, WV 25701. Art history, art teaching, crafts, fabric design, illustration, painting, printmaking, sculpture.

Shepherd College, Shepherdstown, WV 25443. Art history, art teaching, crafts, graphic design, illustration, painting, photography, printmaking, sculpture.

West Liberty State College, West Liberty, WV 26074. Art history, art teaching, crafts, fabric design, film, graphic design, illustration, photography, printmaking, sculpture.

West Virginia University, Morgantown, WV 26506. Art history, art teaching, crafts, graphic design, landscape architecture, painting, photography, printmaking, sculpture. NASAD. ASLA.

Wisconsin

Milwaukee Institute of Art & Design, Milwaukee, WI 53202. Art history, graphic design, illustration, industrial design, interior design, painting, photography, printmaking, sculpture. NASAD.

University of Wisconsin at Eau Claire, Eau Claire, WI 54701. Art history, art teaching, crafts, fabric design, graphic design, painting, printmaking, sculpture.

University of Wisconsin at Green Bay, Green Bay, WI 54302. Art history, art teaching, crafts, fabric design, film, landscape architecture, painting, photography, printmaking, sculpture.

University of Wisconsin at La Crosse, La Crosse, WI 54601. Art history, art teaching, crafts, painting, printmaking, sculpture.

University of Wisconsin at Madison, Madison, WI 53706. Architecture, art history, art teaching, crafts, fabric design, graphic design, illustration, landscape architecture, painting, printmaking, sculpture. ASLA.

University of Wisconsin at Milwaukee, Milwaukee, WI 53201. Architecture, art history, art teaching, crafts, fabric design, film, graphic design, illustration, landscape architecture, painting, photography, printmaking, sculpture. NAAB.

University of Wisconsin at Oshkosh, Oshkosh, WI 54901. Art history, art teaching, arts management, crafts, fabric design, graphic design, illustration, interior design, painting, photography, printmaking, sculpture.

University of Wisconsin at River Falls, River Falls, WI 54022. Art history, art teaching, crafts, fabric design, film, graphic design, illustration, painting, photography, printmaking, sculpture.

University of Wisconsin at Stevens Point, Stevens Point, WI 54481. Art history, art teaching, crafts, fabric design, graphic design, painting, photography, printmaking, sculpture.

University of Wisconsin at Stout, Menomonie, WI 54751. Art history, art teaching, crafts, graphic design, illustration, industrial design, interior design, painting, printmaking, sculpture.

University of Wisconsin at Superior, Superior, WI 54880. Art history, art teaching, crafts, fabric design, film, graphic design, painting, photography, printmaking, sculpture.

University of Wisconsin at Whitewater, Whitewater, WI 53190. Art history, art teaching, crafts, fabric design, film, graphic design, illustration, interior design, painting, photography, printmaking, sculpture.

Wyoming

University of Wyoming, Laramie, WY 82001. Art history, crafts, painting, printmaking, sculpture.

CANADA

Alberta

Alberta College of Art, Calgary, AB T2M OL4. Art history, crafts, film, graphic design, illustration, painting, photography, printmaking, sculpture.

University of Alberta, Edmonton, AB T6G 2C9. Art history, graphic design, industrial design, painting, photography, printmaking, sculpture.

University of Calgary, Calgary, AB T2N 1N4. Art history, art teaching, crafts, graphic design, landscape architecture, painting, photography, printmaking, sculpture.

University of Lethbridge, Lethbridge, AB T1K 3M4. Art history, art teaching, crafts, landscape architecture, painting, photography, printmaking, sculpture.

British Columbia

Emily Carr College of Art & Design, Vancouver, BC V6H 3R9. Art history, crafts, film, graphic design, illustration, photography, printmaking, sculpture.

Selkirk College (Kootenay School of Art Division), Nelson, BC V1L 3C7. Art history, art teaching, arts management, crafts, fabric design, film, graphic design, illustration, painting, photography, printmaking, sculpture.

University of British Columbia, Vancouver, BC V6T 1W5. Architecture, landscape architecture, painting, photography, printmaking, sculpture.

University of Victoria, Victoria, BC V8W 2Y2. Art history, photography, printmaking, sculpture.

Manitoba

University of Manitoba, Winnipeg, MB R3T 2N2. Architecture, art history, crafts, graphic design, illustration, interior design, landscape architecture, painting, photography, printmaking, sculpture.

New Brunswick

Mount Allison University, Sackville, NB E0A 3C0. Art history, painting, photography, printmaking, sculpture.

University of New Brunswick, Fredericton, NB E3B 5A3. Art history, crafts, printmaking.

Université de Moncton, Moncton, NB E1A 3E9. Art history, art teaching, crafts, graphic design, painting, photography, printmaking, sculpture.

Nova Scotia

Nova Scotia College of Art & Design, Halifax, NS B3J 3J6. Art history, art teaching, crafts, fabric design, graphic design, painting, photography, printmaking, sculpture.

Technical University of Nova Scotia, Halifax, NS B3J 2X4. Architecture, art history, art teaching, industrial design, interior design, landscape architecture, photography.

Ontario

Carleton University, Ottawa, ON K1S 5B6. Art history, art teaching, crafts, film, graphic design, illustration, painting, photography, printmaking, sculpture.

McMaster University, Hamilton, ON L8S 4M2. Art history, painting, printmaking, sculpture.

Ontario College of Art, Toronto, ON M5T 1W1. Architecture, art history, arts management, crafts, fabric design, film, graphic design, illustration, industrial design, interior design, painting, photography, printmaking, sculpture.

Queens University, Kingston, ON K7L 3N6. Art history, art teaching, painting, photography, printmaking, sculpture.

University of Guelph, Guelph, ON N1G 2W1. Art history, landscape architecture, painting, printmaking, sculpture.

University of Toronto, Toronto, ON M5S 1A1. Architecture, art history, art teaching, film, graphic design, landscape architecture, painting, photography, printmaking, sculpture.

University of Waterloo, Waterloo, ON N2L 3G1. Art history, crafts, fabric design, film, illustration, painting, photography, printmaking, sculpture.

University of Windsor, Windsor, ON N9B 3P4. Art history, crafts, painting, printmaking, sculpture.

University of Western Ontario, London, ON N6A 5K7. Art history, crafts, painting, photography, printmaking, sculpture.

York University, Downsview, ON M3J 1P3. Art history, art teaching, film, graphic design, painting, photography, printmaking, sculpture.

Quebec

Concordia University, Montreal, PQ H3G 2M5. Art history, art teaching, crafts, film, graphic design, illustration, painting, photography, printmaking, sculpture.

McGill University, Montreal, PQ H3A 2T6. Architecture, art history, crafts, painting, printmaking, sculpture.

Université Laval Cite Universitaire, Quebec, PQ G1K 7P4. Art history, fabric design, film, graphic design, illustration, painting, photography, printmaking, sculpture.

Université de Montreal, Montreal, PQ H3C 3J7. Architecture, art history, film, landscape architecture, painting, sculpture.

University of Quebec at Trois Rivieres, Trois Rivieres, PQ G9A 5H7. Art history, art teaching, crafts, fabric design, painting, printmaking, sculpture.

Université du Quebec a Montreal, Montreal, PQ H3C 3P8. Art history, art teaching, painting, printmaking, sculpture.

Saskatchewan

University of Regina, Regina, SK S4S 0A2. Art history, crafts, painting, printmaking, sculpture.

University of Saskatchewan, Saskatoon Campus, Saskatoon, SK S7N 0W0. Art history, art teaching, crafts, painting, photography, printmaking, sculpture.

22
Professional organizations

At the beginning of this book, I listed the professional organizations, and other groups who were helpful in compiling and editing *Art Career Guide*. They may also be helpful to you. Here are the names and addresses of those organizations.

American Association
  of Museums
1055 Thomas Jefferson Street, NW
Washington, DC 20007

American Association
  of University Professors
One Dupont Circle, NW
  (Suite 500)
Washington, DC 20036

American Craft Council
401 Park Avenue South
New York, NY 10016

American Institute of Architects
1735 New York Avenue, NW
Washington, DC 20006

American Institute
  of Graphic Arts
1059 3rd Avenue
New York, NY 10021

American Personnel
  and Guidance Association
Two Skyline Place (Suite 400)
5203 Leesburg Pike
Falls Church, VA 22041

American Society of Interior
  Designers
1430 Broadway
New York, NY 10018

American Society of Landscape
  Architects
1733 Connecticut Avenue, NW
Washington, DC 20009

American Society of Magazine
  Photographers
205 Lexington Avenue
New York, NY 10016

Art Directors Club of New York
488 Madison Avenue
New York, NY 10022

Artists Equity Association
3726 Albemarle Street, NW
Washington, DC 20016

Association of Art Museum
Directors
Post Office Box 10082
Savannah, GA 31412

Association of Collegiate Schools
of Architecture
1735 New York Avenue, NW
Washington, DC 20006

Bureau of Labor Statistics
Division of Occupational
Outlook
United States Department
of Labor
Washington, D.C. 20212

College Art Association
of America
16 East 52 Street
New York, NY 10022

Foundation for Interior Design
Education Research
242 West 27 Street
New York, NY 10001

Graphic Artists Guild
30 East 20 Street
New York, NY 10003

Industrial Designers Society
of America
6802 Poplar Place (Suite 303)
McLean, VA 22101

Institute of Business Designers
1155 Merchandise Mart
Chicago, IL 60654

Interior Design Educators
Council

Box 8744
Richmond, VA 23226

National Architectural
Accrediting Board
1735 New York Avenue, NW
Washington, DC 20006

National Art Education
Association
1916 Association Drive
Reston, VA 22091

National Council for Interior
Design Qualification
75 East 55 Street
New York, NY 10022

National Council of Architectural
Registration Boards
1735 New York Avenue, NW
Washington, DC 20006

National Education Association
1201 16th Street, NW
Washington, DC 20036

New York/Artists Equity
Association
225 West 34 Street (Suite 1510)
New York, NY 10001

New York Chapter, American
Institute of Architects
457 Madison Avenue
New York, NY 10022

Professional Photographers
of America
1090 Executive Way
Des Plaines, IL 60018

Society of Illustrators
128 East 63 Street
New York, NY 10021

Index